Narrow Is the Way

Also by B. D. Hyman
My Mother's Keeper

Narrow Is the Way

B. D. AND JEREMY HYMAN

WILLIAM MORROW AND COMPANY, INC.
NEW YORK

Library of Congress Cataloging-in-Publication Data

Hyman, B. D. (Barbara Davis)
Narrow is the way.

1. Hyman, B. D. (Barbara Davis)   2. Christian
biography—United States.   3. Davis, Bette, 1908–
I. Hyman, Jeremy.   II. Title.
BR1725.H92A3   1987   209'.2'4 [B]   86-28588
ISBN 0-688-06345-4

Printed in the United States of America

First Edition

1 2 3 4 5 6 7 8 9 10

BOOK DESIGN BY BARBARA MARKS

And it shall come to pass afterward, that I will pour out my spirit upon all flesh; and your sons and your daughters shall prophesy, your old men shall dream dreams, your young men shall see visions:

—JOEL 2:28

And they were filled with the Holy Ghost, and began to speak with other tongues, as the Spirit gave them utterance.

—ACTS 2:4

Narrow Is the Way

Part One

CHAPTER

Justin and I paused on our hilltop, as we so often did when returning from a ride, and gazed out across the hills and valleys that made up our little corner of Pennsylvania. Our farmhouse, which we had renovated ourselves, was snugged into the hillside below us, only the roof visible from where we sat astride our mounts. The barns—an old one where I kept my rabbits, chickens, ducks, sheep and goat, and the newer one where we kept the horses—stood the other side of our dirt road. Beyond and below them was our lake with a screened-in cabin next to it.

Horses, whether I rode them or simply took care of them, had always been a foremost joy in my life. Justin, now six, had inherited my love of animals as well as his brother's pony, Chocolate. Ashley, fourteen, had outgrown Chocolate a few years earlier and, like my husband, Jeremy, was an excellent rider and had his own horse. He had taken formal riding lessons before we left Connecticut but, out here in the wide-open spaces where no such instruction was available, I'd had to teach Justin myself. He had recently graduated from our training ring on the flat hilltop to riding in the woods. He was very excited about it and I was proud of his horsemanship.

I had, perforce, to grind away at my typewriter for most of every day if I was ever going to finish *My Mother's Keeper*, but even so, I managed to take care of my animals, do barn chores, and still squeeze in an hour or so for riding whenever the weather was conducive.

We clucked the horse and pony into motion and descended the hill, crossing one of the hayfields that surrounded three sides of the house. The two horses left behind in the pasture greeted our reappearance with happy whinnies and playful bucking. Being autumn, with the last of the haying done, the fields had that even, clipped look that I found so particularly pleasing. Even the sight of the full hay mows in the old barn afforded me pleasure as we rode past the open doors.

Making the hay was Jeremy's job and he loved every minute of it. The rest of us became involved only at the very end when it was time to pick up the bales and get them into the barns. It was hot, sweaty work, but very satisfying. We needed eight tons for our own stock and sold off the rest when the price was right during the course of the winter. Jeremy had learned a bit of farming when working for a friend of his in England during his late teens. He had not, however, learned much about repairing equipment.

Farm equipment is interesting stuff—it breaks while sitting in the barn doing nothing. It may all have been working splendidly when put away the previous fall but, come spring, the minute each implement is brought out, greased and confronted with the prospect of an honest day's work, it breaks. For the first year or two, Jeremy seemed to spend less time making hay than he did running for advice to the Sharers— our farming neighbors who owned everything around us and as far as the eye could see—and then running twenty miles to the dealer for parts and twenty miles back again.

There was no doubt in anyone's mind that Jeremy's growing proficiency in the operation of the various gadgets had much to do with the more consistent functioning of those gadgets but, nonetheless, it was quite amazing how, among many other such perversities, the tractor ceased getting stuck in two gears once he got the hang of curing the problem in two minutes or less.

One repair I shall not forget. I was seven and a half months pregnant with Justin at the time Jeremy decided the knife in the baler had to be sharpened. He had been warned by Walter, the patriarch of the Sharer family, that getting the knife back in was a real pain in the neck. "You know that little roller you had to take off the plunger before you could get it out? Well—wait till you try to get it back on. You'll lose your religion." To give my husband his due, he did try. After a while, though, a sound I dreaded at such times came wafting up to the house. "Beeeeeeeed! I need you!"

It seemed that the only way to get the offending roller back in was for one person to lie on top of the bale chamber and reach blindly into the innards clutching the roller and its bolt, while someone else got down underneath the whole business and fiddled, equally blindly, with the nut and lock washer. I appreciated the fact that Jeremy's arms would have to be eleven feet long to accomplish this feat on his own, but I was not just pregnant—I was enormously pregnant. Lying facedown on the bale chamber was out of the question, so underneath on my back I would have to go.

With two of us doing it, it did not take long to replace the roller.

How, therefore, had I grown bigger while under the baler? It had not taken much effort to stuff me under there in the first place, so why was I stuck? My husband thought I was kidding at first, but my wails of anguish quickly convinced him otherwise. After considering an assortment of unacceptable alternatives, he got the giggles. "There's only a month and a half to wait. When you go into labor, let me know and I'll call Doc Pete."

We finally got me out by my making myself as thin as possible, no small task in the circumstances, and Jeremy taking me by the ankles and pulling for all he was worth. A dirt road ran right through the middle of our farm and, needless to say, Walter Sharer passed by in his pickup just in time to see both of us howling with laughter as I popped out from under the baler and Jeremy fell on his backside while still clutching my ankles.

As the haying was principally Jeremy's concern, the vegetable garden was mine. Jeremy did most of the picking, cutting, digging and pulling when things were ready for harvest, but the rototilling, planting and cultivating were up to me. The garden itself measured a hundred by sixty feet and was surrounded by a decorative, two-panel oak fence. The Sharers had their own sawmill on their farm and my husband, being English, insisted on building everything out of oak. The Sharers did not mind what we built things out of—they charged the same price regardless of the kind of wood it was—but they were distinctly unnerved when we put a fence around a vegetable garden. I mean, who puts fences around things unless they want to keep one thing in or another thing out?

The produce which we so zealously fenced in, obviously to prevent its escape, was all-encompassing. By fall I had made blueberry jam, thirty-six quarts of spaghetti sauce, pickled beets and, from produce bought elsewhere, a year's supply of marmalade and applesauce. I had also frozen sixty to eighty pounds of French-cut green beans and placed in the cellar enough green tomatoes and squash to last almost until Christmas, and enough onions to last until spring. The harvested herbs hung in great bunches from the kitchen rafters to dry and provided not only the blessing of fresh herbs for cooking but also the most marvelous aromas in the kitchen.

The vegetable garden was my pride and joy and at Christmastime I had enough pickled beets and jars of sage, thyme and savory to be able to include them in my baskets of home-baked goods for friends and neighbors. Another thing I waxed enthusiastic about for a couple of years was grapevine wreaths. Jeremy took the pickup truck and pulled huge quantities of wild grapevines out of the trees in the woods and brought them back for me to weave into wreaths. I went on making them until there was absolutely no one left to whom I could give one. I even mailed them all over the country as Christmas remembrances.

Firewood was Jeremy's department. We used five cords each winter between the big stove in the kitchen and the glass-fronted insert in the living room fireplace. As soon as the weather turned cold enough to make cutting firewood enjoyable, Jeremy cut, split, trucked and stacked until the whole supply for the following year was in the barn. All he cut was oak and it was amazing how much heat was generated by so little wood. By being stacked inside the metal-roofed barn for a year before being used, the wood was essentially kiln dried and converted all of its energy into heat when burned. Green wood consumes a great deal of its energy just in burning and thus produces less heat.

Deer season was also Jeremy's responsibility. The Monday after Thanksgiving is First Buck Day and a statewide holiday in Pennsylvania. The first year we were there, my husband claimed that the deer were much too beautiful to be killed and refused to have any part of it. I loved venison, though, and since Jeremy's birthday fell right at the beginning of deer season, the following year I gave him a deer rifle as a birthday present. He considered it very sneaky but more or less graciously sallied forth to do his duty and bring home food for his family.

By 1983 Jeremy had become thoroughly proficient in the harvesting of "native beef" and had long since learned to stay out of the woods for the first few days of the season. There were, of course, countless locals who were out at dawn on First Buck Day who knew what they were doing but, for every one of the hunters who knew what he was doing, there were scores of crazies who fired their rifles at anything that moved and lots of things that did not. The Sharers lost a Holstein cow one deer season, and our vet, Doc Sullivan, lost a pair of his pedigreed sheep.

The stories were almost as numerous as the hunters. My favorite concerned the local farmer who, every year, placed on his hilltop a life-sized plywood cutout painted to resemble a deer. He loved to watch people shooting madly away at it, on his posted land, and then becoming enraged when they finally realized the hoax, usually a box or so of ammunition the poorer. He counted the bullet holes in his creation at the end of every year.

The out-of-towners were the worst menaces, and the worst of the worst always seemed to be from New Jersey. Despite all the laws, Jerseyites deemed it their inalienable right to go wherever they wanted, posted or not, and fire their weapons out of the windows of moving vehicles while on their way there. We kept our horses in the barn for the entire season lest they find their way to New Jersey as trophies across the fender of some idiot's car.

Our land was posted, as was the land of our neighbors, but the dirt road was a public right-of-way. One day I heard a car skid to a stop almost directly in front of the house. When I looked out of the window to see what was going on, a Jerseyite was merrily drawing a beed on Zelda, my pet goat, who was innocently munching on a rhododendron next to the vegetable garden. When I ran out of the house screaming that the land was posted, that it was illegal to have a loaded weapon on a road and that he was aiming at my goat, he became completely irate and shouted obscenities at me. I ran back into the house with the crazy idea of fetching a shotgun. Fortunately, the sportsman departed, amid squealing tires and a cloud of dust, before I had to decide what I was going to do with the gun, once in hand.

I am a romantic, and a white Christmas had always been one of the great joys in my life. Pennsylvania changed that. I became more than happy to swap a white Christmas for a long, drawn-out fall. This year, which would turn out to be our last on the farm, I got my wish and the weather did not turn nasty until January. As we entered the new year, though, winter arrived with an arctic blast and fierce snows. The horses were driven into their barn, the cats into the haystacks and us to the comfort of the wood stove in the kitchen.

Our routine changed abruptly. The kitchen stove, a handsome old Stanley Airtight #4 made in Vermont in 1845, became the social center of our lives. Going out of doors became a five-minute process of dressing to avoid frostbite, and I spent every snowy or icy day worrying about the safety of the school bus on our tortuous dirt roads. Our bus never had an accident, despite some days when the roads were so bad that I felt the buses had no business being out at all and kept Justin home, but it seemed that at least once a week there was television coverage of a school bus, somewhere in the state, lying on its side in a ditch.

A big storm was predicted for January 19, with the 11:00 P.M. news forecasting at least twelve inches of snow. When my alarm went off at 6:00 A.M., I pried myself out from under our cozy, down-filled quilt, grabbed my clothes and fleece-lined moccasins and hurried downstairs to the warmth of the wood stove. I switched on the lights and the early TV news.

If the storm was going to be a bad one, school cancellations would be announced.

As I pulled on my jeans and ski sweater and waited for the kettle to boil, I heard them saying that the storm would not arrive until evening. I stuffed two great oak logs into the stove, climbed over our enormous Great Dane, Scoobydum, to check the damper and draft settings, then sat down with my coffee to watch the first light through the angle bay window filled with lush green plants to remind me of summer. The air was clear, although a classic snowy gray, and the thermometer outside the window read eighteen degrees.

I woke Justin at 6:30 and he made his usual mad dash to the warmth of the kitchen. He asked hopefully about the snowstorm and was disappointed to learn that school had not been canceled. He brightened at the thought that it was a virtual certainty for the next day. We wondered if Ashley, back at boarding school after a three-week Christmas vacation, was also about to be buried in snow. He was crazy about skiing and worried constantly about the slopes being sufficiently covered.

Bus time rolled around and I bundled us up in our winter gear and began our winding trek to the road. Our house was set on a slope and we had to contrive seemingly senseless routes to get down to the road in one piece, searching out the crunchiest and least icy spots to place our feet. There was usually solid ice everywhere, except near trees or shrubs where the wind caused the slushy, melting stuff to ripple when it froze again. More often than not, when we had any amount of snow, we immediately had a warm day or two to create an horizon-to-horizon skating rink when the temperature dropped again.

Naturally, as soon as there was solid ice everywhere, we would have another snowfall. That was when we began the game of finding footholds to get down to the road. There were times when the only way down was to slide on one's bottom but, fortunately, that did not happen too often.

On that particular day we arrived without mishap and I told Justin to stand inside the barn doors, out of the biting wind, while I watched for the bus. A dozen or so cats of assorted colors and sizes, knowing that breakfast was at hand, came tumbling out of their hiding places to greet us. Justin cuddled Orlando, a huge orange-marmalade tom who was king of the barn. In a few minutes the bus lurched down the ice-rutted road, tire chains clanking their winter rythm, and ground to a faltering stop in front of me.

"Good morning, Dick," I called out as Justin climbed aboard.

"Morning," he replied. "Looks like a good one coming. When d'you think it'll hit?"

"They say evening, but it looks like any minute to me. It might hold off, though."

"Might," he said, looking far from convinced. He closed the door while grimacing and shaking his head.

I stomped my feet with the cold and waved as the bus wended its way along the dirt road and up the steep slope onto the hardtop. As I turned, cats in procession behind me, and found my way around the end of the barn to the lower level and the horses, I asked the Fates to bring my little boy safely home again on yet another worrisome winter day.

The horses, with their sweet warm breath making steam in the morning air, greeted me with nickers and foot stomping from the open center aisle of the barn.

"Hi, guys," I called. The shovel was leaning against the trough as always, and they picked their way carefully toward me as I chipped and bashed at the ice covering their water. When I had made a big enough hole, I hugged their warm silky necks as they took turns drinking. The pecking order never varied: first Ashley's enormously muscled Paint, then Jeremy's Quarterhorse, then Chocolate, finally Pasha, my Arabian. They stood around, noses dripping from their morning guzzle, while I put hay into the racks. Then they began to nip and kick at each other, jockeying for the choicest position. There was plenty of room for all of them at the racks, but they had to go through this morning ritual of proving who the boss was.

After a few more pats and cuddles I went into the barn to feed the cats and shovel out the aisle. As soon as the cat food bag rattled inside the feed bin, more cats came scampering out of every nook and cranny imaginable. In winter the mice went into deep hiding and the cats were hard-pressed to find any natural food. One needed lots of cats during the warm months to keep the rodents under control, so one had to feed them during the winter. I loved to watch their feeding frenzy and I stroked a few favorites before topping up the water dish which sat on an electric warming pan to keep it from freezing.

I left the stable and carefully inched my way across to the old barn and the rest of the animals. A few flakes of snow were swirling in the frigid air and the sky was decidedly darker. It was beginning to look like the weatherman would be wrong again. Drat! Justin was almost at school by this time but he still had to get home that afternoon. I wished the weatherman could be more accurate.

I yanked the sticky old door open and walked inside to my cages of French Lop rabbits, chickens, ducks and more cats. We no longer had the sheep and goat. Marauding dogs had taken the heart out of us with respect to the sheep, and we had become thoroughly fed up with Zelda eating all our shrubbery and had given her away. We had also raised pigs, but they were now butchered and in the freezer.

I fed the cats first, then the rabbits. The latter had all been bred for an Easter bunny crop and they, along with our incubated peeps and ducklings, were our greatest delight as harbingers of spring. When I finished with all the feed dishes, I took care of the assorted water containers and headed for the door.

I emerged at about 8:30 into what was clearly the beginning of a "snow event," as our local forecaster liked to describe a blizzard. The snow had settled into a steady fall and there was no longer any doubt that the storm was twelve hours ahead of schedule. I scrambled and slipped my way back to the house, appreciating the sight of the smoke swirling aloft from the kitchen chimney and the warmth it heralded.

As I was removing the last of my outer clothing and rubbing my hands over the stove—gloves were never enough when it was this cold—Jeremy emerged from the den, where he was editing, and rewriting where necessary, my work of the day before. "Somebody called from the Towanda Jaycees, or something like that. They wanted to know whether anyone would be in all day since they're delivering certificate books. I said by the look of it we might not get out until spring at the earliest, so deliver away if they could. What's the book they're delivering, anyway?"

I reminded him that he knew all about it, that it was a

book of discount certificates for local stores and restaurants, sponsored by the Junior Chamber of Commerce, and that we had agreed to pay them twenty dollars for the book on the basis of his having computed that we would break even at Burger King and Dunkin Donuts alone. Jeremy returned to the den and Scooby mustered enough energy to raise his massive head from the rug beside the stove and thump his tail twice. I gave him a pat and sat down in my favorite recliner, artfully placed between the angle bay window and the stove, and began to focus my mind on the day's writing.

CHAPTER

By 1:30 that afternoon it was apparent that this was not just a blizzard, it was a major one. There was already a six-inch accumulation and it was snowing so heavily that visibility was down to almost nothing. Earlier in the day Jeremy had gone out and replenished the path of wood ash on top of the ice, leading from the kitchen door around the back of the house and down the edge of the driveway. As long as we remembered where the trail of ash was located, it afforded us the chance of getting back and forth without breaking our necks.

I was, as usual, worried sick about Justin getting home from school safely. Jeremy, as usual, reassured me every half hour or so that the bus had chains and was bigger than anything it might bump into; that it was a much worse risk to fetch Justin in our car, even if we did have four-wheel drive.

I had long since dismissed the idea of our coupon book being delivered when I heard what sounded like a car in the driveway. I went to look out of the living room window and there, indeed, was a car. By the tire tracks I could see that it had made it about halfway up before losing its traction, turning sideways and sliding almost all the way back down to the dirt road. The driver was sitting motionless, evidently waiting for his nerves to settle down after his introduction to our snow-covered glacier.

When he opened the door of his car and it became obvious that he was going to soldier on regardless of the hazards involved, I went to the front steps and shouted into the wind, "Work your way carefully to the right edge of the drive. There's a path of ash covering the ice. It'll get you to the kitchen door." He waved an acknowledgment and I ran through the house and around to the kitchen in time to usher in a harried but smiling man. He was round, dark-haired and in his midforties, covered with snow and wet to the ankles. Even his mustache had tiny icicles hanging from it. I commented on his lack of boots on a day like this—he was wearing city shoes—and he explained that he was from West Virginia and had not brought any with him. He introduced himself as Serafino Fazio and said that he was delivering the coupon books.

"Come over to the stove," I said. "We'll hang up your wet things and you can get warm."

"Thanks," he said, "I'm freezing." He took off his topcoat and crossed the kitchen to Stanley Airtight #4. I took his coat and he rubbed his hands over the stove before bending to remove his snow-filled shoes. "I thought I was done for when the car started sliding down the hill. It felt like it was never going to stop."

"I know the feeling all too well," I sympathized. "The storm's going to get worse but a few minutes won't make much difference. How about some hot coffee? Do you like zucchini bread? It'll only take a few minutes to warm some up."

"That would be great," he replied enthusiastically, "so long as you're sure it's no trouble. With all the confusion, I didn't have time for lunch."

I was torn between advising him to get off our hill and back to the flat lands as soon as possible and our ever-present midwinter urge to virtually kidnap any passing stranger just for the sake of someone to talk to. Jeremy had heard our voices from the den, where he had been closeted all day working, and made the decision for me. He came into the kitchen, introduced himself and, reading my mind, said, "Why don't you fix Mr. Fazio some eggs or something, Sweetie? There's no hurry. If he got up the hill in this mess, he'll certainly be able to get down it again." Serafino thanked him but said that coffee and zucchini bread would be fine.

We sat down on the comfortable, leather-covered bar stools at the counter and waited for the kettle to boil and the zucchini bread, which I made in bulk during the summer and stored in the freezer, to warm up.

"What's the confusion you mentioned?" Jeremy asked.

"My delivery boy's car broke down in Camptown," Serafino explained.

"I'm supposed to be on the phones coordinating everything, but the books have to be delivered. Fortunately I've only got a few left and I don't think I've got to climb any more mountains to deliver them."

I could see that expression on my husband's face which signified interest in someone else's private business. He became very intense-looking and hung on their every word. For some reason I could never fathom, he was riveted by the specifics of any business he had never encountered before. "How does this coupon thing work?" he asked. "I know that we, the buyers of the coupon books, get discounts from restaurants, stores and what-have-you, but who benefits from all this? What do the merchants get out of it? What does the Chamber of Commerce get out of it? Do you organize it philanthropically or is it a profit-making business?"

Serafino explained at considerable length the nature of his business and was very charming about it. He did not seem in the least to resent my husband's inquisitiveness and the first time he mentioned being a born-again Christian, it barely registered in my subconscious. A few minutes later, however, Serafino again used the phrase and Jeremy was off and running. "What *is* a born-again Christian anyway? That's the second time you've mentioned it."

I slid off my stool and went to busy myself with the coffee and cake. With a blizzard outside and a holy roller for my husband to bait, this could turn out to be a long afternoon. If there was one thing Jeremy liked more than prying into other people's businesses, it was cornering holy rollers and arguing with them.

Being English, and having been educated in England, my

husband had, perforce, gone to church six times a week and twice on Sunday. He like to say that he had not graduated from school but had escaped from church. Both he and I were devout agnostics and considered religion to be for people who needed something to lean on. We only went to church for weddings, funerals and the odd christening and were happy to keep it that way.

"A born-again Christian," Serafino said, "is someone who's spiritually reborn in Jesus Christ and who commits his life to Him. If you accept Jesus as your personal Lord and Savior and believe that He is truly the Son of God and that He died on the cross for our sins and rose again, then you're born again."

"What happens after that?" Jeremy asked. "What do you have to do next?"

"Love Jesus, worship Him and follow His teachings, and love one another as brothers."

"But what church would I have to join?"

"You don't have to go to church. It's a personal relationship between you and Jesus."

"But whom do I have to give money to?"

"You don't."

Jeremy was patently disconcerted. His standard opening salvos had splashed harmlessly short of the mark and Serafino was smiling encouragingly at him, obviously wanting him to go on asking questions. He did. "If you don't go to church and you don't give money to anyone, what kind of religion is it? What do you call it?"

"It isn't a religion. It's faith. There are born-again Baptists, born-again Catholics, and born-again Jews. Being born again is a matter of faith. Religion is of man . . . faith is of God."

There went the next of Jeremy's and my pet theses: that most of the wars ever fought had been caused by, or at least involved, religion.

"You mean you never go to church and never contribute money to anyone and that's okay with Jesus?"

"I didn't say I didn't go to church. I said you didn't have to go to church if you didn't want to. If you were born again, though, you'd find you wanted to go to church to share the company of other Christians, to fellowship with them. I also tithe. The Bible says that whatsoever you give will be returned to you a hundredfold, and it's certainly been true for me. That doesn't mean you have to do it, though. You'll still go to heaven. You just won't necessarily be rewarded financially during this life."

I had never met anyone like Serafino before. He radiated the sincerity of his words and his answers to Jeremy's questions were direct and without guile. He had an aura of kindness and warmth. This was not a man doing penance or serving a novitiate by banging on doors and handing out tracts. This was a man who really cared. The more he talked, the more intrigued I found myself. My mother had never in her life mentioned God or Jesus Christ except as swearwords, and I had married an agnostic when I was sixteen.

I'd had little or no exposure to matters religious and what little there had been seemed to have been restricted to fanatics, clergymen drumming up business for the biggest business of them all, organized religion, or holy rollers. My greatest exposure had been to the latter since it was they who knocked at my door at the most inconvenient of times and bored me to death with self-serving mumbo jumbo and biblical quotes which meant nothing to me. I had always tended to regard the Bible as a compendium of old wives' tales and fairy stories handed down from generation to generation.

I was convinced that this stranger had no personal ax to grind. With his straightforward answers and smiling confidence in his faith, he seemed to be sprinkling water on a seed that had lain dormant in me, awaiting just such an awakening. Jeremy was far from through, though, and before I could ask a question he took off on his favorite line of attack. "How do you account for the dinosaurs?"

I had seen people get bogged down in the most incomprehensible arguments with my husband over his wretched dinosaurs. He loved every minute of their discomfiture when they tried to explain why there were no dinosaurs on the ark but dinosaur bones all over the world or, alternatively, that no one had satisfactorily proved the dinosaurs to have actually existed at all. The argument generally wound up with Jeremy preaching evolution and the holy roller thrusting tracts at him and rushing off to more fertile fields.

Serafino was not the least disconcerted. He beamed at Jeremy and said, "I don't—but you're welcome to if you like."

"What I mean is," Jeremy persisted, unwilling to accept the lack of an argument, "how do you explain the fact that the Bible says the world began eight or ten thousand years ago, Adam and Eve and all that, while it's an incontrovertible scientific fact that the world has been around for hundreds of millions of years and the dinosaurs came and went a hundred million years ago?"

"Like I said," Serafino replied, almost apologetically, "I don't. I guess I've been too busy to think about dinosaurs. There are lots of things I take on faith. Dinosaurs will just have to be one of them." He brightened. "But if it will help you, it says in the Bible that a thousand years is as a day to God. There's an answer to every question somewhere in the Bible. If that one doesn't satisfy you about the dinosaurs, perhaps something else will. Why don't you read it and find out?"

My husband was left flat-footed and silent. I finally got my chance to ask about something that had piqued my curiosity for years. We had seen Ernest Angley on television a couple of times, mostly by accident while changing channels, and had wondered how the healing of so many people could be a fraud. It did not seem possible that hundreds and thousands of people could be party to such a great pretense without the whole world learning that it was a hoax. Both Jeremy and I had watched in total amazement while children had apparently been healed of congenital deafness and blindness, and people of all ages of everything from withered limbs to cancer. We had found it difficult to believe our eyes, but at least equally as difficult to believe that it was a hoax.

While I was serving the coffee and zucchini bread, I said to Serafino, "There's something I've always wondered about. What's the story behind faith healing? We've seen a guy called Ernest Angley on television once or twice. Does he really cure people of all those things? Can he really cause a cripple who's been confined to a wheelchair for years to get up and walk out of the church? Or is it just mental suggestion, some form of hypnosis?"

"Oh, no,' said Serafino, "it's no hypnosis. Healing is very real. Jesus healed when He was a man on earth and He still heals today. His healing touch comes through prayer or the laying on of hands by someone like Rev. Angley. The healing comes from God, not His servants. Ernest Angley, Oral Roberts and others have a special anointing from God to heal the sick. It's always been God's desire that His children enjoy perfect health."

"Then why is there so much sickness?" I asked.

"Sin. You may think it sounds corny—most non-Christians do—but that's the reason. Man's own sin allows Satan to have his way and deceive man and rob him of all that's good."

"Then why doesn't God stop it, or Jesus for that matter, if He loves us so much?"

"Because He gave us free will. God didn't want robots. He wants us to love and obey Him because we want to. He's there all the time but we have to seek Him out. He won't force His will on us."

"But that doesn't seem fair," I complained, "and why, if God is love, does He permit so much hate and prejudice and killing to be carried out in His name? Look at Ireland! I'll bet every one of those people thinks he's a good Christian. How can he be a Christian and go around killing people just because they're Protestants instead of Catholics? And how could the Protestants have been so prejudiced and treated the Catholics so badly just because they were a minority in Northern Ireland? It's been going on since the beginning of time. If God loves us and wants us to love Him, why doesn't He just step up and make it simpler for us? Put in an appearance, work a few miracles to prove His credentials and then explain the rules and give us a chance to understand what it's all about?"

"You've asked two questions. The answer to the first is Satan again, twisting the things of God to make them look false. The people in Ireland have religion, yes, but not Jesus. They don't follow Jesus' teachings. If you don't exert every fiber of your being to walk in the path set by Jesus, you're a Christian in name only. As I said before, religion is of man . . . faith, Jesus, is of God. Your second question is easy: God *did* appear *and* work miracles *and* explain the rules, as you put it. When he despaired of His chosen people walking in righteousness as He had commanded them, He sent His Son to be a witness to us. The burden is now on us to accept that

Jesus was, is and always will be the Son of God. Jesus bore all manner of sickness, disease and infirmity while He hung on the cross, to give us the gift of health, and then He died to give us everlasting life. From the time of Jesus Christ all people were welcome into God's kingdom, not just the chosen people who had so bitterly disappointed Him. But we can only enter the kingdom through Jesus. Jesus said, 'No man cometh unto the Father, but by me.' Now it's up to us to accept Jesus on faith and inherit the kingdom of heaven, or reject Him and be condemned to hell. It's very simple."

"But that doesn't seem fair," I said again. "What about all the people who worship God in their own way? Lots of them lead blemishless lives and truly believe in some other manifestation of God. Just because they were brought up to believe that Muhammad or Buddha or whatever was the way to go, the true faith, doesn't seem sufficient grounds to condemn them to hell when in all other respects they follow Jesus' teachings without even knowing that's what they're doing. What about them? Don't they deserve consideration on the basis of never even having heard of Jesus Christ?"

"I didn't decide this, God did. The Bible says that sometime prior to the day of judgment everyone will have the chance to hear about Jesus and it will then be up to that individual to decide whether or not to accept Jesus as his Savior. If he doesn't, Satan has him. We either serve Satan or we serve God."

"I'm not a believer and I certainly don't serve Satan. I lead a pretty good, honest life and am very happy in my marriage and with my children. How can you say I serve Satan?"

"I don't say it. God does. I don't want to impose anything on you but you asked. Good and evil are the alternatives. If you don't choose good, you're serving evil by omission."

"What about children, though?" Jeremy asked. "If their parents kept them in the dark, how could the children be blamed?"

"Up to the age of accountability, which most people consider to be around twelve years old, they're considered innocent. After that they're accountable."

"You mean my children could go to hell because I'm an agnostic?" To my astonishment, Jeremy actually looked worried.

"That's right," Serafino replied, "but not exactly because

you're an agnostic. If you were responsible for them not accepting Jesus, then it would be your fault, yes."

"I don't mean to be rude," Jeremy said, "but doesn't every religion on earth believe that its tenets are the only true ones? They all sound more or less equally megalomaniacal, if you ask me, including yours. What on earth convinced you that your religion, or faith if you will, was different, the only true one? I've no doubt the Catholics believe in their interpretation just as strongly as you do in yours, not to mention the Protestants in all their diversity, and all the freaks with their cults. Why are you so sure that you're right? If you've guessed wrong, you know, you might wind up in hell."

Serafino looked like the cat who had swallowed the canary, perhaps because he was causing both my husband and me to think. He said, "I don't know much about denominations and less about cults. The answers to all questions lie in the Bible. We, the born-again Christians, believe in the full Gospel: the Old Testament, the New Testament, Revelation, every word of it. We don't accept any interpretations, whatever the source, only the word of God as reported in the Bible. God's word cannot be changed—He said it Himself—and we accept that as the basis of our faith."

The conversation went on and on, sometimes with me asking questions and sometimes Jeremy. The questions themselves were no longer challenging. Both of us, without yet realizing it, were sincerely seeking understanding. When Justin's bus arrived home at 4:30, we were all startled to discover how late it was. We had not even moved from the swivel chairs. Serafino put a good face on it but was patently alarmed at the prospect of negotiating our hill in the dark with a snow accumulation which, we found on checking outside the kitchen door, was nearing nine inches.

He bundled himself up and I wrote down his phone number in Towanda so that I could call his wife, Joan, to let her know that he was alive and well and on his way to deliver the last few books before returning to the motel. Jeremy went out with him to make sure he made it to the hardtop in one piece. More than once we had used our four-wheel drive pickup and a chain to get people out of our dirt road during snowstorms. Serafino did make it. Jeremy watched his taillights disappear into the blizzard and then went down to the barns to do evening chores.

Later that night, after Justin had gone to bed, we talked. We had both been affected, though in different ways, by Serafino's no-nonsense, direct answers to all our questions. I had even gone to the bookcase to search for the Bible which Ophelia, an old housekeeper of my mother's, had given me for a birthday present years ago. It was still there, on a top shelf, as clean and unhandled as the day she had given it to me. There, too, was the inscription: May 1, 1960.

I felt a strong urge from deep within me to read the New Testament, to try to understand what it was that so moved people like Serafino to such strong conviction. Jeremy felt no such curiosity, but he was deeply troubled at the idea that he was presuming to deny his children the opportunity to make their own decisions.

By the middle of the night we had agreed to call Serafino the next morning to see whether he and his wife would like to come for dinner and talk more about their faith. As my husband and I had gone on discussing the matter, all sorts of questions had popped into our minds and we were eager to find what the answers might be.

We did call them and they did come for dinner. The roads had been plowed early in the day, much to Serafino's relief, and his book deliveries were more or less on schedule. His trip back to Towanda the evening before had been somewhat hair-raising, but he made light of it.

Dinner was a delight. Justin was enormously taken with Serafino and Joan and was most reluctant to go to bed on time. It was quite obvious that he found the idea of a Creator not only acceptable but perfectly logical. When I tucked him in at 9:30, an hour late, he said, "I want to hear more about Jesus and God, Mummy. They have to be real. Where would everything have come from if God hadn't made it in the first place?" I promised to tell him about everything he had missed before he left for school the next morning.

Conversation continued into the small hours. I asked about the concept of the Trinity and Joan explained that it was one of the greatest of all God's mysteries and that one could not really begin to grasp its truth until one felt the presence of the Holy Spirit within one's being. "The Three are One and yet

They are separate. We may never fully understand until we're in heaven."

"Do you really believe in heaven?" I asked.

"Of course," said Serafino. "Don't you?"

"No. To me, heaven and hell are here on earth," I said. "We make our own heavens and hells by the way we live."

"That's true in an earthly sense," said Joan, "but heaven and hell are very real in a Biblical sense. Read the Bible and you'll see."

"Oh, good grief," Jeremy protested. "They made me read the Bible throughout my school life. I didn't get a darned thing out of it except being bored to tears and totally confused. It's nothing but a mass of contradictions."

"What sort of contradictions?" asked Serafino.

"I guess the most commonly mentioned one would be an eye for an eye versus turn the other cheek."

"That's easy," said Joan. "In the Old Testament, God's covenant was with the Jews alone. All His laws and commandments presupposed that the Jews would keep their covenant with God. When they didn't, and God sent His Son as salvation for the Gentiles as well as the Jews, He made a new covenant with all mankind based on love. That's why Jesus said, 'Ye have heard that it hath been said, an eye for an eye, and a tooth for a tooth: but I say unto you that ye resist not evil, but whomsoever shall smite thee on thy right cheek, turn to him the other also.' That's an easy one because Jesus, Himself, answered it directly.

"Most of the so-called contradictions are like that, though; the difference between the old covenant and the new one. The confusion comes about because most people don't read their Bibles. They just talk about the contradictions without studying the historical facts. It's an easy way to justify their lack of faith."

I broached a problem that had begun to bother me a great deal. "What you seem to be saying is that there's no way of understanding any of this without reading the Bible, preferably from cover to cover, at the earliest possible moment. It takes me weeks just to read an ordinary novel. I'd never be able to chew my way clear through the Bible. I won't live long enough."

"Then just read the New Testament," suggested Serafino.

"You could leave the Old Testament until you were in the mood for it."

"You don't have to read the Bible at all to find salvation," Joan hastily interjected. "Plenty of people have accepted Jesus on faith alone. They felt an emptiness within themselves and realized that only an acceptance of God could fill it. Haven't you ever felt that something was missing in your life? That no matter how well things were going, there didn't seem to be a purpose to it all?"

"There have been moments," I admitted, "but I write them off as those mild depressions we all seem to get from time to time."

"They're not depressions in the way you think. It's the lack of fulfillment inside anyone who doesn't have Jesus. Without Jesus and the promise of eternal life, what is there? A few years on this earth and then oblivion? That's not what it's all about. There's a void within us and we must strive to fill it, to find the truth. Money won't do it. Nor will all the other things lost souls turn to: drink, drugs, promiscuity and all the rest of it. The only thing to fill that void is faith, the certain knowledge that there is life after death and that God is with us all the time, that God is watching us and only waiting for us to ask His help with our problems here on earth."

I had enough to think about for the time being. Something was tugging at me but I needed time to myself. I wanted to read a little of my Bible, to see if it spoke to me. I was worried about Jeremy. I could not imagine what it would be like if I accepted Jesus and he didn't. In all the years we had been married I had only known my husband to do one thing emotionally: marry me. This was all too sudden. I wished it were summer so that I could be alone in the woods for a while with my horse.

True to form, although the rest of us had moved on to the discussion of salvation, Jeremy was still worrying away at things in the Old Testament that bothered him. "Doesn't it seem unfair to you," he was asking, "that God ordered Abraham to sacrifice his only son? I know God promised Abraham another son to replace Isaac, but that's hardly the same thing, is it? And, if God hadn't let him off the hook at the last moment, do you really believe Abraham would have gone through with it? I don't think *I* could have."

"Ah," said Serafino, "but you missed the point. It was a test of Abraham's faith. Abraham knew that God wouldn't take his son from him. That's why he went so cheerfully to the mountaintop as God commanded. He knew that God wouldn't do such a thing. We're tested today—constantly—but never beyond our ability to endure. Don't for a moment think that being a Christian is a nonstop picnic. The stronger your faith, the more Satan gets after you. The thing is, you can bind Satan's power in the name of Jesus. You can't beat him on your own, but you can stop him dead in his tracks with God's help."

The questions and answers continued for a long time without my further participation. I heard some of the conversation but, for most of the time, my mind was wandering in fields of its own. When I returned to a full awareness of what was going on, Jeremy and Joan were in deep discussion of God's all-knowingness on the one hand, and His disgust with the Jews every time they let Him down on the other. "How," Jeremy was asking, "could God waste His time getting angry with the Jews whenever they double-crossed Him, when He knew all along that they were going to do it? It doesn't make sense. Either God knows everything in advance, wrote the script, as it were, or He doesn't. And, if He doesn't, how was everything prophesied in advance? If you want to discuss contradictions, how's that for one?"

I caught a little of the ensuing debate, but then my mind wandered off again. There was little doubt that Joan was right regarding the question of depressions versus voids. Until this moment, I had never given any thought to the matter. It had never occurred to me that those mild depressions might be a sense of something lacking in life. The trouble was, I was loath to come right out and admit it to myself. I had been so confident for so many years that I had the best of everything, it was sort of like confessing a huge error of judgment.

I suddenly became aware that the Fazios had dragged my husband out of the Old Testament and into the New, all the way to Revelation, in fact. I forced myself to pay attention as a way of staving off my inner turmoil. Serafino was saying, "All Christians will be caught up in the Rapture when Christ comes to earth again in the end time. All sorts of horrible things will happen on earth while the Christians are up in the clouds with Jesus. Then, when it's all over, we'll be set down again for a thousand years of perfect peace. If you don't read anything else, at least read Revelation. It's John's revelation from God of what will happen on earth at the time of Armageddon. If you can understand it, it'll scare the socks off you."

By the time we all realized that it was three in the morning, I had agreed to read John's Gospel since it is the most straightforward and the simplest for a neophyte to understand. It is also the Gospel that contains the passage about Nicodemus and being born again. Jeremy had agreed to nothing more than listening to me if I insisted on telling him about it. Serafino and Joan thanked us for a lovely evening and repaired to their motel in Towanda. Jeremy and I went to bed after reflecting upon what a novel experience the evening had been and what delightful people the Fazios were.

The next morning Joan rang to thank me again for dinner and to invite us to join them the following night for dinner at a restaurant. "Just because we enjoy your company so much," she hastened to add, "not so we can go on witnessing to you." I laughed as I thanked her and, without even consulting Jeremy, said that we would be happy to join them.

Dinner was just as pleasant, and the Fazios just as great a delight to be with, as the first time. Neither Serafino nor Joan brought up the subject of God or the Bible. I did. And again the conversation went on for hours.

There was something different about the Fazios, something utterly compelling. Joan was a bit of a Bible scholar and prone to quoting Scripture to make her points. Nonetheless, she was interesting. I never felt that she was lecturing at me. Joan was the theologian while Serafino was the all-around enthusiast. It was nigh unto impossible not to be caught up in their faith. Jeremy was still, of course, mumbling about obscure points of law, lore or what have you, but even his interest was obviously piqued.

Dinner ended with my asking one more question. "How do you know when you're born again? What happens? Do you see Jesus, or some bright light, or what?"

"It's different for everyone," Serafino replied. "I was slain in the Spirit. That means the Holy Ghost came upon me and I collapsed with the experience. When I came to, I knew Jesus and felt cleansed. I knew my life would never be the same again. Joan had a similar experience, but a lot of people don't. Some pray and ask Jesus to come into their lives and their hearts. One day they feel His presence and know they're saved. It happens in all sorts of ways, but the key thing is you must want Jesus. You must want to commit your life to Him and be willing to strive to walk in His footsteps. You must read the Bible and know what God promises and what He expects from His children." He paused, then, "Have you read John yet?"

"Yes, I have. Now I'm reading Matthew. I'm not sure I'll ever make it through the Old Testament, but who knows? Maybe I'll feel inspired to try one day."

"That's great," said Serafino with a big grin. "If you keep telling Jeremy about it, perhaps he'll start reading it too."

Two days later I had an experience that had to be shared with the Fazios. I asked Jeremy if it would be alright if we invited them for dinner again. To my delight, he not only agreed but was enthusiastic about it. I called and invited them for the next evening, but they had a prior commitment and could not make it until two days hence, January 25. I was not sure whether I could keep my excitement bottled up for that long without telling my husband. Even though we had never kept secrets from one another, this was one time when I wanted to share my news with others at the same time as Jeremy.

I managed to keep my cool for two whole days. There were times when I was convinced that Jeremy must be able to sense a difference in me but, if he did, he did not say anything about it. Finally, it was time for the Fazios to arrive and I fidgeted nervously until I heard their car. Fortunately for me, the first thing Serafino said after they had taken seats in the living room was, "How are you coming with your Bible reading?"

I almost exploded with excitement as I shared with them what I later learned was called my "testimony." "The Bible reading is going splendidly, but I've something to tell you: I've given my life to Jesus." Joan and Serafino, as one, all but shouted, "Praise God!" They looked ecstatic and both rose to give me big hugs. My husband looked startled. "What brought this about?" he asked.

I felt a warm, happy glow inside as I began to unfold my

story. "Well, I woke up the day before yesterday thinking about what I'd read so far in the Bible. I was thinking about Jesus and the fact that I was not only able to read the Bible, but was also getting all wrapped up in it. I'd devoted every spare minute since our last dinner together to reading the Gospels and found an awareness growing in me of the modern reality of Jesus. I believed every word I read.

"As you know, I began with John and then went back and started at Matthew. The more I read, the more Jesus became real to me. I was gradually seeing the world in a totally different way, a spiritual way, I suppose. I realized, beyond a shadow of a doubt, that we and the universe were created by a living God. I was certain that Jesus was His Son who had died on the cross for us.

"I was still reluctant to make a commitment, though. I liked my life. I treasured my marriage and my children. My friends were important to me. I didn't want any of that to change. We had a carpenter here once who'd become a born-again Christian, or so he said. He'd turned away from his family and his best friend because they weren't saved. There's no way I'd be willing to do that. I couldn't even consider it.

"Then there was Jeremy. If he didn't accept the Lord, what would it do to our marriage? I was drawn to the love of Jesus but there were so many questions. When I was with you," I said to Joan and Serafino, "you answered my questions and made it seem so simple and straightforward. You taught me about the love of Jesus and what God really expects and demands of Christians. But when I was alone, the fears and doubts set in.

"Then I remembered what you said about God recognizing us as individuals first of all and wanting us to go on using our individual abilities; that when the Bible says, 'If any man be in Christ, he is a new creature; old things are passed away; behold, all things become new,' it means that all *wrong* things are passed away, that God doesn't want you to throw away any good things; that God loves *all* people, not just the Christians, and that the difference in God's eyes between Christians and non-Christians will be shown at the day of judgment.

"So, inasmuch as God wanted me to love all men as my brothers, my friends would still be my friends and I would have all of God's family to add to them. You also said it would be inevitable that some of Jesus would rub off on them through me.

"When I woke up I could feel God tugging at my heart. The last thing you said to me, Serafino, was 'Trust in the Lord, He'll never let you down. God cannot fail. He loves you, so lean on Him and trust.' All those things were whirling in my head when I took Justin down to put him on the school bus.

"As the bus pulled away up the road and I waved to Justin, all the turmoil within me was suddenly stilled. A warm light surrounded me and I knew, I *knew*, I was in the presence of the Lord. I could almost feel the stirring of angels' wings. A great peace and joy filled my heart as I was wrapped in the Creator's love. 'Oh, yes, Lord' was all I could think. 'I love you. I *will* trust you. I give you my life. You are my Lord and Savior.'

"I don't know how long I stood there on the dirt road, but there wasn't a sound to distract me. Not a car went by. I worshipped and praised the Lord and thanked him for being so patient with me. I prayed for Jeremy to find Him too." I looked out of the corner of my eye at my husband, but he seemed totally bemused and did not return my glance.

"I felt ten feet tall with the strength of Samson. I floated through my barn chores and caressed each of the animals more than usual. They were more than horses, they were God's magnificent creations. Every silky hair and every puff of hay-sweetened breath on the frosty air was God's creation. The cats too, and all the other animals. I gleefully told them all about Jesus Christ—but they already knew. That day, and each day since, has been brighter. I feel stronger and better able to cope with anything that comes my way."

Joan and Serafino were in tears. They hugged me even harder than before and said how happy they were for me. Jeremy managed a withdrawn sort of smile and said that he was pleased too. It was my one cloud in an otherwise cloudless sky. How would I bear it if my husband, with whom I had been as one for twenty years, would not or could not accept salvation?

After dinner, and much discussion of the Bible in which Jeremy took little part, Serafino suggested that I watch the *700*

Club on television in the mornings while I was getting Justin ready for school. He also recommended modern versions of the Bible that would make comprehension a little easier. They were scheduled to return to West Virginia the following day, so I made a note not only of their address but also an assortment of phone numbers at which they might be reached. We had every intention of staying in touch with one another.

As they were preparing to leave, Serafino turned to Jeremy and said, "How about you? What would it take to convince you?"

"I don't know," my husband replied. "Perhaps I'll take a shot at reading the Bible again one of these days. To be perfectly honest, though, I don't think I'm a very likely candidate. I have to have everything logically laid out before I can accept it, and a lot of this doesn't make any sense."

"Haven't Joan and I been of any help at all? We don't pretend to know the answer to everything, but it's in the Bible somewhere. Like I said, all you have to do is look for it."

"That's all very well," Jeremy said, "but so much of it seems to be a matter of interpretation. A thousand years being as a day to God is fine, but it still doesn't add up to enough years to account for the dinosaurs."

"Why are you so worried about those darned dinosaurs?" Serafino exclaimed good-naturedly. "Of all the arguments for not accepting Jesus, I've never encountered anyone with a dinosaur fixation before. Some things just have to be taken on faith."

"You mean there comes a certain point where God says, 'I've done all the explaining I'm going to do. Now, put up or shut up'?" Serafino laughed and said he would not quite have put it that way himself, but essentially that was the gist of it.

"In that case," Jeremy said, "I'm in a bit of a bind. It's rather like the chicken and the egg, isn't it? One has to have faith in order to accept everything in the Bible, but one has to accept everything in the Bible in order to have faith."

"Don't worry," Serafino said confidently, "we'll pray for you. Something will happen to convince you." Jeremy looked thoughtful for a moment or so, then said, "There's one thing that would convince me—if Beed's back were healed."

My back had been getting progressively worse during the

last few years. It had started with one ruptured ligament which, although extremely painful, could be managed. But, as time passed, more and more of the short ligaments between the vertebrae weakened and ruptured. It had reached the point where I could render myself bedridden, in extreme pain for days, if I forgot to move carefully or bent forward too suddenly. I managed the gardening by doing it on my hands and knees. For the other chores and housework, and particularly riding, I had discovered ways to move my body differently to protect my back. Certain things, like stooping or reaching overhead, had to be avoided as much as possible. That Christmas I had put myself through a terrible bout of pain by reaching up for too long to hang pine roping on the ceiling beams in the house. Virtually everything I did was affected in one way or another and the occasions upon which I had to resort to long periods of reliance on painkillers and muscle relaxers were becoming too frequent by far. There was no treatment for my condition and no surgery could cure it. All I could do was be careful and try to rupture as few additional ligaments as possible. It was likely that by the time I became forty I would be a semi-invalid. Jeremy was aware that, no matter how hard I tried to hide it, I was very frightened.

Serafino did not know what Jeremy was referring to, so I explained. He expressed his sympathy at my plight, then turned to my husband. "Don't forget you said that. God works miracles every day." Jeremy smiled politely and promised to remember.

CHAPTER

3

IT IS A GREAT TRAGEDY THAT SO MANY MOTHERS, MINE AMONG them, love their children so much that they think they own them. They believe their love for their children transcends even the obligation to acknowledge that those children have rights and freedoms. They believe that nothing must be allowed to distract their children from total and undivided devotion to Mother, the only person in the world who truly loves them and unerringly knows what is best for them. Any husband or wife is unworthy and should be driven out like a cancer. The next generation of children is not being instructed properly in anything, and must be shown by Grandmother the error of their parents' ways. Jealousy, hatefulness and absolute absorption with self are all sanctified by this great love. It may not, under any circumstances, be questioned, let alone refused.

So, what does one do? This kind of mother does not accept the gentle hint, the polite request, or even the undisguised threat. This kind of mother throws a tantrum, storms out, marshals her resources—which are always formidable—and returns to the fray. Undaunted and unabashed, she will have her way at any cost.

I had become determined, many months earlier, to force my mother to listen to me for the first time in her life. Letters had done no good—if she did not like the first few words, she tore them up. Phone calls had done no good—if she did not like the words or the tone of my voice, she hung up. Face-to-face confrontation had done no good—the first few words of criticism had sent her wailing and crying to lock herself into another room.

My mother is Bette Davis. I went through years of pain and anguish before being able to put my finger on the root of my problems with her. Unfortunately, understanding the nature of the problem did not constitute a remedy for it. That is why I was writing a book. Once published, it would not go away. Mother would not be able to tear it up, hang it up or run away and wait for it to disappear. I was certain of one thing, and one thing only: she would have but two alternatives. She would probably disown me as a daughter, certainly at first, but there was the other alternative to hope for, at least eventually: that she would finally accept me and my family as we are.

My mother had spent most of my married life, almost twenty years at the time I started to write, trying to ruin my marriage in any way she could think of, no matter how devious. When she failed to come between Jeremy and me, she carried the battle to Justin, spanking him or threatening him whenever I turned my back. Ashley had made a movie with his grandmother a couple of years earlier, when he was almost twelve, and had learned to take care of himself. Justin was defenseless.

She had come to stay at our farm in the spring of 1983, had terrified Justin and done her best to make life miserable for all of us and, as a consequence, I had promised my family that it had happened once too often and that I would never again permit her to stay with us. Publication of my book would solve our problems in one way or another, but I could not tell Mother about it in advance. Far from solving anything, telling her in advance would only make matters worse.

She would become permanently hysterical, probably commit suicide a couple of times, then have a nervous breakdown. During her carryings-on I would be besieged with calls and letters from her lawyer/manager, Harold Schiff, containing everything from pleas to threats of lawsuits. The only remedy for that mess would be my promise not to publish the book after all. Mother would immediately forgive me my aberrant behavior and we would be right back to square one. She would announce that she was coming to visit and, within minutes of her arrival, would drive my husband out of his own home by being intolerably rude to him. Then, the moment I so much as took my eyes off Justin, she would be after him.

No, trying to cure the problem by telling her I was writing a book or showing her the manuscript in advance was not a viable concept. I would send her a copy at publication time. Then it would be too late for hysteria and all the rest of it to change the flow of events. There would be only two alternatives.

Back in November, Mother had called to let me know that she had rejected as "stupid" three scripts for the television series *Hotel*. I had assumed that she felt constrained to tell me about it as a consequence of my having been so strongly in favor of her doing the series in the first place. A couple of days later her secretary, Kathryn Sermak, had called late at night to discuss her personal problems. It seemed that Mother was being even more abusive toward Kathryn than ever, and Kathryn was not sure that she could take much more of it. She also told me that Mother had not even read the *Hotel* scripts before throwing them into the trash bin. Kathryn felt that I ought to tell Harold Schiff what was going on.

I really did not want to become involved in all this again. The writing of my book, the certainty that it would be published, was giving me a sense of release and freedom from my mother's oppressive presence that I had not felt since childhood. But, out of my ingrained sense of obligation and the inescapable fact that, despite everything, I would always love my mother, I rationalized that one call to the lawyer would not constitute getting involved.

I phoned him and reported what Kathryn had told me, not the personal stuff, just the part about not even reading the scripts. He as much as told me to mind my own business and pointed out that my mother knew better than I the quality of a script. I kicked myself mentally for making the call.

My conviction that Mother would never return to *Hotel* had come into being when I visited her at the Lombardy Hotel while she was recuperating from a stroke. She recounted to me a phone call she had made to Aaron Spelling, head of the company producing the series, in which she said, "I never did want to do your lousy show. Now I'm not up to it anymore— and don't let anybody tell you I am—you can take your show and shove it!" She laughed uproariously and then said, "I'll tell you one thing—Aaron Spelling knows who the fighter is now."

That last line, of course, is what led to my recollection of the day my mother had poured out her woes to me when I was a child, and my finally understanding what drove her. It seemed, however, that I was the only person who did not regard her call to Aaron Spelling as an empty threat.

Mother called me several more times during the ensuing weeks to issue *Hotel* script bulletins. Each one she received was either "boring," "absurd," "ludicrous," "completely un-realistic," or made her "look like a fool."

On January 29, Mother called yet again, this time to tell me that Harold had negotiated the termination of her contract to appear in *Hotel*. She went on to say, "Brother! I never wanted to do that piece of junk in the first place. It isn't *honest* to do things just for the money!", and "It's disgraceful how Ann Baxter's let herself go to pot. She's fat and looks old. She's wrecking the show. Brother! Aaron Spelling's really in a mess with *her*!"

I hung up the phone and stared off into space. My mother's typically warped and derisive view of all around her rang in my ears. Here she was, recovered from all her misfortunes and Harold hollering about money after the unbelivable ex-penses of months of private hospital rooms, round-the-clock nurses, doctors and therapists; and there was *Hotel*, $100,000 a day for seven days work per year and Aaron Spelling bend-ing over backwards to be accommodating: special scripts so that Mother could work sitting down, allowing two days for one day's work so that she would not overtire herself and so forth.

And not only that—not only had she walked off the series

for no other reason than to prove that she was a "fighter"—but, having done so, she then had to be derogatory about her replacement and bore everyone with her twisted views.

It had only been six days since I had been visited by the Holy Spirit and had accepted Jesus. Those six days had been of such peace, joy and tranquillity as I had never known. Even my concern regarding Jeremy finding salvation had been laid to rest by my faith that God would work a miracle in answer to the prayers of Joan, Serafino and myself.

Mother's phone call was such a jarring note that it threw me into total confusion. My reaction had been automatic, reflexive: anger at her childishness, frustration at her short-sighted self-destructiveness, resentment at the knowledge that it would only be a matter of time before I received a call from Harold asking me to intercede in some fashion and reminding me of my obligations.

I knew my reaction was all wrong. I knew that Jesus wanted me to love her and try to help and comfort her. I also knew that I was probably facing the greatest emotional struggle of my entire life. I had not yet learned that, in times such as these, one must lean fully on the Lord. All I was able to do, for the time being, was try to put my mother out of mind and resist the emotional release—which was seldom any release at all—of pouring out to my husband my resentment of my mother for constantly involving, or trying to involve, me in problems of her own making.

Kathryn quit but agreed to stay on until Mother found a housekeeper. Seemingly suitable applicants were hired in droves, every one of them to quit within a day or two due to Mother's abusive treatment of them. When Kathryn had had enough, and left without there being a housekeeper on the premises—there were still round-the-clock nurses—Harold called to try to inveigle me into going to California to help out for a couple of days. Knowing full well, from past experience, that the couple of days would be at least a few weeks and, if Mother had her way, the rest of my life, I refused point-blank. I was, as usual, reminded of the state of my mother's health, her fame, my obligations to her, her love for me, and all the other arguments that had in the past broken down my resolve to lead my own life and leave my mother to her own self-made misery and troubles. We had a heated and unpleasant exchange, but my refusal remained unshaken. I had, however, completely lost my self-control. I was not ashamed of my refusal to become, yet again, embroiled in my mother's machinations, but I was most definitely disappointed in the emotional mess these phone calls made of me.

I knew that I was wrong, but it was no use; there was nothing I could do about it, not this soon anyway. I could remind myself of the proper Christian attitude until I was blue in the face. I could tell myself over and over again what Jesus expected of me, but the minute that phone rang and Mother or Harold started on me, it all went out the window. It had gone on for too long to be cured this quickly. I would just have to pray, and keep on praying, that I would be able to rid myself of these lifelong negative emotions.

CHAPTER

4

EXCEPT FOR READING MY BIBLE EACH DAY AND GETTING UP HALF an hour earlier in order to watch the *700 Club,* my life continued much as before. The real change was within me. I felt an inner calm unlike anything I had ever known. I attributed it to my newly found certainty that man's existence had a divine purpose.

I was amazed at the simplicity of it all, and the more I read of the Bible, the more I puzzled over the perpetual debate regarding its truths. Ponce de León wasted his time searching for the Fountain of Youth and philosophers through the ages wasted theirs in the search for the secret of life. But it was so simple. All one had to do was read and, while reading, contemplate the whole. It was no good just reading the Bible and scoffing at the improbable. One had to really read; digest the historical facts and realize the constancy of this extraordinary story. Then one had to look at the world and see what was going on. The proof is all around us if we just open our eyes and ears.

Apart from the times I had watched Ernest Angley for a few minutes and wondered whether his healings were genuine, I had no experience whatsoever with divine healing. The *700 Club*, therefore, was my first exposure to healing since becoming able to accept the supernatural. A "Word of Knowledge," I learned, is a direct communication from God to an individual. The hosts of the *700 Club*, Pat Robertson, Ben Kinchlow and Danuta, receive Words of Knowledge sometime during most broadcasts. Some deal with the healing of physical ailments, some with answers to prayer for spiritual help and some with finances.

I listened to the testimony of people who had benefited from these Words of Knowledge and marveled at their miracles. Watching the broadcast each morning was making my Christian experience fuller and more exciting. I felt no compulsion to go to church and would not have known which one to go to in any event. Pat Robertson bore out what Serafino had told us, that loving Jesus was all that mattered. They quoted Jesus' statement "For where two or three are gathered together in my name, there am I in the midst of them." The show's hosts and I were sufficient and I felt as though I were at church while I watched and prayed.

When the broadcast ended at 6:30 each morning and I got Justin up, I recounted to him all that I had seen that day. He asked endless questions, including why he could not get up earlier and watch with me. He only reluctantly accepted that it would have made his day impossibly long. My one regret was that Jeremy did not exhibit the same interest. I went to great lengths to tell him of the miraculous healings people were receiving every day. I even got him to watch a bit of the show once or twice, but it was no use. He was more intrigued with my tenacious pursuit of God's word than with what the word itself might be. He had lived too long by the maxim "I believe half of what I see, little of what I read, and still less of what I hear."

On March 1, I was watching the *700 Club* when, at about 6:10, there was a Word of Knowledge that a bone spur in an ankle was being healed. I was thrilled. I had bone spurs. They said a woman in the audience was being healed right that minute. Suddenly a doubt crept in as to whether they meant me. Maybe it was the studio audience, not the viewing one. My feet did not feel any different. I reminded myself that where some healings are instantaneous, others are gradual.

I had begun, during the past few years, to get quite decrepit. Not only was I still haunted by colitis—which had begun during a particularly bad period between my mother and me—and the trouble with my back, but I also had a bone spur on my heel and varicose veins. Doc Pete, Wyalusing's version of Marcus Welby, M.D., had told me that the bone spur was operable but that it was a long and painful recuperative process with no guarantee that the spur would not immediately grow back again. The varicose veins were a problem I'd had since I was eleven, the veins of my left leg having been operated on when I was thirteen. Now the right leg was in bad shape and the left one acting up again. Between the spur and the veins, walking far or staying on my feet for extended periods was becoming extremely painful. I made as light of my troubles as I could with my family but, in truth, I was fully aware that I was in dire straits.

Later that day, providentially, Serafino called from West Virginia to see how we were doing. I told him about the Word of Knowledge and he asked if I had claimed it.

"What do you mean?" I asked.

"When there's a Word of Knowledge, you have to claim it. You have to step out in faith. Any number of people can claim the same healing at the same time, but God has to see your faith before He heals you."

"I've blown it," I said, almost bursting into tears. "I didn't know. Do you think God might make allowance for my not knowing? They might not *have* another Word of Knowledge about bone spurs."

"It's a shame," Serafino said, "but don't be discouraged. You can be healed through your own prayer, you know. God wants all His children to enjoy perfect health." I promised to keep all of my physical impairments in prayer, and Serafino promised that he and Joan would pray for me and for Jeremy's salvation as well.

A week later, on March 9, as I was praying along with Pat Robertson, he had another Word of Knowledge that pertained to me. "There's a woman in her thirties with a severe lower-back problem. The ligaments are steadily deteriorating. There is great pain and no cure. God is healing that condition right now. Take your healing. God has healed that back. You are fully restored. Thank you, Jesus! Praise the Lord!"

I cried and thanked Jesus and claimed my healing. "That's mine, Lord! Oh, thank you! I claim it in the Name of Jesus!" I was so excited that I completely forgot to get down from the bar stool carefully. I was crying and thanking Jesus and jumping up and down in my joy when I suddenly realized there was no pain. For the first time in over four years, there was no pain. Just getting off the bar stool quickly, let alone jumping up and down, should have given me spasms at the very least. There was no pain—not a hint of it.

I tested my back carefully. First, I bent over to touch my toes—no pain. Then I tried side bends—no pain. My back was healed! I didn't know it at the time, but it was only the first of many miracles with which we were to be blessed.

I went to wake Justin and, as soon as we were down in the kitchen, I showed him how I could move normally. He hugged me as tightly as he could and we danced around together. When his bus departed and I went to do chores, I threw hay bales around and shoveled out stalls with carefree abandon—not a twinge.

Jeremy had fallen into the habit of working into the small hours of the morning when he was left completely undisturbed. It took a good deal of effort on my part to leave him alone until he awoke of his own accord. I did manage it, however, and when he came downstairs at 9:30 I even kept my cool.

"My back's healed," I said conversationally.

"What do you mean?" he asked, putting the kettle on.

"I mean my back's healed. There was a Word of Knowledge on the *700 Club* this morning. I claimed it and my back's completely healed."

My husband stared at me, mouth agape, his expression more of total bewilderment than anything else. "Are you sure? It's not just mind over matter because you want to believe it?"

"I'm absolutely positive," I cried. "Watch this!" I stretched my arms out sideways and did a few cross kicks, kicking my hands at shoulder height with the opposite foot. For a few seconds he seemed to be dumbstruck, obviously thinking I had lost my mind. Then he busied himself with making a cup of coffee before coming to give me a big hug. "I'm very happy for you, Sweetie, honestly I am, but I'm not sure." He seemed to want it to be true but to be having trouble accepting it. He searched for the right words. "I mean, how do you know it's going to last? It might be just a temporary remission or something."

"It's not temporary," I said with utter conviction and some asperity. "My back is healed, once and for all. I have received a miracle. I've been doing things all morning which should have sent me to bed in agony for days. There's no pain. I'm healed!"

I was used to my husband's skepticism but, this time, I really wished he would accept the evidence of his eyes without such a fuss. "Will you believe it if I'm still bouncing around without any problems later in the day?" I asked in frustration.

"If you're still bouncing this evening," he said, a big grin spreading across his face, "I'll have no choice but to believe it's a miracle." This time he really hugged me, darned near broke me in two he squeezed so hard. "I hope it's true, Sweetie, I really do. I may even try a prayer before the day is out. Who knows, maybe somebody's listening?"

"Somebody is," I said.

The first words out of Justin's mouth when he arrived home from school were about my back. I assured him that I was still alright and that I had, indeed, received a miraculous healing from Jesus. He was thrilled to bits. Evening came and it was Jeremy's moment of truth. To prove to him that I was feeling fine I did some calisthenics. I sat on the floor and did sit-ups. I did toe touching. I did side kicks. I did everything but bend myself into a pretzel and there was no pain.

My husband watched me in awe. When I was finished with my demonstration he said simply, "It's a miracle." There were tears in his eyes.

At 8:30 he called Serafino and said without preamble, "Beed's back is healed."

"Praise God!" Serafino hooted. "How did it happen?" Jeremy told him all about the *700 Club*, how I had claimed the healing and how I had been doing exercises all day long without any ill effects. Serafino shouted out the news to Joan and their daughters and then came back to Jeremy. "Do you remember what you said back in January?"

"I remember," Jeremy admitted, surprisingly without reluctance.

"What are you going to do now?"

"Read the Bible. I'll talk to you again in a couple of months when I've finished it."

"That's great," Serafino exclaimed, "but it'll take you more than a couple of months. I'd hate to wait that long before we talk again. You're bound to have questions—just call us and we'll try to help you."

"O.K.," Jeremy agreed cheerfully. "While I think of it, have you ever been to see Ernest Angley? He's out in Ohio somewhere, isn't he?"

"Yes, we have. His ministry's in Akron. Joan and I went there once. Why?"

"I'd like to go and see him sometime." Jeremy looked at me with raised eyebrows and I nodded encouragingly.

"We've been wanting to go again," Serafino said. "Would you like me to find out about it and get back to you with the details?"

"That would be marvelous. Thank you. Hold on a second, Beed wants to talk to you." He handed me the phone and I told Serafino all over again about my miracle. Serafino then put Joan on and I told *her* all about it. I wanted to tell the whole world about it and, in fact, that's just what I did for the next few days. Anyone who didn't run fast enough heard about my healing whether they wanted to or not.

By the end of our lengthy phone conversation, we had agreed to go to Akron at the earliest moment convenient for all of us. Serafino would get all the information we needed and get back to us as soon as he could. After his commitment to read the Bible, no one tried to pressure Jeremy into anything more.

Mother called two or three days later, all upset about the potential traffic jams during the upcoming Summer Olympics. "It's going to be horrible, B.D., just horrible."

"But you never go out, Mother, so why worry about it?"

"How are people going to get to me?" she barked. "The traffic will drive me mad."

"Just allow a bit more time for them to get from A to B, that's all."

"Brother! You refuse to see the mess I'll be in. Just knowing that I'll be trapped is more than I can bear. I won't take it! I've got to figure out a way to escape."

"Maybe it won't be so bad," I suggested. "L.A. has an exceptional freeway system."

"How do you know? You haven't had to get around out here in years. You never understand. Let's just drop it, shall we? Tell me *your* news. What are you doing?"

An opening at last. I had waited for weeks and weeks until I felt she was able to listen. Now I also had a tangible sign, a miracle, to share with her. I took a deep breath. "I've become a born-again Christian, Mother." I paused—no response. "And as a sign of His love for me, Jesus has given me a miracle. My back is completely healed." I waited.

"Don't do anything stupid now that your back is better. You be careful—and don't tell your husband."

"Didn't you hear me? I said God has restored my back. It's a miracle! I've accepted Jesus as—"

"Very interesting. You must be very happy. Call me soon. I've got to figure out my summer. Tell me you love me."

"I love you, Mother."

CHAPTER

5

FOR AN ASSORTMENT OF REASONS, NOT THE LEAST OF WHICH was that Ashley would be home from school for a vacation, we chose March 30 as the day to go to Akron. Serafino had determined that it would have to be a Friday because that was when Rev. Angley conducted his healing services. One also had to be careful to check with Grace Cathedral as to Rev. Angley's overseas commitments. Serafino had and we were in luck. He was recently returned from a trip to India and would not be leaving for Germany for quite a while. (When he did go to Germany he was arrested for "healing without a permit.")

A gentle spring rain fell throughout the afternoon of the twenty-eighth but, by bedtime, it turned to snow. When we got up in the morning there was a twelve-inch accumulation and it was still coming down with a vengeance. I did not even bother to wake Justin. Jeremy and I discussed whether to go out, here and now, to do some errands which needed doing before we left for Akron, or wait for the plow to come around first. Common sense said wait for the plow but, out in our boonies, one frequently had to ignore common sense in the interests of survival. If the plow operator decided the snow was going to continue, he might not show up until it stopped. Logical from his point of view, but a bit awkward for people scheduled to leave for Ohio at dawn the following day who were out of dog food among other things.

Jeremy decided to wait at least until the visibility improved. This afforded the added chance that the plow would put in an appearance. Floyd Edsel, who owned and operated the plow, except when Floyd Hitchcock drove it for him, also operated a school bus. He might be bored, the schools being closed, and decide to plow even with the snow still falling.

By 11:00 A.M. we knew we were in trouble. The snow was eighteen inches deep, there wasn't a Floyd in sight, and both the phone and the power went out. Our first step was to fill the bathtubs with snow. There was no way of knowing how long we would be without electricity and, apart from personal needs, the horses required about twenty gallons of water a day. The trick was to keep heating water in the iron kettle on the wood stove and pouring it over the snow in the bathtubs.

With this process under way, Jeremy turned his thoughts to Serafino and how to contact him. The wisest course seemed to be to keep our fingers crossed for a few hours and see if we got a break of some sort. We melted snow and waited.

At two in the afternoon, Jeremy determined to do something. He did all sorts of things, but got nowhere. First he put the Scout into four-wheel drive, made it about a hundred feet along the dirt road and went into the drainage ditch on the left-hand side. Fuming but undeterred, he put the pickup into four-wheel and took a tow chain to pull the Scout out of the ditch. He backed up to the Scout, hooked up the chain and, the snow being the soft wet kind, promptly dug all four wheels of the truck into hub-deep icy holes. After trying in vain to go either backward or forward, he tried to unhook the tow chain. Unfortunately, the truck had dug itself in with full tension on the chain and Jeremy could not unhook it.

He considered taking out the farm tractor and another chain to see whether he could pull the whole lot with it but, wisely, he decided that going to the Sharers for help with every vehicle we owned chained together and stuck in the snow was more than his dignity could bear.

We dispatched Ashley to walk the half mile to the Sharers'

for help, then took some tools to knock out the retaining pin from the hook at one end of the tow chain. With this accomplished and a bit of digging, Jeremy managed to free the pickup and return it to the barn. At least he had removed from the scene half of the evidence of his humiliation.

In due course, Ken Sharer hove over the horizon, Ashley in the cab with him, driving their biggest tractor. It had wheel chains and a plow mounted on the front. It was nice having friendly neighbors who owned at least one of every gadget under the sun. If the big tractor got stuck, Ken would mutter into his C.B. radio and another brother would simply bring out the bulldozer.

Ken pulled the Scout out of the ditch, then opened the cab door and shouted to Jeremy, "Where were you trying to go, anyway?"

"Ohio," my husband replied with a straight face.

"Optimist, aren't you?" Ken quipped. "I heard on the C.B. that there are trees and poles down all the way to Wyalusing. Probably all the way to Ohio."

"Is your phone working?" Jeremy shouted through the driving snow.

"I don't know. The power's out but I don't think anyone's tried the phone."

"I'll walk down and give it a try later," Jeremy said. "Your line comes over the hill from the other direction, doesn't it?"

"Yup. Give it a try if you like. Hold on for a minute and I'll plow down to your barn for you." Jeremy knew better than to ask whether Ken had plowed the hardtop on his way up to us. Country mores being what they are, the Sharers wouldn't plow a road maintained by the state unless and until they needed to use it themselves.

Once the Scout was safely and uselessly back in the barn, Jeremy trekked down to the Sharers' to find that their phone was still working, thanks to the phone company, in its infinite wisdom, having routed their line over hill and dale instead of connecting them to the line serving us and everyone else on the hill. He called Serafino and explained our situation. Instead of being put out, Serafino sounded positively elated. "You see the lengths Satan will go to to hold on to one of his own?" he crowed. "You must be making him nervous. That's great!"

day in and day out, but he was not ready to hear that Satan was after him. He related Serafino's comment to me when he got back and even I found it a bit of a difficult concept with which to deal. In any event, Jeremy and Serafino postponed the trip for a week, agreeing to all the same arrangements for the following Friday instead.

We went on melting snow in the bathtubs since Ken had volunteered an opinion, an unusual event in itself, that the power might be out for days. We got out the candles and hurricane lamps and dispatched Ashley yet again, this time to trudge his way down to the cabin by the lake to bring up the gas-operated cooking stove. By the time he got back, wet to the armpits from the drifts in the gulleys and half frozen, he was mumbling about how peaceful and civilized it was at school.

When Justin and I went to do chores we found that Patches, our favorite calico cat, had been kind enough to try to brighten our day by having a litter of five kittens. Of course she had them in the tack room on my best New Zealand horse blanket, but that did not matter. We finished watering and feeding and then spent some time naming the kittens. Naming kittens every spring was almost as much fun for Justin and me as seeing the first flowers come up.

I threw together a makeshift dinner on the camping stove and then we all sat down for a game of Mille Bornes by lamplight. Justin and I trounced Ashley and Dad twice before I had a better idea. "How would you all like it if I read to you from the Bible?" I asked. The vote, to my delight, was a unanimous yes. I read from the New Testament for some twenty or thirty minutes before detecting restlessness in the audience. Not bad, I thought, for a first attempt. The boys went to bed and Jeremy and I chatted about things in general and the Lord in particular.

I had carefully not pushed my husband for any answers regarding faith. I knew he was reading the Bible tirelessly and I was more than happy to give him all the time he needed to find his answers. I was curious though. Had he accepted Jesus as his personal Lord and Savior or had he simply acknowledged the existence of God based upon the miraculous healing of my back? I wanted him to be born again. I felt so differently within myself that I actually felt sad for anyone who rejected what I now wholeheartedly regarded as the center of all things, a center without which there was nothing of a true or lasting value. If Jeremy were to finish his search for truth and reject Jesus, it would break my heart. I prayed constantly that he would receive a revelation, as I had, to make it easier for him, but I suspected he would have to do it the hard way. I also prayed that he would soon find the truth in any way God gave it to him to see that truth.

As we talked, I gained the impression that it was only a question of time. Jeremy was not finished with the Old Testament yet, but it was clear that he had found it possible to accept it as a matter of historical fact. He was no longer worried about dinosaurs and contradictions. He was, in fact, intrigued with the idea that all his questions would be answered by the time he came to the end. "The only trouble," he confessed, "is that there are so many questions, it's difficult to remember when you just found an answer to one. I thought of making notes, but decided it would only distract me." It sounded promising and I became confident that he would accept Jesus when he reached the New Testament.

At 11:30, we were just about to go to bed when the power came on. I checked the phone and found that to be working also. We were more than a little relieved. It had been fun to rough it for a few hours but, by the next day, the question of water for the stock would have required round-the-clock snow melting unless, that is, a Floyd put in an appearance and cleared the road. In that case, since they had their own generator, we could fetch water from the Sharers'. We were not the least bit sorry to be relieved of either alternative. Interestingly enough, although our hill overlooked the village of Stevensville, and although the village lay between us and the source of both our electricity and phone service, the village was without either for two days. I privately decided that working in mysterious ways was not exclusive to the Lord.

I prayed all week that we would not have another blizzard to delay our trip to Akron again. Peculiarly enough, Jeremy grew to like the idea that Satan did not want us to go. It appealed to his sense of the balance of things: no good without evil, etc. I managed to persuade him to leave the Old Testament for a few hours and read Matthew. When he finished he said with a self-conscious smile, "You win. It's true. It may take me a long time to accept it emotionally but, intellectually, the truth is inescapable: Jesus was, is I should say, the Son of God. There's too much evidence to permit of doubt. Between what I've read so far and the healing of your back, I accept it. I don't understand the concept of the Trinity yet—maybe I never will—but I've no doubt that Jesus was what He purported to be and, therefore, still is."

I was overjoyed that Jeremy had found his way to accepting Jesus. I did wish, though, that once in a while he could stop being so rational about everything and just let his emotions run free. Perhaps, I thought, that might change a bit now. We went on talking for an hour or so and he began to wax unusually enthusiastic about our forthcoming trip. I prayed even harder that nothing else would go wrong.

The following Thursday, April 5, was both the day before our second attempt to go to Akron, and my mother's seventy-sixth birthday. I called to wish her many happy returns and learned that Harold had hired the U.C.L.A. (or so Mother said) marching band to parade outside her window and play "Seventy-six Trombones." She was thrilled and it was nice to hear her happy about something. We talked for several minutes and then I returned to my own concerns.

The weather had warmed up a couple of days earlier and the snow, which had eventually amounted to two feet, had been reduced to a rotten, squooshy mess. Then, the night before, it had started to rain. It was still raining and the rivers were rising fast. Had it not been for the problem of changing all the arrangements for the care of our animals during our absence, we would have left for Ohio right then.

Jeremy drove down the hill to see how Wyalusing Creek looked and returned with a very worried expression on his face. We considered all sorts of alternatives and finally decided that if God wanted us to get to Akron, we would get there come Satan *or* high water. We agreed to leave at five instead of six in case we could not cross the Susquehanna and had to run north into New York State and try to go the long way round.

At five the next morning we crossed the bridge over the

roaring creek onto Route 706 and relaxed too soon. We had forgotten the low spot in the road between Stevensville and Camptown. Wyalusing Creek parallels 706 for several miles and this particular spot was very prone to flooding. When we got there our hearts sank. The creek was on our left and the water was lapping at the steps of a house, on our right, which was on higher ground than the road. Jeremy stopped the car and stared at the lake ahead of us for a few moments. Then he put the car in first gear, opened the driver-side door and began to inch forward. I held my breath and prayed.

The Scout was not much good in the snow, but it did have plenty of ground clearance. We crept along, the water getting deeper and deeper, with Jeremy keeping one eye on our direction and the other on the relationship between the water level and the floorboards of the car. By the time we were at the low spot in the road, it was just about a dead heat. Another quarter of an inch and the interior of the car would have been awash. As we started the upslope, Jeremy grinned and let out a sigh of relief. We all looked back, to see again what we had come through, just in time to see a regular, lower-to-the-ground car drown. We felt sorry for the poor beggar but there was nothing we could do to help him. He would have to wade to the house on the rise and call a tow truck.

We wondered whether there were any more trials ahead of us but, with the exception of the Susquehanna having flooded level with one road in one or two places as we headed south to Route 80, our 345-mile trip to Akron was without further excitement. We were comfortably ensconced at a Holiday Inn by noon and looking for the Fazios.

They had intended to be there ahead of us but were nowhere to be found. Since Satan had apparently been foiled in his attempt to keep *us* away, we began to wonder whether any ill might have befallen Serafino and Joan. I dialed their home number in West Virginia but there was no answer. We waited, too excited to take naps, and Ashley getting increasingly argumentative and belligerent.

Among our reasons for wanting to go to Akron so much was Ashley's behavior. I had discussed his symptoms several times with an old family friend, Dr. Arnold Hutschnecker, and it seemed almost certain that Ashley suffered from depressed-child syndrome. It had never been a big problem, either at home or at school, but I bled for the poor boy whenever he went into one of his downers. It was difficult not to become furious when rudeness and belligerence overcame him, and understanding the root of his problem had been a big help. Nevertheless, Jeremy and I had been given to understand that although Ashley might grow out of it, there was a greater chance that his moodiness would become worse without help, perhaps even leading to manic depression by the time he reached his mid to late teens.

Ashley had voluntarily joined the rest of us in accepting Jesus, but I wasn't too sure whether he was truly committed or just going along with the majority. He had been so excited at the prospect of meeting the Fazios, about whom he had heard so much, that their failure to be on time was enough to send him into the glooms.

I succeeded in cheering him up enough to get him to play a game with Justin. I lay down and read my Bible while Jeremy went off to find Grace Cathedral. Serafino had told us about the lines for the Friday services and we had no intention of coming this far only to get lost in the last couple of miles.

We whiled away the next few hours having lunch, catnapping and praying that the Fazios were alright. And indeed they were. At four o'clock they arrived, harried and tired, but safe and sound. They had got away late due to a last-minute business problem. Then they had encountered unusually heavy traffic, a tie-up caused by a bad accident, and assorted other delays. We were so happy to see them that no one heard Serafino's apologies.

The service was scheduled to begin at seven with the doors opening at six. We were there on the dot of six and found the queues already to be of impressive length. There were cars and buses with license plates from every surrounding state as well as Canada and places as far removed as Maryland, Tennessee and Wisconsin. It was quite a sight for people like us who had not, until a few weeks ago, taken seriously the matter of certain people having a special anointing to heal the sick in the Name of Jesus.

Although we had arrived an hour before services were due

to begin, the church was two-thirds full by the time we found seats. The lines had grown rapidly behind us and we learned that when the sanctuary, which held a thousand people, was full, there was room for another thousand on a lower floor who could watch the services on closed-circuit television. Promptly at seven the choir and musicians came out and an assistant pastor led us in song and prayer. Jeremy, a little irreverently I felt, despite it being undeniable that God has a sense of humor, whispered in my ear, "Warming the crowd for the main attraction." I shushed him and chalked it up to nerves.

To our left front, at the foot of the platform, was an alcove that enjoyed a private entrance. We had not noticed it at first but, when we stood for the first hymn, our gaze was drawn to the people assembled there. They were all in wheelchairs or on stretchers, many attended by nurses. By the time Rev. Angley came out at eight o'clock, I was so spiritually filled that I had not the slightest doubt that every single person in the church, including Ashley and me, was going to be healed of whatever ailed him before the night was over.

Rev. Angley spoke for some time on a variety of subjects. I hesitate to say "preach" because he did not seem to be preaching, just talking. Among the topics he discussed was family. He started with love and ended with what to do if anyone, be it mother, father, brother, sister, son or whoever, brought disharmony into the family unit. The essence of his dissertation was that if anyone, no matter how close a relative (he was actually very funny doing impressions of bickering and nasty relatives who came for Thanksgiving dinner), were to bring upset, grief or any form of disharmony into the family unit, and refused upon request to keep their peace, one had, distasteful though it might be, an absolute obligation to cast that person out.

My daily prayers for a sign, a clear, unmistakable sign, as to the right or wrong of publishing my book had been answered. Whenever I focused on my mother's behavior, particularly her treatment of my family, I knew I had no choice but to publish despite the uproar I was going to cause and the accusations that would be hurled at me. Although new births come of pain and although I was acutely aware that no birth of understanding between Mother and me was possible without suffering on both our parts, it hurt none the less knowing that, no matter how loving the reasons, I was about to cause her overwhelming emotional anguish. Jeremy was the only one who had any idea of the soul-searching I had been through and the prayers for guidance I had offered up. As Rev. Angley was speaking, Jeremy looked at me and smiled. He, too, recognized it for what it was.

We had come to this place by design, but on this date by "accident," and I had received the best possible advice on perhaps the most important, certainly the most far-reaching, decision I had ever had to make in my life. Praise God!

At approximately ten o'clock the healings began. We were amazed that we had sat spellbound for two solid hours while Rev. Angley spoke. Jeremy, in particular, was prone to getting the fidgets unless he was truly riveted by whatever he was watching. He had barely moved a muscle during the entire two hours. First, the victims of cancer were called forward. One lady mentioned that she had been there seven years earlier for breast cancer and been healed. Rev. Angley asked whether the same sickness had recurred and the lady said no, it was the other side this time.

Several dozen people stepped out to be healed of cancer. A lady sitting behind us leaned forward and told us she had been healed of cancer two years earlier when the doctors had given her less than a year to live. She said she had never felt better in her life. Each person in turn was asked for the specifics of his or her ailment and, via the cordless microphone Rev. Angley wore on his tie, we could hear every word. Then they were asked if they were born again—not everyone was—and whether they smoked. Whenever someone admitted to smoking, they were healed of that burden also. Rev. Angley reached into people's pockets and removed packs of cigarettes, tearing them in half as though they were single sheets of paper and throwing them on the floor.

Next, people from out of state were called forward. It had been discovered, when Ashley was in third grade, that he had a thirty percent hearing impairment in his left ear. I knew he was going to step out and ask for his hearing to be healed, but I didn't know whether he would, without being pushed, also ask for his depression to be healed. We stepped out into the aisle together and walked slowly toward the line forming at the foot of the platform.

Ashley walked ahead of me, but with increasing apprehension. He had seen person after person collapse into the arms of the waiting ushers at Rev. Angley's healing touch. Now, he whispered to me over his shoulder, "I'm not going to fall down like all those other people."

"It's nothing to do with me," I said. "It's between you and Jesus." Two more steps forward.

"Just so you know," insisted my cool-at-all-costs teenager, "I'm not falling down. You can forget it."

I smiled and said, "Whatever you say." Two more steps.

"I'm not kidding, you know. You can smile all you like, but I'm not falling down." We arrived at the platform, took our places and awaited our turns.

People with the most extraordinary range of afflictions were healed. There was a girl, accompanied by a guardian, who suffered with five personalities. After Rev. Angley had cast out four demons, the girl looked around and asked where she was and how she'd got there. Standing next to Ashley, on his left, was a man who asked to be healed of acute deafness. The deafness was dealt with but then Rev. Angley noticed the man's hand. It was withered and deformed.

"What happened to your hand?" the reverend asked.

"It was crushed in an industrial accident thirty years ago," the man answered.

"Don't you want it healed?"

"I didn't think it could be." The man looked puzzled. "There are bones missing and everything. It was such a mess when I had the accident, the doctors just removed all the bone splinters and fragments and sewed it up." I looked carefully, as did Ashley, and saw that the back of his hand was completely concave where the bones were missing.

"Don't you think God can replace missing bones if He wants to?" Rev. Angley asked.

"Well, yes," the man answered hesitantly, looking shamefaced.

"Well, let's let Him heal it, then," said the reverend. He reached forward, took the man's wrist in both his hands and began to massage it. He worked the wrist back and forth and then rubbed the hand itself, his thumbs in the palm and his fingers on the back. The expression on the man's face was of absolute wonderment as there came a quiver in the fingers and the most awful cracking noises echoed over the microphone.

"What's that noise?" the man gasped.

"Don't you think God is entitled to make a little noise when He's replacing bones?" Rev. Angley asked with a big smile toward the congregation.

Ashley and I, standing right next to the man, saw it all. The most hideously deformed hand I had ever seen, gradually, in a matter of thirty seconds or less, resumed its normal form. The man flexed his fingers for the first time in thirty years.

"Hallelujah!" I cried aloud for the first time in my life.

It was Ashley's turn. If he'd had any doubts before this, I knew they had been dispelled by what he had just witnessed.

"What can God do for you, son?"

"I have diminished hearing in my left ear and I suffer from depression," Ashley blurted. I said a quiet prayer of thanks.

"Are you born again?"

"Yes, I am." It was the first time he had said it in so many words.

"Do you use tobacco in any form?"

"No, sir."

"Let's take care of the hearing first." The reverend placed his hand on Ashley's left ear and cried, "In the Name of the Lord, come out!" Then he stood back, leaned against the edge of the platform and stared into Ashley's eyes. My son later described the experience to us as follows:

"He stared straight into my eyes. First I could see red lines running from his eyes into mine and there was a burning sensation in my head. He stood there, with his arms folded, and stared at me. Then, the red lines turned blue and my head suddenly felt cool. Rev. Angley stepped toward me, tapped my forehead gently with the palm of his hand and shouted, 'Yayah.' "

I saw Ashley touched on the forehead, two ushers standing behind him as they had for each person in turn, and watched as my son went as stiff as a board and collapsed backwards into the waiting arms of the ushers. They laid him gently on the floor. His eyes were closed and there was a look of complete peace on his face.

"That's my son!" I shouted in my excitement. I was crying and laughing at the same time and tried to thank Rev. Angley.

"Hallelujah!" he said. "Now what can God do for you, Momma?" I gave him a list of my woes. "I have colitis, varicose veins, calcium in both ankles—"

"Hold it," he said. "That's a powerful lot of burden. We'll just ask God to heal you from the top of your head to the bottoms of your feet. Are you born again?"

"Yes."

"Do you use tobacco?"

"No."

Rev. Angley touched my forehead. "Yayah! In the Name of Jesus." I didn't pass out cold as Ashley and some of the others had, but I was suddenly too weak to stand. The ushers caught me and laid me down beside my son. I knew I was healed. I knew Ashley and I had received miracles. I was on my feet within a minute and was about to touch Ashley when one of the ushers told me to leave him alone until he came to. "Some healings take longer than others, especially when they're to do with the brain."

Ashley came to in about four or five minutes and we returned to our seats. He was gazing about him as though seeing things for the first time. He said he could hear clearly and, somehow, the church looked brighter. He noticed a couple of cute girls looking at him and smiled back at them, something he never would have done before.

Back in our pew, he gave us his testimony, the Fazios hanging on every word. While unconscious he'd had a vision. (Jeremy and I later double-checked with Ashley that he had never actually read or heard about this particular part of the Bible story.)

"Did anyone ever walk across a sort of big lake, Dad?" he asked.

"Yes," his father replied. "Jesus did. He walked across the Sea of Galilee."

"Well, it was Jesus I saw, then. I saw Him walking on this big lake. It was great. Then I saw Him on the cross and then I saw Him go up to heaven. It was beautiful. His arms were outstretched and He was all white and shining like a bright star; His robe was fluttering like leaves on a tree. Then I saw heaven. It was fantastic, all flowers and fields and this huge city shining in the distance. Boy! I hope I go there some day."

"You will," I said, hugging my son and shedding still more tears. "Praise God, you will."

When all the out-of-staters had been ministered to, the reverend took a breather in the form of another short address to the congregation. It lasted some ten or fifteen minutes, and then he walked up the aisles receiving Words of Knowledge. As he specified the disease or ailment that was about to be healed, he pointed into the area of the church where the sufferer was seated. In almost every instance someone quickly arose right where he was pointing and claimed the healing. In a few instances, and I felt terrible for the poor souls whose faith was insufficient, the healings went unclaimed.

The reverend then returned to the platform and asked if there was anyone else to be healed. A considerable number arose and made their way to form another line. Serafino and Joan, Jeremy, Ashley and I were still enthralled with every aspect of the service, though we had by this time been seated in Grace Cathedral for nigh unto five hours. Justin, poor little guy, could not hold out any longer. Ashley slid over a little to make room and Justin almost instantly fell asleep with his head on my lap and his feet on Ashley's.

When the last of the healings, except for those waiting in the alcove, had been completed, there was an altar call. Jeremy went forward and pledged his life to Jesus. I thanked God for all the miracles my family had received that night and for the answer to my most fervent prayer: that my husband would accept Jesus as his personal Lord and Savior.

After the altar call and a period of prayer, everyone who had stepped out in faith returned to his seat and Rev. Angley went to the alcove. The first healing was received by a man in a wheelchair who was paralyzed from the waist down. Rev. Angley commanded him, in the Name of Jesus, to get up and walk, and rise from the wheelchair and walk he did. The next was a lady who had been carried into the church on a stretcher. She had been in a coma for six weeks and was on an intravenous drip. The reverend asked permission of the attending nurse to remove the I.V. drip. With the needle removed, he laid his hands on the lady. She was, I would guess, in her sixties. He commanded her to arise and walk. He helped her slowly into a sitting position, then to place her feet on the floor, then to stand up. Albeit with the nurse helping her, the lady walked.

At this point the congregation spontaneously went into what Serafino later told us was called a "praise." Prayers of thanks broke out everywhere and within seconds we could hear nothing more of the healings. It was a few moments before Jeremy and I realized it but, all around us and throughout the church, most of the congregation seemed to be praying in all sorts of weird-sounding foreign languages. Most were so strange that they did not sound like languages at all. Serafino explained that this was "speaking in tongues."

The gift of tongues is received by born-again Christians after they receive the baptism of the Holy Spirit. It is a private prayer language which not even the person using it understands. It is the Holy Ghost speaking to God in behalf of that person and only God understands what is being said. It also happens from time to time that during the course of a church service a member of the congregation will suddenly and unexpectedly break out in tongues. When this happens, all remain quiet and wait, for it is a message direct from God. The interpretation will be given to another person who will speak it aloud. It is most likely to occur when there is a heavy anointing on a particular service and it is very exciting. (There is also, of course, the further meaning of "speaking in tongues," as when Jesus addressed a multitude from many nations and all understood Him. Jesus bestowed this gift on Paul for *his* ministry.)

The acceptance of the gift of tongues by Pentecostal Christians as not only very real but also as a fulfillment of one of God's promises to His children is one of the things that sets them apart from all other denominations and faiths. Pentecostals accept *everything* in the Bible, from Genesis to Revelation, and do not pick and choose the bits they like, disregarding or explaining away the parts they do not. The whims of spiritual leaders over the centuries and the prejudices of religions and cults, not to mention the founders and hierarchies thereof, have no place in faithfulness to God's word. God's word cannot be changed and the Bible contains His word. That's it. No need for a conclave of holy men to figure out what we can or cannot do. Just look in the Bible. The answer to every question is there. If you cannot clearly understand what the Bible is telling you on any given point, or you do not agree with someone else's opinion in the matter, listen to your own conscience. If you are truly born again, the Holy Spirit will be your conscience, and a harder taskmaster He is than any spiritual leader ever dreamt of being. You might be able to fool your pastor, but you will never fool your own conscience.

We stayed only a little longer and then joined the early leavers. It was after midnight and we thought we ought to get some sleep before rising early again for the long trip home. As it turned out, we were all so spiritually uplifted and excited that none of us could go to bed. Serafino went for doughnuts and coffee and we sat around and talked. Justin had woken up refreshed by his nap and contributed his version of the happenings of the evening until he conked out at 2:00 A.M. Ashley followed him at three. The rest of us kept at it until 4:30.

The first thing I mentioned to Joan and Serafino was the extraordinary answer to my prayer for guidance with respect to the publishing of my book. I explained the problem of my total inability to communicate with my mother in any normal fashion, her habit of tearing up letters, hanging up the phone, or locking herself away in other rooms when she did not want to read or hear what one had to say.

Joan drew my attention to a verse in Paul's Epistle to the Romans: "Let us not therefore judge one another any more: but judge this rather, that no man put a stumbling block or an occasion to fall in his brother's way." She did not deny that Rev. Angley's sermon had been a blessing to me, but pointed out that I could have found the answer myself had I but looked in the Bible. "Right in Genesis 2 it says, and Jesus Himself cited it later, 'Therefore shall a man leave his father and his mother, and shall cleave unto his wife: and they shall be one flesh.' You see, the commandment to honor your mother and your father ends when you get married if, as in your case, your mother has become a stumbling block. Stumbling block or not, your first loyalty, once you're married, is to your spouse. The family unit is holy and no man must put it asunder. That includes your mother."

We talked and we talked and we talked. Every question Jeremy or I put forward was answered, usually by Joan knowing where to look in the Bible. We absorbed all we could concerning the faith we had so recently found and about which we knew so little. My husband and I had been spellbound by the healings we had witnessed during the service that night, but the Fazios rejoiced far more over all the people, including Jeremy, who had answered the altar call and accepted Jesus. The Fazios were right, of course—a soul saved is far more important than a body healed—but, at that time, we were so overwhelmed by the miracle of God's healing power that we scarcely gave a thought to much else. We were to be taught a sharp lesson in this regard in the very near future.

When we finally went to bed at 4:30, I tossed and turned until 5:30, then woke up, charged with energy, at 7:30. I read my Bible until Jeremy awoke at 8:00, then we both went to rouse the boys in the adjoining room. We found them wide awake and recounting the events of the previous evening to one another. Ashley was bubbling with joy and insisted on giving us his testimony all over again. His attitude and demeanor were entirely different than they had been before. He was not on one of his short-lived highs that we were used to, and which would succumb to foulness of mood the minute some little thing annoyed him or went wrong. He was genuinely filled with joy at the world around him. Even little Justin came into our room, while his brother was taking his turn in their bathroom, and commented on the difference in Ashley. We said yet another prayer of thanks.

We met the Fazios for breakfast and extracted from them a promise that they, and their daughters, would come and spend a long weekend with us during the summer. Before we went our separate ways at 11:30, we joined hands and thanked God for bringing us all together back on that snowy day in January.

By Sunday morning I had proof that I was healed. The burning sensation in the veins of both my legs was gone. The aching of the legs themselves and the numbness in my toes were gone. Even the deep purply-blue discoloration of the veins was noticeably diminished. There was some flexibility in my ankles where there had been none for the past year. I had been walking duck-footed with the ankles stiff. Jeremy and I prayed together and thanked God for healing Ashley and me— and we have continued to thank Him ever since.

The completion of my healings took time, but over the next several months became complete. I have never again had an attack of colitis, the calcium in my ankles has not recurred, and my varicose veins have remained healed. The one curiosity I feel constrained to mention is that, although the discoloration of the veins disappeared, the swelling did not. My legs still look terrible. Nor, despite much prayer, has my metabolism been healed. My inability to lose weight, a result of the hormone treatments I had to undergo in order to be able to get pregnant, is still very much with me. Diets of six hundred calories a day for weeks on end have made no difference. Since both these problems are cosmetic only, it would seem that God differentiates between what is needed for perfect health and what is only a matter of looks. On the other hand, it may be nothing more than a test of my faith.

CHAPTER

A MONTH OR SO EARLIER, MOTHER HAD TOLD ME THAT SHE HAD
been invited to be a presenter on the Academy Awards show
on television and that she was going to do it. She had also
given me a bulletin on the further postponement of *The Aspen
Papers*, but it had been postponed so often for so many reasons that I seriously doubted whether it would ever get produced, let alone with Mother in it.

As the date of the Academy Awards show neared, Mother
told me how excited she was about making her first public
appearance since the beginning of all her illnesses. I told her,
quite sincerely, that I thought it was wonderful and that there
could be no better forum for her triumphal return than the
Oscars.

On the day, Jeremy and I watched the show with great
interest. We were curious to see how Mother looked and how
she would carry off the moment. We watched the whole
show—no Mother and not so much as a mention of her name.

Three days later she called. I asked why she had not been
on the show, but her doorbell rang—I could hear it in the
background—and she said "Oh, Brother! Hang on for a mo-

ment, sweetheart." There was a thirty-second pause before her hairdresser came on the line and spoke in a whisper. "Miss Davis will have to call you back."

Weird, I thought.

Half an hour passed and then Mother called again. She would not tell me why she'd had to leave the phone and only answered my question about the Academy Awards after I repeatedly pressed the point. First, she said, "I just couldn't do it. Everyone backstage would have made such a furor when they saw me, I'd have had no strength left by the end of the evening. Brother! I'd have been dead!" A little later in the conversation she said, "Anyway, I don't know why you're so concerned about the Academy Awards. The important thing is that I'm fully rested for *The Aspen Papers*."

"That's great," I said. "I didn't know the picture was finally going to get started."

"Well, it is," Mother blurted. "In Italy—in July."

Regardless of my determination to be more compassionate toward my mother, I found myself wondering. What on earth was going on? First, there was the oddity of the abbreviated phone call. It was so totally out of character for Mother. She had never done anything like it before. Oh, sure, she would do it when I was saying something she did not like, but if that had been the case, she would not have called back. Then, the double-talk about the Awards. Knowing my mother's predilection for turning everything backwards, I wondered whether she had actually been afraid that no one would make any special effort to celebrate her appearance; that she would arrive expecting a triumph, only to received a "Hi, how are ya?"

Then there was the change of story. She must know that *The Aspen Papers* was as unlikely to start in July as it had been at any other time and, even if she did not, how could the strain of presenting an award be such that she would need three months to recuperate from it? She had frequently bugged out of things she did not want to do on flimsier pretexts than that, had done it all her life, but something about this felt different. I put the puzzle to my husband.

"Maybe she's lost her nerve," he suggested. "Sort of battle fatigue." I pondered on that for a while. "It's possible, I suppose. Do you think she'll get over it?"

"How the heck would *I* know?" Jeremy replied. "I've never understood her—even at the best of times." He paused to think. "If nobody *makes* her go to work, she may well convince herself she's too old and feeble to do it anymore. You and I know she has the constitution of an ox, but even Harold buys her 'worst cold in the history of man' performances."

"But what'll she live on? You know she's always broke."

"I really don't know. Harold should have laid down the law to her over *Hotel*."

I suddenly fell prey to the most depressing of scenarios. The only thing in the world my mother had ever truly cherished, by her own oft-repeated admission, was her career. If she abandoned that, then what? I could not conceive of Harold taking care of my mother financially for the rest of her life. I had never doubted for a moment his devotion to the best interests of his client, but how far could that devotion extend? Could Mother wind up in the Old Actors' Home, or whatever it's called? Could Jeremy and I find ourselves responsible for her? The mind boggled. My mother could fritter away half a million dollars a year without even trying.

I blanked the questions from my mind as too depressing to contemplate any further. At the end of Ernest Angley's discourse on disruptive family members, he had said, "You are not responsible for that person's spirit, but you must pray for their soul."

I started to pray and, as I did so, a realization came to me: if my mother and I were ever to find reconciliation, she would have to read my book and understand what I had been trying for so long to tell her—that was why I was going to publish the book, after all—but, and this was the realization, for Mother to truly hear me at last would be a miracle; and, for God to work that miracle, Mother would have to accept Jesus, would have to find salvation. There was no way in which Bette Davis would ever forgive me for what I was doing unless she found salvation. For her to change enough in spirit to be welcome once again in my life, she would have to find Jesus. Such a transformation of personality and temperament could only be achieved through God's intercession.

My prayers took on new form and the book far greater import.

CHAPTER

FRIENDS OF OURS BY THE NAME OF HOWARD AND SUE ROEDIGER lived some thirty-five miles away in Windham Center. Theirs was a May–December marriage and a great success. Howard, a horse trainer and trader by profession, was also scrupulously honest. This may seem strange, as it did to Jeremy and me at first, since horse dealing and honesty are all but mutually exclusive concepts. Nonetheless, it was so.

Sue was a born-again Christian but Howard was not. Howard believed in God, but privately. God was not a matter for open discussion and certainly not to be considered in conjunction with the everyday events of our lives. Were anyone so importunate as to beard Howard on the subject of Jesus Christ he would, most likely, take a big bite of chewing tobacco and remain silent until the offender took his leave.

Howard was a cowboy. He looked like a Remington sculpture of a cowboy. Face seamed and weather-beaten, skinny—under a hundred pounds soaking wet—he personified the Old West. His knowledge of horses and touch with them was extraordinary. There was in Howard, however, an anguish of spirit about which Sue constantly prayed. In addition, Howard had been suffering from emphysema for a long time and, during the past year, it had become extremely bad. He had great trouble breathing and had been forced to give up training altogether. The doctor had warned him against spending another winter in our climate, and had gone so far as to say that Howard might not live out the year.

We had, of course, shared our newly found faith with them, and Howard, to Sue's delight, had actually found it possible to accept from Jeremy thoughts he would have shunned had they come from anyone else. We had made a point of seeing them more often than usual. When we knew we were going to Akron to the healing service, we broached the matter to Howard. At first he was dubious and noncommital but, one evening, Sue called and said that he had agreed to come with us.

When the blizzard caused the postponement of our trip, Howard lost interest. We tried to convince him to accompany us a week later but to no avail. We later found out from Sue that an importunate door-to-door sermonizer had stopped by their ranch and bombarded Howard for two hours with a lecture on the subject of sin, hell and damnation. Howard had become so angry at the man's presumption, and so dismayed at the thought that he might have to associate with such people, that he clammed up and refused to discuss Akron or anything to do with God, even with Sue. Even the possibility of a miraculous healing with no strings attached was not open for discussion.

When we returned from Akron, we went to visit them and tell them all about it. Sue was enthralled with our testimony, but Howard listened with half an ear. A few days later, Sue called from Towanda and asked if we would come over again. She thought that if Jeremy were to tiptoe gently around the subject of healing, Howard might listen to him just once more. I promised that we would go over that very evening.

Conversation languished in generalities for a while until Jeremy could no longer contain himself. "Howard," he said, "you're as stubborn as a mule. There's a pool of crystal-clear water out there and you're thirsty but, just because someone's trying to lead you to it, you won't drink! What do you have to lose . . . a few gallons of gas and a day of your time? What's that against the chance of being healed of emphysema?" So much for tiptoeing gently.

"I don't know," Howard mumbled. "I sure don't. There's so much to do around here and I've got sales to go to the next couple of weekends. Sue keeps on at me about this, same as some other people, but I sure don't know." He brooded for a moment, then, "You know that funny little guy you met here the other day?"

"You mean the one who talks about money all the time?" Jeremy asked.

"That's the one alright. Well—he says he's a born-again Christian. Says his life was a mess but now it's all straightened out. Trouble is, I knew him before and after and he's just the same as he ever was. He sure is. Still talks about money all the time. Says he belongs to some Christian Businessman's Fellowship or something and that everything he touches turns to gold. What I can't figure is, if everything's so good, how come he spends all his time worrying about money, the same as before? I know how he got the money he had when he moved here. He's lucky he's still alive. He sure is."

"Look," Jeremy said, "I don't know nearly as much about all this as I should. I haven't been at it very long. The one thing I know for sure, though, is that you can't look at other people and try to make decisions based on them. Maybe this guy's a phoney. Maybe he's really born again and just taking a long time to see himself clearly enough to know he has to change. I don't know and frankly, Howard, he's not my immediate concern. You are. You're a good guy. You're an honest man. You believe in God—you've admitted it—and Sue's going to have a baby. You're sitting here with emphysema, worrying about all sorts of extraneous problems, when all you have to do is take a day of your time to go to Akron and be healed. You're already a better Christian than most Christians, but you won't accept what God is willing to give you."

"But I've got to go to these sales and get some more stock in here," Howard argued. "Maybe later on—when there's less to do."

"What good will more stock do you if you're flat on your can, too sick to do anything with them?" For a moment it appeared as though Jeremy had scored, but then Howard said, "Well, I don't know. I sure don't."

"Boy, I wish Serafino were here!" Jeremy exclaimed. "He'd know what to do with a stubborn old mule like you. Listen— if other people matter to you so much, look at Beed and me. We still have the same old worries. The only difference now is that we know everything will come out right if we keep on striving and praying. Beed's still struggling not to dwell on the hate part of her relationship with her mother. She's trying to put it out of her mind once and for all and think nothing but kind thoughts, but she needs time for such a huge emotional adjustment. Thank heavens I sold out of the trucking business last fall. The way I felt about my ex-partner, I never could have accepted all this. I despised him so much there were times I'd have liked to kill him with my bare hands. Now I wonder how I could have let him get to me so badly. But that part's easy for me, not hating him anymore, I mean. It's a thing of the past and I honestly wish him well.

"But it's different for Beed. Her Mother is an ongoing anxiety. It's easy for me to forget the bad and remember the good. I don't have to go on living with the bad. Beed has to, though. She has to make a conscious effort to purge her system of the bad memories. God knows she's trying, but it's going to take time. It will undoubtedly be easier for her when the book is finished. At least she won't have to keep on reliving the past every day.

"What I'm trying to say, I guess, is that it's different for everybody. Serafino, to use his own words, was a rascal before he was saved. He drank like a fish and ran anywhere and everywhere to hustle a buck. He walked into a Full Gospel Businessmen's Fellowship meeting one day—he never understood what led him there—and was slain in the Spirit. When he came to, everything was changed for him. He felt differently, saw everything differently, and his whole life changed in the instant.

"I wish it could be that way for me, but I know it won't. I'll have to read and study and reason every step of the way. The clincher for me was the healing of Beed's back. I accepted the healing as a miracle and I'm working my way from there. All I'm asking you to do is go to Akron and see for yourself. If you'll just—"

It was obvious that Jeremy was embarked on an all-or-nothing attempt to get Howard off the fence of indecision before the night was out. Sue beckoned and Justin and I followed her out to the barn. She showed us Farrah Fawcett, her ferret who had just had babies, and a wild mustang which a lady had adopted under a government program to thin the western herds. She had sent it to Howard to tame and train. The baby ferrets were adorable, climbing and tumbling all over the place, but the mustang had conformation that only its mother could love. Justin was much more taken with the ferrets. By the time we got back to the house some twenty minutes later, Howard and Jeremy were chatting about this and that and neither of them referred to the real purpose of our visit.

As soon as we were in the car and out of the driveway I said to Jeremy, "Well, how did it go after we left?"

"I honestly don't know. It's tough to read Howard. The only thing I'm certain of is that he's thinking. I'd say that Akron and those sales of his are about even money."

"I guess that's better than nothing," I said, looking on the bright side. "At least he didn't say no, and I sure mean no." We both chuckled.

The saddest part of the situation was that Howard could no longer handle anything physical. He made decisions and gave directions, but Sue and Caroline, Howard's eighteen-year-old daughter from an earlier marriage, did all the work. We were afraid that Howard was so frightened he was unable to see the forest for the trees. We felt that perhaps he was trying to deny the fragility of his health, even his mortality, by refusing to seek help. Jeremy decided that, if it came to another go-round with Howard, he was going to lean more heavily on the upcoming baby.

The next day Sue called to tell me that Howard had agreed to go with her to Akron the following Friday. Jeremy was out and I told Sue how thrilled and relieved he would be. We talked about Howard for several minutes, said a few hallelujahs and shed some tears of joy together over the phone. When Jeremy returned I gave him the good news. He let out a huge sigh. "Praise God!"

I fully expected to hear from Sue late Saturday or Sunday to let me know how things had gone, but it wasn't until Monday that she called. "I'm so sorry, B.D., but I just couldn't bring myself to call you till now." She sounded utterly distraught and on the verge of tears. "After all you went through, all the time you spent with Howard, and then, at the last minute, he wouldn't go. He said he wouldn't know what to do when he got there and it probably wouldn't work anyway. I didn't know whether to laugh at his helpless act, or cry out of pure frustration at his stubbornness. I think he'd go next Friday if Jeremy went with him, but I feel so guilty asking him to do it."

I was stuck for a moment. I was unwilling to say no, but I could not bring myself to say yes. Jeremy was out, so I used his absence as an excuse to postpone a decision. The trouble was that the coming weekend was Easter and we had made all sorts of plans. Ashley would be home from school again and we intended to do things together as a family. I did not feel that dragging the kids off to Akron again was exactly fair, but I did not want to leave it to my husband to go alone. We almost never did anything separately and, on the rare occasions we did, we were both miserable. It always sounded dumb when I tried to explain it to people, so I did not try anymore. It was, however, the reason that neither Jeremy nor I ever joined clubs or participated in activities that were exclusively for men or women.

"There's no need to feel guilty," I said. "It's not your fault Howard's so stubborn. I wouldn't go so far as to say it's his most endearing trait, but he is what he is and we all like him that way. Give me until Jeremy gets home and I'll tell him what's happened. One of us will call you later."

I broached the matter as soon as Jeremy walked in the door.

"I have to go," he said without hesitation. "You and the boys don't have to come too, but I have no choice but to go. I took it upon myself to witness to Howard and convince him to go to Ernest Angley for a healing. If I have to go with him, so be it." I started to say something but he held up his hand to stop me. "You know, Sweetie? The more we talk to people about our experiences, the more we witness to people, the more this kind of thing is likely to happen. Serafino mentioned being tested all the time. Well, I think we'll be tested in this as in everything else. If we undertake to do God's work, it has to be an absolute undertaking, not just something you take a passing shot at when convenient."

"I know that," I said. "You'll get no argument from me. But why Easter weekend? Why can't I just tell Sue that next weekend's no go but the following weekend's fine? What difference could it make?"

"Only one that I can think of: Howard's ready to go now. Postpone it for a week and another door banger may get at him. Don't forget what Serafino said about Satan. He hates to lose."

Jeremy was right, of course, and I had known it all along. It had been nothing more than a feeble hope that I wouldn't have to sacrifice a weekend to which I had been looking forward with anticipation. "O.K.," I said, albeit grudgingly, "we'll all go. But you explain it to the boys. I haven't the heart."

"No problem," Jeremy said. "Ashley will be home Wednesday night. I'll explain it to both of them at once. You tell Sue it's on and that we'll make the motel reservations."

At dinnertime on Wednesday, a remarkable and heart-warming thing happened. Jeremy explained the circumstances of Howard's aborted trip to Akron and told the boys we were all going again two days hence. Instead of the grumbling I had expected, both Ashley and Justin were enthusiastic about seeing Ernest Angley again. Justin had the only slight reservation. "Will we be back in time for the Wyalusing Easter egg hunt on Saturday, Dad?"

"I'm afraid not, son," his father answered. "It's a shame, but we won't get back till late in the afternoon or evening, the same as last time."

"Oh, well, it's not that important. I'd rather see Ernest Angley again."

And that was that. I would have to learn to trust more in the Lord's perfect plan and stop worrying about selfish details.

Due to our determination to partake of an offer of all the fish and chips we could eat for $4.95 per person in the dining room of the Holiday Inn, where the food was fine but the service atrocious, it was 6:10 P.M. by the time we arrived at Grace Cathedral. If the queues were impressive the first time we were there, this time they were mind numbing—if you had to get at the end of one with a sick friend, that is.

There were buses everywhere. The parking lot was full of

them and they were ahead of us looking for spaces, behind us and beside us. Cars were skittering about like water bugs on a lake with no apparent purpose in mind, although the purpose of all of us was to find a parking space. The queues stretched around the building and out into the lot, further impeding the progress of the vehicles toward their illusive goals. Jeremy stopped our car, Sue glued to our tail in theirs, and told Ashley to get into what looked like the shortest line to wait for the rest of us.

When we had disposed of the cars, Sue, Howard, Caroline, Justin and I went to join Ashley while Jeremy made a circuit of the church to see if there was a shorter queue somewhere. There wasn't. For half an hour our line inched forward while my husband and I grew more and more desperate in our fear that there would be no room left in the main sanctuary by the time we got there. We threaded our way up stairs and around corridors, inch by nervous inch, until, at 6:40, we were into the sanctuary.

There was not a single seat left. Our hearts fell as we stood, in utter despair, and watched ushers steering people off to a descending staircase which led to the lower level and the T.V. monitors. The Roedigers were not aware of the situation and neither Jeremy nor I had the courage to explain. We took a few steps forward, out of the still-moving line, and stared in shock at the packed pews. I would not go so far as to say that I was actively praying for a miracle—my mind was too numb for that—but that's exactly what we received. Or so it was to us at the time. Some ushers appeared carrying folding chairs which they set up behind the last row of pews. We took another step forward and were seated.

The service began as before with Rev. Angley again making his appearance at eight. He spoke for a time on the subject of Jesus suffering on the cross to heal us of all our sickness and cleanse us of all our sins; of His dying to redeem our souls. It was a beautiful sermon, rendered more so by the obvious intensity of the reverend's emotion while delivering it. It was not that he shouted or gesticulated or indulged in any form of histrionics; it was an emotion that welled up from within him and communicated itself to all of us. There were few dry eyes in the congregation when he finished.

Next came the Words of Knowledge. Rev. Angley made his way up and down the aisles and many healings were claimed. I prayed that one such would be for Howard, but it was not to be. Things were going very smoothly until a lady, healed of a lung problem, raised her arms and shouted, "Thank you, Jesus!" Such a reaction is perfectly normal and frequently begets sympathetic words of praise and thanks from others in the congregation. This time, however, the anointing on the service was all but destroyed.

An extremely tall black lady, with a shrill, high-pitched, southern accent, jumped up and began to howl, "Thank you, Jesus! Thank you, Jesus! Thank you, Jesus! . . ." On and on and on she went. After some thirty or so seconds of this, her seated companion tried to get her to stop by tugging a few times at her dress. Rev. Angley returned to the platform and waited. "Thank you, Jesus! Thank you, Jesus! Thank you, Jesus! . . ." Louder and louder. Rev. Angley began to speak but his words were completely drowned out. Not even his microphone could overcome the shrillness of the woman's howling. "Thank you, Jesus! Thank you, Jesus! . . ." Five minutes . . . ten minutes . . . "Thank you, Jesus! Thank you, Jesus! Thank you, Jesus! . . ." The reverend continued to speak without trying to silence the woman. No one could hear him. Howard was mumbling and muttering to Sue, "I told you we shouldn't have come . . . no different than those southern churches . . . bunch of fanatics . . . can't stand these holy rollers . . . sure can't . . . complete waste of time . . . sale at Unadilla . . . work to do . . ." "Thank you, Jesus! Thank you, Jesus! Thank you, Jesus! . . ." Fifteen minutes.

We have since learned that almost all pastors will put a stop to a disruptive demonstration such as this. It is accepted that no one praying in the Spirit will ever do so in a fashion which disrupts an ongoing service. Consequently, a pastor confronted with such a situation will say something like, "You're praying in the flesh, not the Spirit, and that's enough. Please sit down and be quiet." For whatever reason, however, Rev. Angley did not tell the woman to sit down. "Thank you, Jesus! Thank you, Jesus! Thank you, Jesus! . . ."

Twenty minutes. Finally! We were not so much aware of the howler having stopped as we were of our sudden ability to hear what the reverend was saying. "We're only going to do a few healings tonight because we're here to celebrate Christ's sacrifice on the cross at Calvary. . . ."

He went on to call forward two people, who had evidently made arrangements ahead of time, and all the people who had come on a bus from a senior citizen's home. As they made their way to the platform the realization hit me like a lead weight in my stomach: this was it—we'd blown it! It was Good Friday and there was not going to be a full healing service. I wasn't even sure, after the howler, whether there would have been in any event. But, there wasn't, and that was that. We had dragged Howard all the way here, mostly against his wishes, and we had blown it. It was all I could do to stop myself from crying aloud. What had we done wrong? Why should Howard be punished for something Jeremy or I had done? What *had* we done?

Then I remembered something Pat Robertson quite often said: "God rewards perseverance." I leaned across to Sue. "Take Howard down *now*. Just mingle with the other people down there. But don't waste any time—grab him by the elbow and drag him if you have to, but take him down *now*."

The urgency in my tone must have conveyed itself to Howard since he put up but token resistance before getting up and permitting Sue to help him down the aisle. By the time they got near the platform, a considerable crowd had formed behind the huddle of old folks. We were unable to see what was happening but we could hear various healings taking place. Approximately ten minutes elapsed; then we saw Rev. Angley climb the steps back to the platform and cross it to the alcove.

The crowd which had gathered uninvited, including Howard, was not to be ministered to. Howard and Sue made their way slowly back to their seats. Howard was quite winded when he sat down and Caroline, seeing his condition and assuming that her father was not going to be healed, burst into tears. Ashley, very sweetly, tried to comfort her and told her not to give up hope, but in vain. Caroline put her head on his shoulder and sobbed her heart out.

While Rev. Angley was talking to his assistants in the alcove, Howard began to talk about leaving the church and Sue began to cry. Jeremy and I whispered back and forth to each other in a slough of hopelessness. We wanted to do something but we could not figure out what. Our attention was drawn back to Rev. Angley when his voice came over the microphone. He was talking to a man in a wheelchair who, we learned, was an old, retired miner who had been crippled by a cave-in twenty years earlier.

The reverend reached forward and took the man's hands. "In the Name of Jesus, I command you to walk." The old miner stood up and Rev. Angley instructed him to walk with him up the steps and across the platform for all to see. The miner was a little unsteady and leaning heavily upon the reverend, but they made it up the steps and a few paces along the platform. The miner was staring determinedly at his feet.

"Look up," Rev. Angley commanded. "Look up to Jesus."

"I need someone on the other side to help me," the miner said.

"Jesus is there to help you if you'll reach out to Him. Look up."

The miner continued to stare downward and began to relive the moment of the cave-in and the hours during which he was buried alive and crippled.

Rev. Angley told him that he must put all that behind him and reach out in faith for Jesus if he wanted to be healed, that Jesus was trying to heal him but he was blocking his own healing with doubts. They continued to walk together, the miner continually stumbling, being held up by the reverend, and staring at the floor. "I can't do it!"

"You're walking *now*, aren't you?"

"Yes, but—"

"No buts—just look up and accept your healing."

"I can't!"

"Yes, you can. Look up!"

It was no use. The miner gave up altogether and collapsed on the floor. Rev. Angley called two ushers over to return the old miner to his wheelchair. With tears in his eyes he turned to the congregation and said that it was the most extreme lack of faith he had ever tried to deal with. He pulled himself together and went to the alcove once more.

There was another man sitting in a wheelchair who had

not walked for two or three years. The attendant said that he had a brain tumor. The instant Rev. Angley touched him, he was out of the chair and not just walking, but jumping up and down and praising God.

"Now there," said Rev. Angley, "is a real miracle. Look at this! Look what the Lord can do if you have the faith to receive it!"

With all the healings God had performed through him during the thirty years of his ministry, he actually seemed relieved. It was difficult to believe, but there it was. Many, many times since that night my husband and I have discussed the events and wondered about them. It has been our absolute belief that the "howler" so upset the service, and indeed the reverend, that the anointing of the Lord upon the proceedings, which is so vital, was missing. There has to be unanimity of purpose and of faith for there to be a heavy anointing at any given time. The howler had destroyed it.

Rev. Angley left the alcove, and all the other waiting sick and disabled, and returned to the center of the platform. He delivered a sermon on faith, pointing out that we can all be healed by our own prayer if we have sufficient faith.

This was too much for Howard, who had been paying attention during the incident of the miner and the subsequent healing, but was now determined to leave. Despite Sue's tearful protests, he got up and made his way toward the main entrance. Sue whispered that she was sorry and hurried after him. Caroline cried harder than ever and Jeremy and I were at our wits' ends.

"You go after Howard and get him back here," I said. "I'm going to talk to someone. There has to be something we can do."

Leaving Rev. Angley preaching, Jeremy took off after Howard and Sue while I went to seek I knew not whom. I wandered around the corridors until I bumped into an usher who seemed to have nothing immediate to do. I explained our predicament to him and asked his advice. He was most sympathetic and kind and suggested that I go down to the area of Rev. Angley's office, and seek out the usher on duty there and present the problem for his consideration. I asked directions but was so overwrought I found them impossible to follow. There were just too many ups, downs, lefts, rights and can't-miss-its. I decided to return to our seats, make sure that Howard had been brought back, and then ask Jeremy to take care of the next phase.

Howard, Sue and Jeremy were indeed back in their seats. Howard looked grim and irritable, Sue was sniffling and my husband had his head bowed and his hands clasped in prayer. The choir was singing hymns. I tapped Jeremy on the shoulder and explained what I had discovered.

"Did the usher say we had a chance?" Jeremy asked.

"He didn't say anything definite about chances. He just seemed to imply there was a chance of doing something by giving me the advice he did. I mean, why would he send me off to bother the usher on duty by Rev. Angley's office if there weren't some purpose to it?"

"Well, anything's better than sitting here chewing my fingernails to the bone. I'll find out where the office is and give it a try."

Jeremy left and I began to pray. "Oh, God," I whispered, "guide my husband to the right usher and put a burden on him to understand our dilemma. Grant, Lord, that the usher will know of some way that Howard can get the healing he so desperately needs and which is being denied him because of some fault of mine. I don't know what we did wrong, Lord, but Howard . . ." And suddenly I knew what we had done wrong.

In all our talks with Howard, mostly Jeremy's, we had been so careful not to upset him by sounding like religious fanatics that we never mentioned Jesus. We mentioned God from time to time, but almost exclusively we talked about miracle healing. Because of our weakness, our fear of losing Howard, we had permitted him to come here, not in faith, but as a welfare recipient demanding his due. We had overlooked that although Jesus performed miracles and then preached, He did both together. He did not heal the sick and then wait a week or two before preaching to them. That is what we had done. We were relying on Ernest Angley to bring Howard his healing, believing that we would then be safe to witness to Howard without fear of losing him. We were the ones short in faith, not Howard. Howard had not received a true witness from us because we had not trusted in God's word. We had thought to finesse Howard into a healing first and faith later.

And look what a mess we had made: Caroline crying endlessly on Ashley's shoulder, Sue weakening in her faith and Howard rapidly and, perhaps, irretrievably, losing what little faith he had before we blundered in and presumed to advise without sufficient understanding. I prayed again and asked God's forgiveness for Jeremy's and my failure. I also asked Him to take mercy on Howard and not punish him for our wrongdoing.

When Jeremy returned he was beaming with pleasure. "There's an usher down there who'll take care of the whole thing for us. All we have to do is get Howard down there. The usher will give Howard and Sue a little cubicle to wait in. As soon as Rev. Angley comes to the end of the services, he always exits by the door leading to his office. The usher will have Howard waiting right there. Apparently the reverend never leaves anyone standing flatfooted in the corridor. You were right, Sweetie. God rewards perseverance." And also forgives us our shortcomings, I thought.

Jeremy and Sue took Howard between them and left for the nether regions of the church and the corridor leading to Rev. Angley's office. The choir continued to sing until communion was served and Rev. Angley delivered his final address. I must admit that, until Jeremy returned and indicated that everything was under control, I didn't hear a word—I was too busy praying.

After his sermon, the reverend led us in prayer and praise. The prayer continued for a long time, although not breaking into a spontaneous praise in tongues as it had the first time we were there. People started to move into the aisles and depart while others were still praying.

"Let's go," Jeremy said, "or we'll never make our way through the crowd to where Howard is."

We joined the exodus, Jeremy firmly clutching Justin's hand lest we lose him in the crowd, and wended our way through the ups and downs and circuitous corridors to the cubicle where Howard and Sue had been left with the usher. I do not know whether Rev. Angley returned to the waiting sick in the alcove or not. Once people had started to leave their seats all over the church, it was impossible to see.

There was no sign of anyone in the cubicle or the corridor which led to the reverend's office, so we headed for the car. When we got there we were greeted with the most amazing and uplifting sight. Howard, with Sue hugging his arm, was sitting behind the wheel of his car grinning from ear to ear. "He healed me. He sure did. I felt the power go right through me." We agreed to leave the rest of the story until we got back to the motel.

Ensconced in our room with coffee and doughnuts that we had picked up on the way, Howard gave us his testimony. "That usher sure was a nice guy. He had several heart attacks four years ago. He was supposed to die if he had another one. He was healed right here. He's been fine ever since. He was so grateful, he's been working for Ernest Angley for the last few years just to be near him. He talked to me until the reverend came out of the auditorium and then took me into the corridor that he had to pass through. When he saw me he said, 'What can God do for you, brother?' I told him I had emphysema real bad and he asked if I was born again. I said no. He asked if I smoked and I said no." Jeremy gave Howard a look that spoke for itself. Howard continued, "I know I chew, but he didn't ask that. He sure didn't. He asked if I smoked and I don't.

"Anyway, he touched my forehead and I felt a kinda chill. He said, 'In the Name of Jesus, I command your lungs and your whole system to be free of disease. Yayah!' Then I went right out. I sure did."

"He just sprawled on the floor and lay there," said Sue. "I helped him up after a few minutes. He was just grinning and happy, but wouldn't say much. I asked him if he felt better and all he said was, 'God healed me.' It's no use trying to get Howard to talk when he doesn't want to, so we came out here to wait for you."

"Praise the Lord," Jeremy said fervently. "Do you actually feel any different yet, Howard, or is it going to take time?"

"I don't really feel any different, but I know I'm healed," Howard replied. The faith was there. Howard was healed. We hoped that the healing would become apparent quickly, for Howard's sake.

* * *

Early the next morning, Sue knocked on our door. "I'm sorry if I woke you up but I had to tell you. After we left your room last night, Howard sat down on his bed and started to cough. I've never heard him cough so bad. It frightened me to death. Then he started to spit up the most horrible-looking stuff. There was so much of it he had to go in the bathroom and hang his head over the toilet. He coughed and spit out junk for a whole hour. I prayed and prayed. I thought he was dying.

"When it was all over Howard was exhausted. He lay down on his bed on his back and slept like a baby. Do you know how long it's been since Howard could lie down on his back? Years. He hasn't been able to sleep on his back for ten years. He slept like a baby—on his back."

CHAPTER

DURING MY NEXT FEW CONVERSATIONS WITH MY MOTHER I TRIED to tell her more about my faith and our miracles. I had no success, Mother only being interested in her staff problems. One day, however, my persistence brought an explosive response: "I've rebroken my hip!" Caught by surprise, my reaction was, "Oh, good heavens! Did you fall again or what?"

Mother had broken her hip early in January. Although extremely painful, the break had been shallow and a pin had been inserted without surgery. Mother was out of the hospital and back in her condominium at the Colonial House in four days. She used a wheelchair and a walker, the break mended quickly and well, and the wheelchair was dispensed with in a few weeks.

"No, no. Nothing like that," she replied. "It's just terribly painful and I know it's broken again." She paused. "So—now I'm stuck in L.A. despite the Olympics. Brother! Does that make you happy?"

There was not a doubt in my mind that this was nothing but a red herring, but the thought did not occur to me until sometime later that Mother now felt constrained to compete for my attention, not only with my husband and children, but also with God.

She steadfastly refused to go to the hospital for X rays, but insisted that the hospital send a doctor and technicians, with all their equipment, to her apartment. Since this was patently impossible, one of the nursing staff—Harold had kept them on to keep Mother company until the servant problem became resolved—eventually succeeded in inducing her to go to the hospital. X rays were taken and showed nothing untoward. The hip had mended splendidly and there were no complications.

Mother called me and said, "Brother! The doctors in this town are all idiots. Not one of them gives a hoot about me." I said I was sure they knew what they were doing and congratulated her on the good news regarding her hip.

"Good news?" Mother exploded. "Brother! They're just too stupid to figure it out. My hip's in big trouble."

The next time Mother called, I again tried to tell her what was happening in my life. "Guess what I did Easter weekend?"

"I don't know what *you* did," she said peevishly, "but at least *I* didn't have to interview anybody for a few days. Gawd! I've interviewed enough cooks to last me a lifetime."

"Who's doing the cooking?"

"The nurses. Who else? We're living on Stouffer's frozen dinners. They're better, I might add, than most of the so-called meals these high-priced cooks have to offer."

"Why don't you just get a decent housekeeper, then, and live on the better-class frozen dinners? Goodness knows there are enough of each."

"Are you kidding? Brother! Housekeepers cost a fortune!" She seemed to muse for a moment. "I suppose they don't cost any more than the cooks and the food they ruin."

"We went to Grace Cathedral again on Good Friday. It was our second time in two weeks."

"That's fascinating. Pray for me to find a decent cook. I can't take much more of this."

"Alright, I will. But you should have been there. Jesus healed dozens of people and I took communion for the first time in my life."

"What! You aren't a Catholic, are you?"

"Communion isn't just Catholic. It's a Christian commemoration of the death of Christ. It was wonderful." I was trying to answer her in short sentences in the hope that she would ask more questions.

"Were *you* healed of anything?"

"Not this time. We took a friend who was healed of emphysema. He was dying of it."

"You mean you've been there before? Where did you say it was?"

"Akron, Ohio. It's Ernest Angley's healing ministry. We were there the first time on April 6."

"April 6? You didn't tell me you'd been to Ohio on April 6."

"You never gave me the chance. Everything that was wrong with me was healed."

"What do you mean, everything that was wrong with you? What was wrong with you?"

"Oh, come on, Mother! You know perfectly well that I've had bad ankles, colitis and varicose veins. As well as my back, that is. You've known about it all for years. Well, it's all been healed."

"*Ha!* Maybe *I* should go some time and get all fixed up. Brother! If God will do it for you and all those other people, He'll certainly do it for *me*."

"Yes, He will," I said, taking a deep breath, "but you have to go there repentant and at least *seeking* Jesus. If you don't go in—"

"I'm very happy for you, dear. Just pray for me and love me a lot. I have to go now—love you."

It was an improvement. A very big one, in fact. She would not listen beyond a certain point, but at least she had listened up to that point. She had even been polite at the end of the conversation instead of just hanging up. For the first time I felt that I really had a chance. I prayed intensely for God to use this tiny opening to reach Mother's heart.

On May 4, we were still waiting for spring to arrive in our corner of Pennsylvania. March had ended with a blizzard, April had begun with two feet of snow on the ground, a thaw and a flood, and since then we'd had nothing but rain, freeze, rain, freeze and more freeze. Nothing but gooey mud or frozen mud. Fruit blossoms were severly damaged and the corn crop was so late in getting planted that many farmers were verbally writing it off even as they were planting. The Sharers were so late that there was no time left to plant any oats before haying had to begin.

Jeremy and I made a decision. We had long been discussing moving to a warmer climate, preferably an island. We had been to Jamaica twice and loved the island culture. Unfortunately, Jamaica itself was out of the question because of its economic and other problems. We began to discuss where we would like to live and quickly became agoraphobic. The very notion that we were only governed by the availability of schools, water and whimsy nearly threw us into a panic when we started to contemplate how many islands there were. The number of prospects diminished rapidly, however, once we got out an atlas and studied the trouble spots in the world and took into our considerations what was too close to which.

We sent for brochures, wrote to friends and friends of friends, communicated with real estate agents and read about tax laws and civil laws. Tortola was a possibility for a while but, the more we read about it, the more it sounded like a fish preserve with a Victorian dress code. Jeremy fell in love with the notion of having the Dry Tortugas as an address. He thought it sounded very piratey—it's a shame there's nothing there but turtles. And so it went, one island or group of islands after another. We were not to settle on the Bahamas, and Grand Bahama in particular, for months.

Mother's next phone call led me to believe that she had actually been thinking about God. "Tell me how you decided to become a Christian," Mother said. "Is that what you call it—a Christian?"

"Yes, a Christian, actually a born-again Christian. We met a delightful man one day. He was delivering something we'd ordered and he mentioned that he was a Christian. Jeremy started asking his usual cynical questions and Serafino—that's the man's name—had very good answers for all of them. One thing led to another and we wound up having dinner with

Serafino and his wife a couple of times and learning about Jesus. I became convinced and started reading the Bible. Then my back was healed and Jeremy accepted it as the miracle it was and also accepted Jesus. We—"

"Yes, yes." Impatiently. "But why?"

"Because of the love and joy He offered and—"

"*Ha*! So that's what it's all about. Brother! Your husband doesn't love you anymore so you've gone and got religion. You can't say I didn't warn you. I'm just surprised it's taken you so long to admit it, that's all."

"Oh, for heaven's sake, Mother! Will you please be serious? I'm talking about the love of God and Jesus. On top of that, I'm not talking about religion—I haven't 'gone and got religion.' I needed God; we all do. I—"

"What do you mean, we all need God?"

"You know that feeling of loneliness we all get, even depression at times? The feeling that there's no purpose to it all, that life is just one big hassle after another and that there's no point to it? That's what I'm talking about—that void within each and every one of us. That void is the lack of God. Without God, we're not complete. But He won't force Himself on us. We have to seek Him out. Jesus is the way—"

"I don't get it. Are you saying it's all *my* fault because I didn't make you get all dressed up and ship you off to Sunday school when you were little? Brother! If I'd known you were going to blame me for that too, I'd have made you go."

"I'm not blaming you for anything, Mother. It wouldn't have made a scrap of difference if I *had* gone to Sunday school, or even church. None of it means a thing unless there's an awareness of Jesus as one's personal Lord and Savior. The world is full of people who go to church every Sunday and that's all they do. They don't read their Bibles, they make no effort to live the lives that Jesus wants them to—far from it— on Monday mornings they go right back to boozing, lying and cheating on their wives or husbands. What we're discussing is being right with God. Going—"

"But weren't you always a Christian? You were brought up in the Episcopal Church. You were even married in the Episcopal Church. Doesn't that count for anything?"

"No, it doesn't. And anyway, I wasn't brought up in the

Episcopal Church. I never went to church in my life. As for choosing All Saints for our wedding, that was only to have a traditional wedding and you know it."

"Then what did I go to all that trouble for? Brother! It cost a fortune."

"And I've always been grateful. It was a beautiful wedding and I loved every minute of it. But so did you. You wouldn't have settled for anything less. But we're getting away from the point. The point is Jesus Christ and our obligation to accept or reject Him. There's no in between. And if we accept Him, we must accept the Bible in its entirety. The Bible is God's word and it cannot be changed."

"Do you mean to tell me you believe all that stuff about the Immaculate Conception? Brother! You can't convince *me* that Joseph didn't do it to Mary. Jesus!"

"He's the guy, Mother. If you believe in God, you believe He can do anything. He created every grain of sand in the universe and all of *us*. Through the Holy Spirit he placed the embryo of His Son in Mary's womb before she married Joseph. An angel of the Lord visited Joseph to put his mind at rest about—"

"*Ha*! That's a laugh! She got knocked up before she was even married, for Christ's sake. Some virgin! I don't believe you can actually swallow all that rot. Jesus!"

"He's the guy."

"I suppose you'll tell me next that heaven and hell are real."

"They certainly are—very, very real. That's why it's so important for every man, woman and child to accept Jesus. You're either for or against Him. There's no middle ground, no wait and see. We all—"

"Heaven and hell are right here on earth. Don't tell *me*!"

"In certain respects that's true, but only in the worldly sense. On the day of judgment we'll all go to one or the other for all eternity. I intend to go to heaven. Most people seem to think they're going to heaven, but they can't be bothered to find out about the entrance exams—it's too much bother. Well—"

"Didn't you say that Jeremy had become a Christian too?"

"Yes, I did. He—"

"Well! If *that* bastard's going to heaven, I don't want to go!"

* * *

Sue Roediger and I talked several times during the weeks following our trip to Akron together. We kept trying to get a dinner organized, either at their house or ours, but there always seemed to be something that one of us had to do on any night convenient to the other. I did learn that Howard was telling everybody about his healing and attributing it, as he should, to Jesus. His old, God-is-private-and-not-to-be-discussed-publicly attitude was gone. Sue was elated over the change in her husband and asked that Jeremy and I keep him in our prayers. We fixed a date for dinner at their house some ten days hence and swore that this time we would let nothing upset it.

When we drove into the yard at the ranch, the difference in Howard was thrilling. He was bustling about, busy as a beaver, and promptly took us on a guided tour of the new stock in the barns. It was just like the good old days. The expression in his eyes told it all: there was joy where there had been fear.

During dinner we learned that he had been to the doctor with a chest problem. The doctor had confirmed that there was no remaining trace of emphysema and diagnosed Howard's current problem as a touch of bronchitis. He had warned Howard not to get overconfident, since he would remain susceptible to chest colds and infections, and again suggested that he move away from the harshness of our winters.

"The trouble is," Howard explained to us, "I put the ranch on the market when Sue and I went to Arizona for a year a while back and had no luck. On account of the indoor ring, I have to get more money for it than people are willing to pay. Unless somebody comes along who wants to run a horse business here, I can't afford to leave. I sure can't."

"Howard," I said, "have you ever heard the expression 'Put you trust in the Lord?' You, of all people, should now know what that means. Start praying for something to turn up and it will. Don't ask me what—I don't know. Just pray for help and guidance and you'll get it. God won't let you down so long as you have faith in His Word."

"I sure saw what lack of faith can do," Howard said. "Do you remember that miner, that old man who refused to be healed? Wasn't that something? I mean, he actually got up and walked. He sure did. But he refused to look up and accept his healing from Jesus. He just stared at the floor and said, 'I can't, I can't.' Wasn't it something? It was just like Peter walking a few steps on the water and then saying 'I can't' before he sank. Darnedest thing I ever saw. It sure was."

And to think that Jeremy and I had believed the old miner to be largely responsible for almost putting Howard off. Far from it. Of all the things that happened that night, the old miner was the most important to Howard's faith. There is no doubt that God was sorely disappointed that the miner refused his healing—for God wants perfect health for all His children—and there is also no doubt that, had the miner accepted his healing, God would have found some other way to bring Howard around. The fact is, and one must always remember this, God gave us free will and it is up to us to have the faith to stand on God's promises.

We were beginning to learn, slowly but surely, how great a mistake it is to question God's methods or His plan. If your prayers do not seem to have been answered, persevere but be patient. In the fullness of time you will find that God has done what is best for you—even though you may not immediately recognize it as such.

Howard went on about the old miner at considerable length. According to Sue, it had been his main topic of conversation for weeks. More often than not, he told his listeners about the miner's lack of faith before mentioning his own healing. The only cloud on Sue's much-brightened horizon was that she had not yet been able to talk Howard into going to church with her. Jeremy suggested that she leave well enough alone. "Beed and I don't go to church. We haven't felt any pressing need to. But, who knows? One of these days we may decide to go. Maybe Howard will surprise you. If he doesn't, though, I don't think it matters. It's one's faith that counts, not going to church. Just don't let Howard forget. If you think he's starting to waver, remind him of the old miner."

The entire Fazio family came to stay for the weekend of June 22. It was a wonderful few days, just like having one's favorite, but long lost, relatives show up en masse. The three girls, Rhonda, Michelle and Christine, were as charming as their parents. Ashley, in particular, was very taken with them since it was his first chance to discuss his faith with members of his own peer group.

Justin and Ashley had not been baptized, nor had my husband or I since becoming Christians. Serafino had checked with his pastor and confirmed that it was entirely scriptural for anyone who is born again to conduct baptisms. Armed with the appropriate Scripture, he had arrived ready to dunk the lot of us in the water of our choice. We picked Sunday as the day on which to do it and spent much time debating the relative merits of Wyalusing Creek versus our swimming pool as the place.

The creek undoubtedly bore a stronger resemblance to the River Jordan and we were leaning in its favor, mud and all, until Sunday dawned. Miserable, cold, pouring rain. Even the thought of getting in the pool gave us the shudders. The creek lost out. Serafino donned his trunks and baptized each of us in turn. Despite the wretchedness of the weather, the chlorine, and Serafino's appearance being antithetical to that of John the Baptist, it was a most marvelously uplifting experience and one we shall never forget.

I would not go so far as to say that I believed my attempts to witness to my mother were on the verge of bearing fruit, but I was beginning to feel there was hope if I could stay the course. Our next phone conversation led to Mother asking, "What do I have to give up if I become a Christian?" I crossed my fingers and plunged right in. "Swearing, lying, being cruel, getting drunk—"

"I don't *get* drunk, you bitch! And as for—"

"I'm not *accusing*, Mother. You asked a question and I was trying to give you a straight answer. I was beginning to list the things that God proscribes in His children's behavior. Swearing, for instance, is an—"

"I hardly ever swear. *Jesus!*"

"He's the one alright, but *you* only mention His Name as a swearword. You're no more aware of how much you swear than I was. It was just part of my speech."

"*Well! I'm* not changing for God *or* man. *Christ!* I can tell you that much right now. No *man* is going to be in charge of *me!*" I was still trying to think of what to say next when Mother continued. "How do you know God is a man, anyway?"

"Because throughout the Bible He's referred to as Him."

"Jesus!"

"That's right."

"That stinks!"

"Not at all. It's beautiful."

"You're nuts! Brother! What do you see in all this, anyway? You're just knuckling under to some man who claimed to be the Son of God. What do you get out of it? I've lived my life *my* way this far, and nothing's going to change me now. You don't make any sense."

I was beginning to understand why so many people quoted from the Scriptures when trying to make their points. I had been inclined to scoff at the argument that one had to be armed with God's Word. Perhaps, after all, they were right. Perhaps the only way to avoid the sort of dead ends at which I kept finding myself with my mother was to quote Scripture. The trouble was, I could not do it. Oh, I could do it if I set my mind to it, but it would take years of work. Mother was now— I did not have years. I decided to try something new. I did not hold out much hope with respect to reading matter, but I might get her to watch the *700 Club*. Despite her protestations to the contrary, Mother did watch a lot of television.

"Look," I said, "I'll send you some magazines to read. They contain all sorts of miracle testimonies. You don't have to read everything, just skim through them and read anything that catches your eye. All of it's true and maybe something will make an impression on you. Besides that, you could watch the *700 Club* on television. You'd understand more of what I'm trying to tell you if you did."

"What's the *700 Club*?" I explained what it was, including the reminder that it was due to a Word of Knowledge on that program that my back had been healed.

"I still don't understand," Mother said, "why God healed your back but won't listen to *me*. Brother! Have I prayed!"

"Prayer alone won't do it, Mother. Healing comes from Jesus and we have to accept Jesus as our personal Lord and Savior before we can expect answers to our prayers. You can't just say a prayer one day and expect results, let alone a miraculous healing, without first doing what God demands of you."

"I've always believed in God."

"That's great, but you have to do your homework and make a commitment. Read the magazines I'm sending and watch the *700 Club*. I think you'll better understand what I'm talking about."

"We'll see."

Once I was off the phone my subconscious must have gone to work. Why it had not occurred to me before that my book would have to be torn up if Mother accepted the Lord, I do not know. I can only assume that I found it so improbable that she would listen to me about this, when she had never before listened to me about anything else, that I simply neglected to give the matter any thought. Now I had to. "We'll see" was a very positive statement coming from my mother. I had never known her to equivocate when she was dead-set against something.

I broached the matter to Jeremy after dinner that evening. "Have you given any thought to what we'll do if I succeed in witnessing to my mother?"

"Of course I have," he replied. "Quite often, in fact. But I came to the conclusion the odds were so long against your succeeding, it wasn't worth considering. Why? Do you think you're making progress?"

"I wouldn't exactly call it progress, but she *is* asking questions. She never seems to accept anything I say without a rebuttal or an epithet but, nearly every time I talk to her, the conversation comes around to Christianity. It's usually Mother who brings it up, too."

"Well, praise the Lord. Maybe she'll come around. It would be one heck of a miracle but we both know God's in the miracle business."

"I agree. The question is: what do we do if she does? Accept Jesus, I mean?"

"I assume you mean what do we do about the book?" Jeremy said.

"Right."

"That's easy. We can't publish it. You'll just have to pretend you wrote a long letter but never mailed it."

"I know, but suppose we have it finished, delivered to Jay [my agent, Jay Garon] and he's sold it to some publisher—then what do we do?"

"Punt."

"Come on! I'm serious. If Mother accepts salvation after we've sold the book, what do we do?"

"That's the point at which I stopped thinking about it. If you want an answer, give me a few minutes to think. Matter of fact, you wash the dishes and I'll go for a walk. Maybe I'll have an inspiration."

And off he went to search for inspiration. The truth of the matter was that he did have his best ideas when he went for a walk. He also avowed that alone at night in the great outdoors was when he felt closest to God. He always went for a walk before going to bed in order to pray.

I was finished with the dishes and ten minutes into a television show by the time Jeremy returned. He was grinning broadly. "You'll write another book."

"What do you mean, write another book? What good will that do? How does that help if we've already sold this one to a publisher?"

"We'll tell the publisher what's happened and say that this one is no longer relevant, as is, and that you have to just use bits and pieces of it to set the scene, and then tell the story of how a couple of dumb agnostics came to Jesus and brought the great lady with them. They'll love it—it'll have a great ending.

"And, as far as writing another book goes, you ought to do it anyway. How many agnostics can put their testimony in writing and stand a chance of it being published? If My Mother's Keeper has been published, it'll be a sequel. You'll have a whole constituency out there wondering what happened next. Let's tell them.

"In a nutshell, it'll either be two books rolled into one if your mother accepts Jesus in time to pull MMK, or MMK and a sequel if she doesn't. Hopefully, the sequel will include her salvation. If it's part of God's plan, it will include her salvation." Jeremy had paced back and forth the whole time he was talking. He flopped into an armchair, raised his eyebrows expectantly and added, "As Spyros Skouras used to say after the screening of every new Fox picture, 'Tell me how much you love it.' "

I could only see one loophole. "I love it except for one thing: what happens if Mother accepts Jesus before actual publication of MMK but too late to pull it? Suppose it's on the presses or something."

"It's such a long shot we have to ignore the possibility. We'll put our faith in the Lord's perfect plan."

"O.K., I love it. But—who's going to write the sequel? You've been around during the time frame involved, just as much as I have, so why don't *you* write it?"

"Except for conversations with your mother, I suppose that's true, but it's better if you're the author of record. Who cares what a son-in-law thinks?"

"We can argue about the cover credit another time. I'm talking about actually doing the writing. Are you willing to at least co-write it with me?"

"Sure—it'll be fun."

CHAPTER

ONE AFTERNOON HAROLD SCHIFF CALLED TO SAY THAT HE NEEDED my help in inducing Mother to finally write her book. I did not know too much about it, but Mother had signed a contract with a publisher at least two years earlier. A ghostwriter had spent significant time with her and had produced at least one, if not two, complete books which Mother had, apparently, decided she did not like. The publisher had run out of patience, the ghostwriter was miserable, and Harold had become very anxious and—in order to avoid Mother having to repay the advance she had accepted—had made a deal with a new publisher to take over the old contract.

Mother, it seemed, had long since derailed the original concept with which she had been approached—a memoir of her love life to be called *Husbands, Lovers and Other Strangers*—and had refused to countenance anything more than a reworking of her 1959 autobiography, *The Lonely Life*. I was not at all clear as to what she was supposed to be writing for the new publisher but, with her ongoing financial problems, it seemed the least I could do to put in a word for Harold's cause.

I did not have to conjure up a means of broaching the matter to Mother, for she called me and launched right into her grand plan for the summer. "B.D.! I've just got to write this lousy book and I can't stand my apartment in summer. Weeps! Besides that, you know I'll go mad with all the Olympic traffic. I'm renting a beach house in Malibu. I need it for my soul— and anyway, walking on the beach every day will be good for my hip. Tell me you approve."

"Mother," I said as calmly as I could, "I keep praying that one day I'll be able to talk to you without getting angry about something. Wasn't it you, a couple of weeks ago, telling me how panicked you were about money? Didn't you say, to use your own words, that you were flat broke? Isn't the only reason you're even considering going back to writing your book that you need the money? That was you, wasn't it, or am I confusing you with someone else?"

"Yes, but—"

"But me no buts, Mother! You have a huge, beautiful condominium in Los Angeles, and half an hour away you rent a beach house that has to cost a fortune. Considering the fact that you're writing the book solely for the money—which you always resent and are only doing because Harold's got you frightened—I'm completely baffled."

"I'm doing the book because I have a new, and far better I might add, deal with a new publisher. Brother! I'll be the judge of what I can and cannot afford. How can you be so mean? You never think I make any sense. You don't *want* to understand me. Sometimes I wonder how I managed to raise you."

Even though I wanted desperately to blurt out, as usual, my frustration at Mother's refusal to contemplate practicalities, I bit my tongue and tried to see her point of view. I did not do very well and wondered whether this conflict within me would ever cease.

"Well," I said, "at least put my mind at rest about one thing: since you're determined to rent a beach house in Malibu at the height of the season, are you going to finish the book this time? Have you even begun it?"

"Of course I've begun it. Brother! But I can't write here, B.D., I can't! My writer is flying out to work with me and Kath is coming back to be my secretary."

"Are you back to writing the same book you started with?"

"Yup. All about the hell I've been through with my stroke and all the hysterical cooks and housekeepers and staff problems. Brother! I *had* to get away from those people. All they wanted was a dirty book—which you approved of, I might add—about all my affairs and marriages."

She was partially correct, at least. I hadn't exactly approved of the idea that was to have become *Husbands, Lovers and Other Strangers*—my private sentiment had been that it would be one of the shortest works on record—but I had helped talk her into doing it. I had been complying with another of Harold's requests for assistance.

"Whether or not I approved of it isn't exactly relevant, Mother. You agreed to write an intimate book—at the time you were all excited at the prospect. You signed a contract with that understanding and accepted money for it. *You* changed your mind, not the publisher. You can hardly blame them for being a little put out."

"Let's drop it, shall we? Brother! I'm writing *my* book now. I'll stay in Malibu until it's finished and then I don't want to hear about it anymore. Writing is murder. Don't ever try it."

"Has your new publisher set a time limit on finishing the manuscript?"

"Get off it, B.D.! I don't get any dough until it's done. That's my problem, not yours. Brother! I'll be fine. I always have been, for Christ's sake! You're mean! You want me to feel guilty about the house. Well, I won't!"

"Mother," I said, coming close to the brink, "I love you but, in all honesty, whether you feel guilty about anything is the farthest thing from my mind. If you hadn't demanded my approval, I wouldn't even have proffered an opinion. I do care, and a great deal, when you use the Lord's name as a swearword. Do you think, as a simple courtesy, you could cut it out?"

"*Ha!* Now the way I speak isn't good enough for you. Jesus! You're really something." She hung up.

There was no doubt in my mind that I had to examine

what was left of my relationship with my mother. I had no illusions about the amount of time it would take to get my book into print—the finished manuscript was now in my agent's hands—and I had to get through at least another six months before *MMK* could hit a bookstore. Instead of my faith in the Lord making it easier for me to deal with my mother, it seemed to be making it more difficult. I did not realize, at that time, that I was making a mistake in praying for patience. I wasn't to learn, until several months later when talking to our pastor in the Bahamas, that God sends us tribulation as the means whereby we may learn patience.

What I had said on the phone was perfectly true: I kept praying that I would be able to talk to my mother without getting angry about one thing or another almost every time. All my life had been spent, it seemed, arguing with her over what I considered to be her excesses and just plain stupidities. I hardly ever wanted to be involved in her business. I became embroiled through Harold, or his predecessors, demanding my intercession, or Mother asking for my approval whenever she was in her little-girl mood and needed me to tell her everything was all right.

Only since beginning to write my book had I realized just how bitter I was. The bitterness had always been there, but I had kept it buried, or, at least, under control. Now that I was examining every facet of myself in order to measure up as a Christian, the need for a solution to the problem my mother represented in my life was becoming of paramount importance.

I was succeeding in becoming more tolerant of other people, in giving up my propensity for harboring grudges—and I felt much better and happier for it—but, and it was a monumental "but," whenever my mother entered the picture, all my good intentions went up in smoke. I was in a bind, and a tough one at that. I seemed to be completely incapable of dealing with my mother and keeping my temper and equilibrium. I was now, because lying is a sin, even denied the ability to appease her demands—and thereby avoid argument—by telling her the lies she wanted to hear.

Perhaps I could mumble inanities and beg the issue entirely. If I—

My reverie was broken by the harsh sound of the telephone ringing. It was Harold. "How can you have done this, B.D.? After all the work I went to to convince your mother to go to work, far from being a help, you go off on a tangent and get her upset. You should have checked with me first."

"Checked with you about what?"

"The beach house in Malibu. What business is it of yours where your mother spends her time? All I asked you to do was help to reinforce her resolve to write her book, not criticize her or presume to interfere in her personal life."

"Why, pray tell, should I check with you to find out whether a woman, who you yourself told me was 'desperately short of money,' should rent a top-dollar beach house for goodness knows how many thousands of dollars a month? I expected you to be grateful, not all over my case about it."

"That's beside the point. Your mother has to write and she has convinced me that this is the only way she can."

"That's no surprise. She convinces you of everything. How on earth can you permit her to spend all that money, when you say she's broke, and then have the nerve to ask me to help you, because she needs money, to get her to do something she apparently doesn't want to do."

"Stop interfering in matters that don't concern you. You must—"

"Interfering? I must? *You* called *me*—remember? You ask my help to get Mother to make sense, then you make less sense than she does. Why can't the two of you lie to each other and leave me out of it? You can live happily ever after in your client's fantasy world. I was fed up with this kind of nonsense before this particular mess began. I'm sick of it! This is the last time you get me involved in one of your machinations. Period!"

I found it difficult to believe at the time, but he completely ignored me. It was as if I had not spoken. "You must call and tell your mother that you approve of the beach house and that writing her book is all that matters at this point. No one else is even talking to her about any projects."

"Didn't you hear what I said, Harold? I have no—"

"She needs you to tell her that you think this house is a good idea and that she should go ahead with it. She's in a very precarious state of mind and it's difficult to keep her attitude productive. You must undo the harm you've done. You owe it to her."

I almost choked, but I managed to speak calmly. "Yes, Harold. I've heard it all before—too many times to count. I'll make this one phone call—not because I owe either of you anything—but to put paid to this whole dreary episode. But remember what I said: this is the last time I play. Is there anything else?"

"No. Just be sure to—"

"Good-bye, Harold."

I repaired to the barns to do chores and compose myself before calling Mother. The composure was quick in coming once I was among my animals. A solution to my problem was not. The best I was able to come up with was a determination to try mumbling inanities without actually going so far as to tell a lie. By the time I got back to the house it was getting quite late and I had to start dinner. What with one thing and another, I did not get around to calling Mother that evening.

At nine the next morning, six o'clock Mother's time, she was on the phone. "B.D.! I've lain awake all night with the sweats. Brother! I haven't slept a wink. I don't understand why you're so mean. I can't *stand* this apartment during the summer. You *know* that. All I want to do is get out of the traffic and the heat and you try to break my heart. *Jesus!*" I gritted my teeth—ignore it B.D., and let her finish. "I can't write my book here, I just can't."

Carefully measuring every phrase and nuance, I said, "I'm sorry that I've caused such a to-do. If I'd known that money wasn't your foremost problem, I would never have said what I said. Obviously, it's best if you do whatever will make you the happiest."

"Oh, *thank* you, sweetheart!" she cried. "I *knew* you'd understand. I love you. Talk to you soon."

She had not heard a single word I'd said after "I'm sorry . . ." I knew it as certainly as I knew my own name. It was the twilight zone. The bitterness sank once again to its position in the depths of my subconscious. I was overcome with a new emotion, one of overwhelming sadness. There was nothing. She was my mother and I loved her because of it, but there was nothing. It was all fantasies and role-playing. Whatever substance there once had been was gone, buried forever beneath the dominant force that was Bette. Ruth Elizabeth was gone, perhaps never to be seen or heard from again.

For a long time I sat and allowed free rein to my emotions. At first I was angry with Harold. He used me, lied to me and manipulated me, all with the single purpose of furthering the interests of his client. Whether he truly believed that I owed it to my mother to do his bidding, as he so frequently contended, I had no way of knowing, but every time he invoked my debt to her my stomach churned. I owed her nothing but my love and, with every passing year, that had become more and more difficult to give.

I did not relish the knowledge that there were times when I felt sorry for myself. Self-pity is so demeaning. But why couldn't I be left alone to lead my own life in peace and harmony with my family? Why did I have to protect myself and my children against the demands of a selfish and irrational woman who happened to be my mother? Why did I have to make a choice between my mother and my children? It just was not fair that I be forced into such a position. And beyond that, even when she was thousands of miles away, she still wouldn't leave me alone. She wanted me to be her Mommy, to tell her what a good little girl she was whenever she was behaving at her worst. I couldn't deal with it and didn't see why I should have to. If I hadn't cared about her at all, I could have made a game of it and laughed at her absurdities. But I did care—and that was my problem.

The lawyers and managers and agents were so quick to remind me of my duty and my debt to my mother, but always when it furthered their interests by furthering her income. If they walked away from her out of anger, or simply because she was not earning enough to warrant the amount of their time she was taking up, no one criticized them. They were free to do whatever they wanted. What about their duty, their obligations? Their peers probably chuckled and wondered why it had taken them so long to throw in the towel. Mine condemned me and reminded me of my duty. Nuts!

But, Harold did not have much of a bargain either. Certainly he earned significant sums from being Mother's lawyer/manager, but at what cost? He had to live with his client's tantrums and vileness too. He had stuck by her through thick and thin, even, I believe, to the extent of lending her money when she was truly broke back in the sixties. I had no right to get angry at him. His first obligation was to his client and, were I in his shoes, I would probably do just as he did: bring pressure to bear wherever it could be brought.

And poor old Mother. She had not been taught to be civil to other people. She had been pandered to by her mother, catered to by her sister, and manipulated by everyone during their pursuit of the almighty dollar. It was no wonder she was a mess. Nobody had ever insisted that she say please or thank you, let alone apologize for anything. They had turned her into an idol to be worshipped. At first she had merely accepted it as the inevitability of stardom. Then she had demanded it as her due. There was nothing unusual about that—most famous people succumb to the same weakness.

But—and here lay the problem—she insisted that it was her inalienable right to be nasty, cruel, vindictive, intolerant and abusive—the very monster, in fact, that she occasionally accused me of thinking her to be—and equally her right, despite her treatment of them, to demand adulation from the people around her. What a miserable way to live—no real love, no real happiness, no real anything.

It hurt me to think of my mother in these terms, but loving Ruth Elizabeth, the mother I knew to be buried beneath the character traits that constituted Bette, did not protect me from having to deal with the reality of Bette. We are taught to separate the sin from the person, to hate the sin but love the person. I could, and did, love my mother, but I had not the ability to keep all the parts separated, let alone be scriptural about it.

I realized that I could keep up this kind of directionless thinking until I went crazy. The question was simple: *MMK*, when published, would draw the battle lines, but what would I do in the meantime? I was resolved to avoid any further senseless and unproductive arguments with Mother. Refusing to talk her into or out of any particular course of action, at Harold's behest, would help in that regard. I would not play the game of mumbling inanities and talking in circles to avoid lying. It made me feel soiled somehow. I would, however, do my best to short-circuit conversations that would lead to confrontation. The only thing about which I was prepared to go to any lengths with Mother was the question of God.

Only if I could convince her to accept Jesus Christ as her personal Lord and Savior would there be any chance whatsoever of our ever again having a relationship. There was no other way in which Mother could change sufficiently in temperament and personality. It would take a miracle, and miracles come from God. It was not only my Christian duty to try to bring this about; I also wanted to have it happen. She was my mother.

Lonely and virtually alone. Well along in years and encountering the health problems of the aging. All but friendless. Money troubles yet again. Not the remotest idea of what happiness is all about. Not even a glimmer of understanding of the meaning of the word "love." Most of it of her own choosing, but some of it not so. This was my mother. An idol alone on a pedestal, the fans only buying tickets when it suited them, and I—"the only thing I've ever truly loved," in her own words—forced to resort to the public forum in order to make her listen to me.

A waste? No, not in the earthly sense. Mother had achieved great fame and brought pleasure to millions. But, what of herself? What about her private life? Who knows? Perhaps if Ruth Elizabeth had thrived, there would have been no fame, no actress—no Bette. Perhaps it was meant to be this way. But what about the spiritual sense? Is it too late? No, it's never too late. It's sad that a person can achieve so much and have so little, but it's never too late. It's sad that my mother is all alone and I have to leave her that way.

It's sad—oh, God, it's so sad.

I pulled myself together. I knew what had to be done and all the meditation in the world was not going to change the facts. My book would be published—I had no illusions that I would ever convince Mother of anything without the use of *MMK* as the two-by-four wherewith to attract her attention. I would keep on trying, though. I would try to communicate whenever the opportunity afforded. I would keep on talking about Jesus until I was blue in the face. Somehow, someday, I would find the chink in Bette's armor that would allow me to get through to Ruth Elizabeth. Before publication, after publication, if she lived to be a hundred, I would keep on trying. She was my mother.

CHAPTER

JAY GARON PHONED THE FOLLOWING TUESDAY TO SAY THAT HE and his staff had all read my manuscript and loved it. I was relieved that the first hurdle had been overcome and looked forward to hearing what a publisher might think. Jay confirmed that he was going to submit it.

A week later, he called again—the book was sold. He spoke enthusiastically about the publisher's reaction. I heard most of what he said, but not all. My mind kept wandering.

It's done, I thought—for better or for worse, it's done. I mused yet again on the pain Mother would feel and the reaction that would be forthcoming from her: the rage, the invective, the contention that it was all a pack of lies. All of that would have to come and go before she would even read what I had written, let alone understand why I had written it. It was inevitable and I would have to live with it. That, together with the hostility of the press and the fans, was the price I had to pay. And it had to be paid—there was no other way.

Jay was talking about contracts, editing and a spring publication date. I thanked him for his good work and agreed that Jeremy and I deserved a few weeks' rest while the contracts were being prepared. We exchanged a few more pleasantries and hung up. I would have to wait until lunchtime to give

Jeremy the news since he was on the far side of the next mountain, helping the Sharers with their haymaking.

We were beginning to become accustomed to "coincidences" and accept them as a fact of Christian life. It was quite extraordinary how often they happened, and always beneficially. Not earth-shaking miracles, as it were, but little things. Like being at Grace Cathedral a week later than planned and hearing Ernest Angley's dissertation on disruptive family members; like the fellow we only saw once or twice a year, who dropped by unannounced at exactly the moment we were looking for a literary agent, and asked if we needed one since a friend of his had a very good one, Jay Garon; like Jeremy bumping into an old friend, whom he had not seen in twenty years, who had been part of developing Grand Bahama and who recommended it for our serious consideration. This sort of thing kept happening. Whenever there was a serious need of any kind, sometimes ones we were not yet even aware of, a "coincidence" would occur to fill the need. We were learning about God's perfect plan.

I was feeling an increasing need to go to church and enjoy the fellowship of other Christians. The trouble was, I had not the faintest idea of how to pick a church. I discussed the matter with Serafino and he recommended Assembly of God, if I could find one. As it happened, there was one some twenty-five miles from us but, speaking to its pastor, I learned that the congregation was quite old and there were almost no children, hence no youth groups or youth activities. I was unable to locate another church even approaching Pentecostalism and was about to go to the one twenty-five miles away, and risk my children's first exposure to church being boring—not to mention my husband refusing ever to go to church again— when another "coincidence" happened.

It was 7:30 and we were just finishing dinner when there was a knock at the door. Justin went to open it and ushered in two men. One of them, Denny DeWitt, we knew slightly from meeting him and his wife at Parent Teacher Group functions. The other, another young man introduced by Denny as Pastor Larry Burke, was the pastor of the Wesleyan Church in Herrickville, some eight or nine miles away. Denny and Pastor Larry, as he liked to be called, had heard about our becoming Christians and were stopping by on the chance that they might be able to interest us in joining their congregation. Jeremy and I who, only that day—the same day that Jay had called with the news about the book being sold—had been discussing "coincidences," exchanged knowing smiles. God's perfect plan at work again.

We chatted comfortably and pleasantly for close to two hours and learned much about the Wesleyan Church. It did not sound quite as Pentecostal as we would have liked, but the youth program sounded fabulous—not surprising given the fact that Pastor Larry was little more than a big kid himself. Jeremy asked the children what they thought about giving it a try. Ashley—typical fifteen-year-old—was cautiously optimistic. Justin—seven and slightly starved for playmates on our mountaintop—was bursting at the seams with anticipation. We said we would go to the service the following evening.

Wednesday services were short, followed by Bible study for the adults and assorted activities for the different age groups of children. We, including our teenager, thoroughly enjoyed ourselves and went again the following Sunday morning, and almost every Wednesday and Sunday thereafter. Serafino had been right: the time is not long in coming when one begins to instinctively crave the company of other Christians.

It is difficult to explain but, once one is born again, one feels a sorrow for people who have not discovered, or will not accept, the truth one has found. One is constantly torn between the urge to enlighten and the fear of being boorish and importunate. It is one's Biblical and moral obligation to be a witness to the unsaved, but all too easy to be branded a fanatic. It takes a delicate touch to sow the seeds; it takes patience to find if they have fallen on fertile soil.

Newly born again Christians tend to be like reformed drunks, fired with a fervor to let no ear go unbent. They must be careful lest they do more harm than good. Getting together with other Christians a few times a week becomes an absolute must, not only for the pleasure of their company and conversation, but for spiritual fulfillment and, occasionally, as a tempering influence if one's enthusiasm becomes unbridled. There are times and places for the joyous outpouring of one's faith and praise of God. There are other times when quiet reason is called for.

CHAPTER

11

SEVEN ARTS PRODUCTIONS, THE COMPANY FOR WHICH JEREMY had worked until the mid-sixties, had been a partner in the Grand Bahama Development Company. Jeremy had visited Grand Bahama on business twice during 1962 and his memories of the island were of a flat, almost uninhabited, virtually treeless atoll. It was for this reason that he had dismissed the Bahamas as a possible new home for us. Not that Grand Bahama was the only island—it is only one of many populated Bahamian islands—but we had no interest in becoming part of the hurly-burly of Nassau, nor of becoming recluses on an island devoid of good schools or any modern conveniences.

It was for this reason that it was so fortuitous that Jeremy had encountered the old friend of twenty years earlier who had been directly involved in the development of Grand Bahama. His description of what the island had become was so far removed from my husband's image of it that we determined to get a publication called *The Bahamas Handbook* and see what it had to say. Far from the least of the considerations in choosing an island, Caribbean or otherwise, is fresh water. Most islands do not have plentiful water supplies and conservation is not just a fact of life—it's a way of life. Grand Bahama, Jeremy discovered—he felt silly for not having remembered this most salient of factors—is almost unique among islands in that it has an inexhaustible water supply.

There also seemed to be good schools, the church of our choice, a fully integrated society and all the modern conveniences. We were warned that living in a tourist-oriented locale held certain drawbacks but were assured that, due to the topography of Freeport/Lucaya, it was possible on Grand Bahama to almost entirely avoid the areas frequented by tourists.

Jeremy decided to talk to the pastor of what would become our new church, if we were to move to Freeport, to see what he had to say about bringing up children there and so forth. He called Freeport information and asked for the phone number of Calvary Temple, the local Assembly of God church. He then dialed the number he was given, had a long talk with the assistant pastor who answered the phone, and became totally confused. This church didn't accept miraculous healing, the gift of tongues or anything else that Pentecostals take for granted.

He called information again and verified the number. It was as he had dialed it. Determined to get to the bottom of the mystery, and it was a mystery, he started to chat with the Freeport operator. After thirty seconds or so of asking about the weather, the fishing and other illuminating subjects, Jeremy asked if the girl went to church.

"Of course I do," the girl replied. "I'm a Christian."

"That's great," said my husband. "So am I. That's why I called information in the first place. I'm thinking of moving to Grand Bahama and I'm trying to get the phone number of Calvary Temple, the Assembly of God church in Freeport. I called the number I was given, which you confirmed, but got someone who doesn't even believe in healing. Can you—"

"Oh!" the girl exclaimed. "You want Ernie DeLoach. His number is five-five-five–six-nine-three-seven."

"Who's Ernie DeLoach?" Jeremy asked.

"The pastor of Calvary Temple."

"Is that his home number or the church?"

"Home. Do you want the church too?"

"Yes, please." She gave it to him . . . a completely different number than had been discussed before.

"How did you happen to know the pastor's home phone number without looking it up?"

"Because he's my pastor. I go to Calvary Temple."

"How nice," Jeremy said. "Are you sure the pastor won't mind my calling him at home on a Saturday?"

"Oh, no, mun! Everybody always call him at home."

Jeremy thanked her for her help, hung up and pondered on the whole transaction. He made, thereby, a serious mistake—one we were to learn to avoid very soon after we actually moved to Freeport—he tried to make sense out of it.

Another phone called reached Pastor Ernie DeLoach at home. This time there was no doubt that Jeremy had located the right pastor of the right church. He sounded charming and enthusiastic about what we would think of the island. He confirmed that the schools were good but pointed out that the children would have to go to the mainland for college. When Jeremy got off the phone he was full of excitement for the first time in weeks. He felt that we had found our new home. We discussed the matter at length and agreed that he would have to go down there at the earliest possible moment. Unfortunately, the earliest possible moment would not be until the publishing contract was signed and my editor had had the chance to meet with me.

The wait seemed interminable. As it turned out, Jeremy could have gone to Grand Bahama, done what he had to do, and returned with weeks to spare, but we did not know that at the time. We had been led to believe that everything was just a matter of days, not the two months it turned out to be. I busied myself with organizing the move we now felt to be a certainty, and Jeremy kept out of trouble by continuing to help the Sharers with their haymaking.

There were innumerable phone calls from Mother during the period but no progress whatsoever in my attempts to witness to her. I stuck to my resolve to avoid confrontation and, for the most part, was successful. She told me that *The Aspen Papers* had been postponed again and, later, that she had signed to do a movie in London called *Murder with Mirrors*. Even as she was voicing her pleasure at the thought of doing a class movie again after so long, my heart was growing heavier.

To get from Los Angeles to London, Mother would stop over in New York. Once in New York she would announce that she was coming to the farm for a few days. She had never, in all my twenty years of marriage, passed within two hundred miles of me without coming to visit. I had been so complacent while she was in California, and even more so when she rented the beach house in Malibu for an indefinite period. I had simply assumed that *MMK* would be on the stands before I had to contemplate this situation again.

My faith in God's perfect plan should have been stronger. I suddenly awoke to what Mother was saying. "It's a crime. Brother! Because of this lousy book, I won't have the time to come and see you. I have to work on it until the last minute. I don't know how Harold expects me to get it finished even then. It's impossible! I'll only have an overnight in New York. I'm sick about it. Weeps! Maybe you could come and see me at the Lombardy for the day?"

"I'll be thrilled to," I said without hesitation. And that was the truth—it sure was.

As it would turn out, my fear of having to tell Mother that she was not welcome at the farm would be replaced by a new concern: that she not pass through New York before we winged our way south. Until she signed to do *Murder with Mirrors* there had been no problem; I had intended to tell her of our move as soon as our plans became firm. Once she committed to a movie, though, everything changed. There was no way I could tell her we were leaving the country. I knew her too well—I could hear it all: "I am *not* going to London while my daughter is in this mess. Brother! They can take their movie and shove it!"

Terrific.

If things weren't already bad enough, that would really tear it.

The contract was finally signed, my editor came to spend a few days at the farm, the work to be done on the manuscript was agreed upon, and Jeremy was free to go to Grand Bahama. He called a local travel agent and found that Bahamasair flew direct from Newark—the closest international airport to us—to Freeport. There were a few things the agent forgot to mention.

The foremost thing the travel agent forgot was to tell Jeremy that Bahamasair was not listed anywhere as even existing; not on the billboards listing the various airlines and their locations in the terminal, not on the terminal itself, not on any door to anywhere constructive, and not at or over any ticket counter. In addition to all of that, no one in the terminal building seemed to have heard of Bahamasair.

Jeremy studied the paperwork he'd been given and found nothing enlightening: Bahamasair, October 2, 9:00 A.M., Newark–Freeport. Carrying his overnight bag, he methodically began at one end of the terminal and questioned his way to the other. Unfortunately, he began at the wrong end. After talking to airlines, car rental agents, cops, information desks, candy stores, bookstores, people in the men's room and anyone just standing around looking bored, he was advised by an airport security man that the illusive Bahamasair was disguised as Piedmont, at the other end of the building.

Since it was then ten minutes to takeoff time, Jeremy ran flat out to the Piedmont counter—where there was no mention of Bahamasair—and asked where it was. A girl told him that it was at the Piedmont desk on a lower level, adding that he need not hurry since the flight was delayed. He hurried anyway.

Craftily hidden around a corner and within one of those artistic circular constructions—which are dotted about in modern airline concourses and which house anything from men's rooms to Bahamasair—there were more Piedmont desks. At the very end of one desk, looking very harried, were two girls with Bahamasair emblazoned on their jackets.

Jeremy tried to check his bag in but learned that this was a carry-your-own-luggage-to-the-door-of-the-plane situation. He wondered whether the sight of the plane tended to scare people away and the airline preferred that they take their luggage with them. He was given a boarding pass, which he found reassuring. It at least indicated the existence of an airplane somewhere. When and if that plane would ever take off was another matter.

He was told that there would be "a slight delay." That was nothing unusual with airlines but, in this instance, the girls were very noncommittal about how slight the delay might be. One said half an hour, the other an hour. A nearby prospective passenger mumbled that they had told him two hours.

Jeremy got a cup of coffee and sat down with his book to read. It was only an hour before the flight was announced and only a half hour after that that they fired up the engines. He was puzzled, therefore, at the obvious disgruntlement of the lady sitting next to him. "An hour and a half late isn't much," he said with a cheerful smile. "Why are you so upset?"

"An hour and a half for you, maybe," she replied. "I've been here since eight o'clock yesterday morning. They kept us waiting till noon and then announced that the flight had been canceled altogether."

"Holy smoke!" Jeremy exclaimed. "No wonder you're so teed off. I would be too."

"That's not the worst of it," the lady added. "When the cancellation came over the loudspeaker we all went to the desk to see what was going on and what the airline intended to do about putting us up or whatever. There was no one at the desk—they'd left for the day. There wasn't a single Bahamas-air employee anywhere in the terminal. It was cheaper to go home for the night than to stay at a hotel, so I went home. It cost me thirty-five dollars each way."

Once the plane took off—my husband reminding himself several times that the pilot would not have done such a thing if he didn't think it was safe—Jeremy tried to tilt his seat back. It would not move an inch. He asked the disgruntled lady, who was still muttering to herself, whether her seat worked. It didn't. He looked around and found that the plane was only about a third full. He excused himself as he stepped across the lady and wandered about the plane, pushing buttons and seat backs until he found one that worked. It was the eighth one he tested.

When the stewardess came down the aisle he mentioned the seats to her and suggested, politely he insists, that the airline do something in the way of maintenance.

"What for?" the stewardess replied airily. "De passengers just break 'em again if we fix 'em." Jeremy kept any further constructive criticism to himself and prayed that the same theory of maintenance did not apply to the engines wearing out.

He happily minded his own business and went back to reading his book until brunch was served. Croissant, orange juice, coffee and so forth, all in plastic cups and shrink-wrapped to a plastic tray. No problem until he tried to lower the fold-down table from the back of the seat in front of him—the supporting arms were broken. He looked around to see whether it was worth changing seats again, to one with a usable table ahead of it, but only saw people spilling things all over themselves as they tried to balance their brunches on broken-armed tables. He forwent the table, balanced the tray on his lap, skipped the coffee, took the orange juice at one gulp after opening it, munched the croissant, and congratulated himself on learning to cope with Bahamasair's idiosyncrasies.

The plane landed at Freeport ahead of schedule, if one counted time in the air only, and thus proved Jeremy's theory about the pilot not being a fool. He cleared customs and immigration, rented a car and went to the hotel to check in. From his room he called Pastor DeLoach, who invited him to come straight over to the church for a chat. He bought a road map of Freeport and began his combination of fact-finding and arrangement-making. He explained to me on the phone that night that although he did not know much yet, he felt we were supposed to be there.

He found the flora particularly interesting. Wherever developers had been at work there were huge rubber trees and banyans, scheffleras, frangipani, oleander, bougainvillea, royal palms, coconut palms, banana palms and palms he didn't recognize. There were flowers he had never seen before and lime, lemon, orange and grapefruit trees in people's gardens, as well as avocados. Where no road, store or house had been built it was as nature had designed it: Caribbean pines, thatch palms, poisonwood and goodness knows what. He was told that there were wild orchids and bromeliads if one could survive the poisonwood while looking for them. The island was still the same featureless atoll he remembered, but the developers had markedly improved the landscaping.

Jeremy liked the pastor on sight. There was an effusive warmth about him that my husband found irresistible. They talked for a considerable time, the pastor telling Jeremy much that he needed to know, particularly about schools. The one he recommended for us ran from kindergarten through high school, which meant that both Ashley and Justin could go to the same school. He also recommended, at Jeremy's request, a real estate agent and a car dealer, but hastened to point out that he did not know either of them very well. The pastor mentioned that there would be services the following night, Wednesday, and Jeremy said that he looked forward to being there.

He went straight from the church to the school, met the vice-principal, discussed the curriculum, discovered that there was room for both boys at their different grade levels provided they could pass the entrance exams, obtained entrance application forms and returned to the hotel to call the real estate lady. They arranged to meet outside the hotel at eight the next morning. Since it was too late to do anything else of value, he drove around for an hour to get the feel of the place before having dinner and repairing to his room to watch TV for a while. The reception was so bad that he gave up trying, called me to give me a bulletin and went to bed early.

Punctually at eight the next morning, Jeremy was in front of the hotel. At 8:35 the real estate lady showed up, all smiles and no apology. It was my husband's first exposure to the difference between real time and Bahamian time, though he did not realize it yet. The lady's name was Louise and Jeremy explained to her, very carefully, that we had no desire to buy anything until we knew more of the island. What we wanted, for the time being, was to rent an apartment, town house or condominium or, better than that, to rent a house with an option to buy if he could find a house that he liked. A one-year lease for any of the above was acceptable.

He also carefully explained that we needed three bedrooms as a minimum and would prefer four since we expected guests even during our first year. When Louise said she knew just the place and drove off, Jeremy was pleased. She took him to a house that had two bedrooms, was half renovated and was, generally speaking, an unprepossessing mess. My husband, unusual for him, felt constrained to measure his words. He said that the house was interesting but not quite what he was looking for. Louise said that was a shame since it was her house and she wanted to move to Nassau.

Jeremy reminded her of the bedroom requirements and they were off again. After meandering around several back roads,

Louise headed east on a lovely divided avenue with magnificent plantings. They turned into a new developement and pulled up in front of a white house with a white roof. Along both sides of the road were other white houses with white roofs. The one they entered had only two bedrooms, which Jeremy quickly pointed out, but Louise assured him that some of the others had three. Jeremy asked how much they were renting for and Louise said they were only for sale.

The next stop was further along the avenue, again down a side road. This time all of the houses were lovely. The one they looked at was nice enough—it even had three bedrooms—but Jeremy did not like the layout and did not ask about price. The next stop was to gaze at a massive pile across a canal—there are man-made canals all along the south shore and many houses are built beside them—because Louise thought the view of the mansion to be better from afar. Jeremy was not sure why she was showing it to him since it could patently house an army. Louise insisted on going around for a close-up inspection, although admitting that she did not have the key. They wandered around the house, boat house and dock and back to the house. The whole thing was absolutely enormous.

"Well," said my husband, still wondering why they were there but trying to be polite, "at least this one has enough bedrooms."

"Actually it only has two, but they're very large. It has three dining rooms, though," Louise said, as if that were the reason they were looking at this monstrosity. "You could always make bedrooms out of two of the dining rooms." Jeremy was not sure what to say to that, so he asked how much the owner was asking.

"Seven hundred fifty thousand, but they'll probably take a bit less."

"I'm relieved to hear it's negotiable," my husband commented, keeping a straight face. "What's next on the agenda?"

What came next were three or four houses, ranging from a broken-down wreck to another mansion. None of them was for rent and Jeremy did not like any of them anyway, but he was beginning to wonder whether the real estate lady understood English. It was, by that time, early afternoon. Louise had another appointment to keep and they agreed to meet at nine the following morning and try again. Jeremy spent the rest of the afternoon at Immigration, finding out what the rules were and obtaining the appropriate forms to file for residency, and wandering about from store to store to see what was available on the island.

At seven o'clock he went to the evening service at Calvary Temple. There was a full house and the service was a lot more like that which Serafino had described to us as a full Pentecostal worship.

There were praying in tongues, and prayers for healing; a couple of people accepted Jesus; and Pastor DeLoach fulfilled Jeremy's expectations. As he said to me on the phone later that night, "You may not find all of his sermons riveting, but you'll never manage to sleep through one."

After the service the pastor invited my husband to join him and his family for a quick snack at Burger King. Jeremy found them all to be charming and friendly, but the most interesting event of the evening was an impromptu baptism. A Bahamian boy, seemingly in his early twenties—with a terrible weight problem, probably glandular, and slightly retarded—came over to their table and asked the pastor to baptize him. Jeremy expected the pastor to tell the lad to come to the church the next day, but not so. He led him to the quietest corner, produced a small bottle of water and baptized him on the spot. When he returned to the table, the pastor said, "Praise God! We'll have to see what we can do to help that poor boy. He has no one." Jeremy was very moved by the incident. He could not help but think back to the staid and stolid Church of England days of his youth. What a difference.

Louise was almost on time the next morning, arriving at 9:15, and the morning was spent on an approximate replay of the previous day. Jeremy was beginning to lose his sense of humor when they arrived at a house which the real estate lady, with a certain air of smugness, described as available for rent. Jeremy looked it over and, although it was not anything he would want to buy, decided that it would serve as an acceptable rental for a year. He was becoming less choosy by the hour since one and a half of his three days had already gone by with hardly any progress to show for it.

"What's the rent?" he asked Louise.

"I don't know," she replied. "I'll have to get in touch with the owners. They really want to sell it, but I know they'll rent it if they have to."

"How long will it take to find out?"

"Well, they're somewhere in Europe." She looked thoughtful. My husband did his best not to let out a scream and strangle her on the spot. She brightened. "They'll be back before Christmas. I could ask them when they get here."

"Look, Louise," Jeremy said, wanting to give it one more try before writing off the time invested and searching for another agent. "I told you before we started that we wanted to move next month. What good is it discussing someone who might or might not rent me a house two months from now?"

"But you're so picky," she complained. "There just aren't that many houses available for rent."

Jeremy wanted to say that he had no way of knowing since he hadn't seen a single one yet, but felt it to be a waste of words. Instead he asked, "What about all the apartments and condos? Everywhere we go, I see 'For Rent' signs. We haven't looked at any of them."

"They're all one- and two-bedroom. Three- or four-bedroom are almost nonexistent."

"If that's the case, I better stop wasting our collective time and start looking on another island." Either the words or the touch of asperity in his tone galvanized Louise into action. Fruitless action, but at least different.

She showed him townhouses that would not be finished for three or four months; other townhouses that were tied up in litigation while various heirs disputed ownership after the death of the contractor/builder; apartments that were too small; condos that were available on time-sharing; nothing whatsoever that could, by the broadest stretch of the imagination, be of any conceivable interest.

The afternoon, too, was wasted and Jeremy was at his wits' end, kicking himself for not trading Louise in at lunchtime. As she was dropping him off at his hotel she said, completely offhandedly, "I'll be showing you an apartment in the morning which I know you'll like. It's two apartments made into one, actually. It has four bedrooms."

126

"Why in tarnation didn't we look at it yesterday, or even today?" Jeremy exploded.

"Because another agent has the key. I can't get it until later this evening. Anyway, I thought you ought to see some other properties to get a better perspective." My husband regretted, if only for a few seconds, his Christianity. He wanted to tell the agent where to park her perspective.

"Ah," he said, "that makes sense." He didn't care whether it did or did not so long as the apartment suited. Neither did he care to ponder his next step if the apartment were no go. Somehow, he had always assumed that Grand Bahama was where we were meant to be. He had not even considered the possibility that it might not work out. "What time shall we meet?"

"I'll call you first thing—as soon as I finish breakfast."

"Could you give me a guesstimate?" Jeremy persisted. Fixed appointments were nerve-racking enough; a loose one was too much to contemplate.

"Boy, you sure are nervous!" Louise said. "You'll have to get used to the pace of the islands. We don't do things the way you do on the mainland. I'll call you by eight o'clock." With a wave and an ingratiating smile, she drove off, leaving him to wonder why an expatriate Frenchwoman, who had given him a two-day runaround, was delivering lectures on island custom.

Louise was late the next morning, both in calling and in arriving, but the apartment was eminently satisfactory. The deal was made and the other agent returned to his office to prepare a lease. Louise dropped Jeremy at the hotel and arranged to meet him at the office in two hours. Jeremy then began a circuitous trek in the attempt to get things like the power and phone companies to cooperate.

He went to the power company first and explained that Apartments 205 and 206 at the Richmaur were now one apartment, that he had rented it and that he wanted the power turned on on November 1, the date upon which the lease began and on which he had decided we would move. Papers were pushed around, a computer was consulted, he was sent to stand in line at another window to post a cash bond, he returned with a receipt and was assured that the power would be on when he arrived with his family. He neglected to read the receipt carefully.

His next stop was the phone company. Unlike the power company, their first request was for his address. He told them 205–206 etcetera.

"No, sir," he was told, "your post office box number."

"Do you mean I have to have a post office box in order to have a telephone?"

"That's right. How could we bill you, otherwise?" Jeremy did not bother ask why, but went straight to the post office to rent a box.

While the lady in a back room of the post office was writing up another series of forms, however, he made so bold as to ask if there was mail delivery to one's door on Grand Bahama, or if a box was the only way to receive it.

"Oh, yes," said the lady reassuringly, "we deliver to de door."

"Then why do I need a box?" Jeremy asked, more than a little perplexed.

"Well, it depend when you want to get your mail, you see."

"You mean you don't deliver door to door every day. Well, how frequently *do* you deliver?"

"Well now, dat depend."

"What on?"

"When somebody going dat direction."

Back at the phone company everything went swimmingly. In exchange for the name of our Pennsylvania phone company as a credit reference, our post office box number and a sizeable cash bond, Jeremy was assured that our phone would be connected on November 1. It being almost noon and almost time to be at the agent's office to sign the lease—and foolishly believing he had taken care of the utilities—he made a quick stop at a bank to see if banks, also, had any quaint requirements. It was a good thing he did. No bank in town would even open a checking account for you until you produced a reference from some other bank attesting to its having known you personally for a thousand years or so and guaranteeing your integrity.

At the real estate agent's office Jeremy read the lease carefully, found no problem and everybody signed it. They had a cup of coffee, chatted about things in general, and then Jeremy mentioned his adventures with the utility companies and the post office. "Are you sure the power company understood they were to turn on the electricity in both apartments? There are two meters, you know?" Louise looked worried. My husband pulled the receipt out of his briefcase. "See? It says right here, 'Apartments two-oh-five and . . .' Oh-oh! No two-oh-six. I'd better go back and make sure." They stood up and Jeremy asked if he could have a set of keys to the apartment.

Louise looked at the other agent questioningly, and he went into a song and dance about not turning them over until the inception date of the lease. Louise then promised to obtain the keys on November 1 and meet us at the apartment at any time of our choosing. She gave my husband all the numbers at which she could be reached and then said, "If you send me a cable telling me your flight and arrival time, I'll meet you at the airport and help with your luggage." Jeremy thought that very civil of her and agreed to send a cable as soon as he made the flight bookings.

It was 1:00 P.M. He was booked on the 7:00 P.M. Bahamasair flight back to Newark and needed to be at the airport at six. He went straight to the power company, but they were closed for lunch until two. He went to see Pastor DeLoach, told him that we were going to be numbered among his flock the following month and thanked him for his kindness and help. He returned to the hotel, packed his things and left them ready for a quick checkout.

Back to the power company. "I was here earlier and asked for the power to be turned on at two-oh-five–two-oh-six Richmaur Apartments on November first. I paid my bond but just noticed that the receipt only shows Apartment two-oh-five. I wanted to make sure there's been no misunderstanding." The girl punched some things into her computer. "We show an outstanding bill. Until that's paid, we can't turn the power back on."

"I'm not asking you to turn it back on. I haven't even moved in yet. I'm asking you to turn it on when I do move in—on November first."

"Until the outstanding bill's paid, we can't."

Jeremy scratched his head. He was not sure whether he was dealing with standard computer idiocy or island custom. Getting angry at the former is perfectly acceptable anywhere in the world; losing one's cool in the face of the latter is inadvisable; it will unquestionably lead to far greater delay, perhaps even to the need for one's own generator. He went for the simpler answer first. "Punch it up again—see if it comes up the same." It did.

"What address are you putting in?"

"Two-oh-five Richmond."

Jeremy breathed a big sigh. "It's two-oh-five–two-oh-six Richmaur, not Richmond." The girl gave it another try. Success. She looked at the receipt my husband was holding. "No problem. The order to turn on two-oh-five is in. Is that what you wanted to know?"

"No, it isn't," Jeremy replied, bending his every effort to keep a smile in place. "What I asked was, has the order gone in to turn on two-oh-five *and* two-oh-six? They are one apartment now—the dividing walls have been removed. I paid my bond, but the receipt only shows two-oh-five. That's why I came back."

"Oh," said the girl. She punched again. "There are two meters. You'll have to pay the bond to get the other meter turned on."

"But it's only one apartment," Jeremy protested, "with one family about to live in it. Why do you need two bonds?"

Stupid questions deserve stupid answers. "Because there are two meters." Big smile of encouragement. Jeremy could not think of anything with which to refute such impeccable logic, so proceeded graciously to the cashier's window to ante up yet another hundred dollars. This time he read the receipt carefully.

Two thirty and oodles of time. Out to the airport to talk to Customs about things to beware of when moving to the island. *Everything.* Everything except the shirt on your back is dutiable. Old, new, borrowed, blue—dutiable. At what rates? Dat depend. What on?

Well . . .

He wished he hadn't asked.

The car dealer had gone out to lunch at 12:30. Jeremy was

advised to wait since he would have to be back at any minute. He read magazines, looked nervously at his watch, walked around the premises, read more magazines, and reminded himself that this was the Bahamas. At 4:30 the dealer returned. Jeremy introduced himself, mentioned that he had to catch a plane and had little time to spare, and then listened to the dealer discuss some Little League baseball game for ten minutes on the phone.

When they finally got down to business, Jeremy said that he wanted a good secondhand car with air conditioning, something to meet our requirements until we were sure of what kind of vehicle we really needed. They looked at a Ford Fiesta that was in good shape. The price was right and Jeremy said he would take it. The dealer, very considerately my husband thought, suggested that they leave the paperwork until we arrived on November 1. He volunteered to meet us at the airport with the car if we would advise him of flight and arrival time. They shook hands.

Jeremy dashed back to the hotel, got his bag, checked out and stopped at a boat dealer on his way to the airport. There is no point to living in an island paradise unless one owns a boat. My husband had never owned one and knew less than nothing about them. He found the owner of the establishment, Colin Rose, doing some late paperwork, and sought to get a full-scale education on yachting in half an hour. At twenty to seven, Colin reminded him that he had a plane to catch and shoved him out the door, armed with a diversity of pamphlets on boats and their appurtenances.

The return flight left but ten minutes late and arrived on time. The first seat Jeremy sat in worked, although the fold-down tray had both arms broken, and left him with a sense of disappointment. He missed the adventure of the south-bound trip.

CHAPTER

JEREMY, TIRED BUT ELATED, GOT BACK TO THE FARM AT 1:45 IN the morning. He had T-shirts for the boys that said IT'S BETTER IN THE BAHAMAS and a bottle of perfume for me. I was brimming over with questions and trying not to fire them at him all at once. We were about to move to a place I had never seen and, although I had a strong feeling for tropical islands and great trust in my husband's judgment, I was nervous.

His first words were of warning. "You're going to have to do some major adjusting, Sweetie. Patience has never been your strong point and you're going to have to learn it. They have a philosophy of their own when it comes to time. There's real time and Bahamian time and fighting it gets you nowhere."

"That's no problem," I said cheerfully. "I intend to get just as relaxed as everybody else." I had no way of knowing, then, just how relaxed one had to get in order to cope with Bahamian time and custom. As I was to learn the hard way, a firm commitment to meet at a certain place at a certain time is, to a Bahamian, native or adoptive, nothing more than a nonbinding agreement to consider doing whatever it was if nothing else crops up in the meantime. The other party does not, necessarily, even feel obliged to let you know if he won't be there.

As Jeremy unpacked his briefcase and made piles of paper and forms around the dining room table, one pile for immigration forms, one school forms and others for minor matters, I asked about the people. "What is the population made up of? What are they like? Are they friendly, standoffish or what?"

"There are two basic groups, Bahamians and ex-pats. Each—"

"What are ex-pats?" I interrupted.

"Expatriates—people who moved there from other countries. The Bahamians come from all over the islands and are black, white and everything in between. There are lots of mixed marriages. The ex-pats consist of Brits, Americans, Canadians, Germans, a few Swiss and the odd Frenchman, Italian, Indian and what-have-you. Everyone is extremely friendly, couldn't be more so, although I heard that some of the old entrenched Brits are a bit standoffish. I didn't meet any so I can't say. The marvelous thing is there's no prejudice . . . absolutely none. Well . . . almost absolutely none. The *Grand* Bahamians, those born and bred on Grand Bahama—and they're probably too thin on the ground to make up a bowling league—would make my father proud. He always said, 'Never trust a foreigner.' From what I'm told, the Grand Bahamians consider anyone not born on the island a foreigner, even when they're from Abaco or Bimini only fifty miles away. All in all, I'd say it's as close as you're going to get to a fully integrated society."

"It sounds neat. How much of the island is developed?"

"Not much, comparatively speaking. Most of what is developed is quite pretty, but the bulk of the island is just forest. Scrawny-looking Caribbean pines, thatch palm, ferns, sea grapes, poisonwood and so forth."

"What are sea grapes?"

"Odd-looking shrubs that turn into trees and bear some kind of edible fruit late in the summer. The fruit is in clusters like grapes—hence the name, I guess."

I asked lots of questions about the trees and flowers and

learned that one of my all-time favorites, hibiscus, was everywhere. Jeremy summed it up by telling me that everything I so diligently nurtured in pots around the house was growing along the roadsides in Freeport. Even our apartment building, which was not an entry in any landscaping contest, was surrounded by several varieties of hibiscus, bougainvillea, oleander, sea grapes, a few palms and schefflera. He neglected to mention poinciana, and that was an extra treat the island held in store for me.

The building had a nice pool and was located on a canal where we would be able to keep our boat. With a big grin, Jeremy produced brochures of the type of boat he thought we ought to buy. I thought he was exaggerating a bit when he said that lobster would replace venison as the freebie in our diet but, when we got established, it turned out to be no exaggeration at all. I would wind up with a full dozen ways of preparing lobster just to stop it from becoming boring.

Jeremy had told me a great deal on the phone. I knew that the whole south shore of the island was one long, sandy beach and that the stores had all the commodities we took for granted, although at significantly inflated prices. There were, however, certain things that worried me despite his confidence and reassurances. Foremost among them was the school situation. "Are you absolutely certain," I asked, "that the boys won't have trouble adapting to a new school system? I mean, from what you've told me about your own upbringing, the English system is awfully different from what they're used to."

"They call it English system," Jeremy explained, "but it's really a crossbreed. It's somewhere between English and American. They won't stand still for ill-behaved kids, but they don't throw them out for looking cross-eyed at a teacher either. The curriculum, too, is a crossbreed and a bit more advanced. Both boys are going to have to work like crazy to catch up and stay up, but the school is used to ex-pat kids and makes suitable allowances."

"But how can you be so sure they'll pass the entrance exams? What on earth will we do if either of them fails?"

"They won't fail . . . either of them. Some things we're just going to have to take on faith. To tell you the truth, we're making this whole move on faith. Why worry about one thing when there are so many that could go wrong?"

"What about immigration? Is that another of the things that can go wrong?"

"In a way, yes, but it's not to worry about either. The rules are a bit weird. If our applications for residency are approved, it'll mean that once a year we have to request extensions for another year. If I understand it correctly, once you have annual residency status the extensions are all but automatic. If you're not granted residency, it only means that you have to leave the island every eight months and come back to start another eight months. It's the first thing on my agenda Monday. I have to get a bank reference, two personal references, a police report—which means Les Cunningham, the Laceyville police chief, and I'll bet he's never done one of these before—more passport photos of each of us, and fill out those ruddy great forms in that pile over there. That, together with a check for a thousand and sixty dollars, is the first step."

"Are you sure we're doing the right thing? I mean . . . you have covered all the bases?"

Jeremy looked thoughtful for a few moments, then, choosing his words carefully, said, "As far as covering all the bases goes, yes, I'm pretty sure I've thought of everything. Are we doing the right thing? I believe we're doing what's right for us. Ever since Grand Bahama sort of recommended itself to us, I've had the feeling we were being led there . . . that God wants us to go there. I don't know why. I do know that everything keeps falling into place. Take the school as an example: they don't have many vacancies, yet there's a vacancy in both the third and the eleventh grades, one each for Ashley and Justin. We're meant to go there, that's all there is to it. God will show us why in His own good time."

I prayed very urgently before going to bed and was still nervous when I fell asleep. When I awoke, however, I felt nothing but excitement and anticipation. We were going to do it. We were actually going to do it. We had taken months and driven thousands of miles, looked at countless properties, before moving to our farm. Now, with Jeremy spending a mere three days in a place none of us had seen before, he had made all the arrangements and we were going there to live. I was a little awed by his ability to organize. He seemed to take my

trust in his judgment for granted. Perhaps he was right—
perhaps we were being led there.

I had many phone conversations with Mother during the
few months leading up to our November 1 departure for our
new home. During the course of a few of them she asked
about my faith. I even thought we might make some progress,
break new ground, a couple of times, but it was not to be.
Incredibly, her biggest stumbling block at that time was that
God was a man. "No *man* is going to be in charge of *me!*"
There was nothing one could really say to combat such a per-
verse point of view so, in keeping with my determination not
to provoke her, I permitted the conversation to fizzle out
whenever we arrived at that particular dead end. I did, finally, hear that she would be in New York on October 22,
staying that night and leaving for London the next morning.
I arranged to spend the afternoon with her and prayed that
she would not, this time as so often, be delayed for a week or
so. It was only nine days before our own departure, of which
she still knew nothing and of which she would not learn until
she was safely at work in London.

There were also three phone calls from Harold Schiff. The
first one was exploratory. He had heard rumors in the street.
"What's this I hear about a *Mommie Dearest* book you've written?" I foomfled with things like, "I don't know. What have
you heard?" and "How could I possibly write a book like
Mommie Dearest when my mother in no way resembles Joan
Crawford?" I managed to put him off without telling a lie, but
knew full well that he would be back with a vengeance.

The next time he called, his opening line was, "B.D., the
rumors won't go away and several people I know in the publishing business insist that you have written a book about your
mother." I admitted that I had, but stated categorically that it
in no way resembled Christina Crawford's book about Joan.
Harold said that I had no right to do such a terrible thing and
asked whether I had any love or compassion for my mother.
I assured him that I had an abundance of both and that that
was my reason for writing a book.

Harold's next tack was to allege that my book would hurt
the sales of Mother's book. He then launched into his tried
and tested old rhetoric. "Your mother is far more important

than you are. Her needs and desires must come first. Look what she's given the world. After all . . ."

To the total of his thrusts I stated that: yes, I had finished my book; yes, I had made a publication deal; no, there was no way he could dissuade me from publishing; yes, I had not only given the matter careful thought, but more thought than any other decision I had ever made; no, I would not tell Mother about it, nor would I, under any circumstances whatsoever, let her, or him either, see the manuscript prior to publication. Harold said he would prefer that I told her about it but that, if I refused, he would have to.

"It is my intention, Harold," I said stiffly, "to present Mother with a *fait accompli*. It's the only way in which my purpose will be served. Whether she knows ahead of time that I've written a book will make no difference. Whether or not you tell her is entirely up to you. The only thing I will tell you about it is that it's the story of a mother and a daughter and I want her to read it."

Harold called me one last time and pulled out all the stops. "B.D., I ask you again what it will take to get you to stop this book."

"Nothing will stop it, Harold, absolutely nothing, and I don't like your implication. We've been through all this before."

"Then perhaps there's something you ought to know." Here it comes, I thought. "Your mother's health is far more frail than you realize. The shock of this book could kill her."

"Not a chance, Harold! It won't work this time. You've used that frail-health ploy too often, and then followed it, when it suited your purposes, with the hale, hearty, indomitable constitution gambit."

"She hadn't had a mastectomy and a stroke then, B.D. This is different."

"Whoa! Wasn't it you who told me, when you wanted her to get back to work, how strong and well she was? You're getting your stories crossed. The guilt trip doesn't cut it this time. My book will be published and I don't care whether you know or understand my motives."

"At least delay publication for a year. Your mother proba-bly won't live out the year anyway and that way, even though what you're doing is wrong, she'll be spared the pain."

"You're not listening as usual. The whole point is to have her read it."

"What is it about? At least you owe her that much."

"I've already told you! It's a relationship between a mother and a daughter, a very real one."

"Why won't you let her see it? I can stop you if I want to, you know? All the rumors are that it's another *Mommie Dearest*."

"Take your best shot, Harold. Everything in the book is absolutely accurate and true. There's not a thing you can do . . . unless you're far more foolish than I think you are. Rumors or no rumors, it is not *Mommie Dearest*. Frankly, I'm surprised that you, of all people, set such store by rumors."

He was silent, his favorite tactic to get the other person to go on talking and, perhaps, say more than they wanted to. I waited patiently. Suddenly, "How can you do this, B.D.? How can you look at yourself in the mirror?"

"With no trouble at all. I answer to God and my conscience, and I've no trouble with either. As a matter of fact, I'm more at peace with myself now than I've ever been."

"I will have to tell her, B.D. It's the right thing to do."

"Do whatever you feel you must, but remember one thing: if you do tell her, she'll promptly take to her sickbed. She always does when something upsets her. She'll refuse to go to England to make the picture until she gets her own way. Well, this time she can't have her own way. You can call me until you're blue in the face, Harold—I will not budge. If you break it, it's up to you to repair it. Think hard on that point and what's really in the best interests of your client."

"I've never heard you speak like this, B.D. What's come over you?"

"A sense of priorities; perhaps even just plain sense."

"I guess there's nothing more to say . . . unless—"

"No unlesses, just nothing more to say."

"Well . . . good-bye then. I hope you know what—"

"Good-bye, Harold."

I was still, two days later, feeling both satisfied at the way I had handled the inevitable confrontation with Harold and relieved that it was over. I should have known that he would make at least one more attempt and he did. My brother, Michael, phoned me from Boston, where he was involved in politics and practicing law. He told me that Harold had called and told him about my book and asked him to do his best to talk me out of publishing it. Failing that, Harold wanted him to persuade me to tell Mother about it and, failing that, he wanted Michael to tell her. Michael did none of the above.

Having related the underlying purpose of his call, he simply said that he hoped I knew what I was doing and, to my assurances that I did, said that he trusted my judgment. A very friendly chat ended with each of us extending love and best wishes to the other's family. During my subsequent conversations with Mother, it was obvious that no one had told her. Harold, despite his protestations regarding what was right and matters of conscience, was clearly keeping his counsel. This would be one bearer of bad tidings who, even if he did not get killed, might well wish he were dead. And every insider was all too well aware of it.

During the course of the three-and-a-half-hour drive to New York City on October 22, I reflected yet again on God's perfect plan. Twenty years of marriage and not once, until now, had Mother passed by my home, in one direction or the other, without allowing a few days to come and visit. This time, with *MMK* to be my last-ditch attempt to make her listen to me—I just could not bring myself to admit to her that she had forced me into the position of promising my family that they would never have to see her again, at her house or ours—and with my whole family moving to the Bahamas in nine days, and not wanting her to find out about any of this because it would interfere with her work, this time she didn't have the few days for a visit to the farm. It was beyond extraordinary—it was supernatural. I did not doubt that to most people it would appear to be nothing more than a stroke of luck, a "coincidence," but I knew better. For twenty years Mother had planned her life around coming to visit me, and this time, this most critical of all times, she could not do it. My prayers had been answered.

I concentrated on blotting all past unpleasantness from my mind, on looking only forward, forward to the day when she would read my book and, overcoming her initial rage, would find it in her heart to forgive and accept forgiveness, forward to the day when she would choose the narrow path.

I had with me a present for her, a copy of the Living Bible, bound in green leather with "Ruth Elizabeth Davis" engraved in gold leaf at the bottom right of the front cover. I did not expect her to sit down and read it from cover to cover, but I hoped that she might peek at it from time to time and, having peeked, find it as interesting and compelling as it truly is.

Armed with my present and my determination to let Jesus' light shine through me, I knocked at her door. I determinedly set aside the thought that, if everything went wrong, if I had completely miscalculated the effect of my book, this might be the last time I would ever see my mother face to face.

Mother threw open the door. She certainly did not look sick. She was thin, yes, but spry and perky. Beautifully dressed, with high spike heels indicating no residual problem with her hip. There was great animation in her face, and no sign whatever, after her flight from L.A. earlier in the day, of fatigue or frailty. She was the picture of health and moving briskly as she always had. I thought of Harold's attempts to convince me of her failing health.

"*God*, you're late!" she cried, holding her arms wide for a welcoming hug. "I was worried."

"You look absolutely marvelous!" I said, giving her a big squeeze. "It's wonderful to see you looking so well after all you've been through."

"Yes," she said, turning to lead me into the suite, "it's been murder, but I've made it."

As we entered the living room, two men arose from opposing armchairs. One was Harold, grinning smugly, the expression in his eyes speaking volumes. I rushed straight at him, hand extended. "How nice to *see* you," I emoted, smiling broadly and, I hoped, ingenuously. "It happens so seldom. Are you joining us for dinner?"

"No, I'm afraid I can't. I have another engagement, but I wanted to wait and say hello." I might have been kidding myself, but I was sure I detected a note of disappointment at my lack of unease at his presence.

"What a shame," I said. "But it was awfully nice of you to wait. Thank you." I beamed at him.

Mother introduced me to the other man, whom I had wrongly taken to be an associate of Harold's. He was young, about thirty, and a walking advertisement for Brooks Brothers. Feeling Harold's eyes darting steely icicles at my back, I shook hands with Mother's new editor. It was all I could do to stop myself from collapsing into a puddle of laughter. The whole scene could have come straight out of an afternoon soap opera.

The lawyer knows what the daughter has done.

The editor knows what the daughter has done, and also knows that the lawyer knows, because it was probably he who told him in the first place.

The daughter knows that the lawyer and the editor know.

The lawyer and the editor know that the daughter knows they know.

Everybody knows everything, except the mother, who doesn't know anything because the daughter won't tell her and the lawyer and the editor are afraid to.

We all took seats and engaged in the most vacuous of conversations. We did five minutes on how wonderful Mother looked and another five on her book, still not finished, and her about-to-be-made movie. Then Mother, completely unaware of the electricity in the room, did a ten-minute monologue on how wonderful I was, my farm was, and my children were. She finally mentioned having an early dinner because she was starving, which Harold and Brooks Brothers took as their cue and left. I wondered what Harold had made of my performance. I also wondered what Young Editor had made of the daughter who chatted chummily with her mother the legend while on the brink, in Young Editor's opinion no doubt, of crucifying the legend for nothing but selfish gain.

I was relieved that they were gone, if only because I was able to stop being so disgustingly charming and sit back and relax. Kathryn entered to fix us drinks and she and I exchanged warm hugs. I gave Mother her gift and was happy that she seemed pleased with it. As she riffled the pages I marveled again at how well she looked, far better than I had dared hope. She strode about in her spike heels like a young girl, looked radiant and exhibited nothing but vitality.

"The Living Bible," I explained, "is an accurate interpretation of the Bible, but more in the vernacular. I thought you might enjoy it more if you could just sit back and read whenever you have a few spare minutes without having to concentrate so much."

"That's great. I'll try to read it sometime." I had not expected her to be overwhelmed.

"Would you like me to read a bit out loud so you can see what it's like?" I asked.

"Why not?" she replied. "Kath! Come and sit down. B.D.'s going to read to us."

I chose the Sermon on the Mount, read for a few minutes, and then shared Pat Robertson's teaching on the Beatitudes. When I was finished, Mother said she could see a difference in me, a kind of excitement and enthusiasm that she had not seen before. "That's my faith," I said. "When you suddenly discover that someone loves you and that that someone is absolutely all-powerful, how can you help but be excited and enthusiastic?"

"Hunh," Mother grunted.

"I'm serious. We can have victory over all of life's troubles through faith in the Lord. God wants to love all of us. That's the joy you see in me. But we have to reach out to Him; He won't force Himself on us. Jesus suffered to heal us of our sickness and infirmity and died to redeem us. Think about it!"

"I have. It doesn't make sense. If God is so much love and it's automatic for Jesus to heal everyone, why do I still get pain in my hip? I prayed and prayed."

"But it's not automatic. You don't suddenly decide you want something, offer up a quickie prayer and expect an answer. If that were the way it worked, there wouldn't be anyone anywhere lacking anything, would there? Before God will answer you, you must reach out for Him. You must make a commitment, accept Jesus as your personal Lord and Savior. Dialing 1-800-GET-WELL won't do a thing for you, no matter how often you try. And, apart from that, you could start out by thanking God for the blessings you've already received. Can't you see that He's giving you another chance, more time, to realize your need for Him? Your cancer was localized, your stroke was mild and—"

"*Mild?*" Sudden anger. "You think my stroke was easy? *Jesus!*"

"He is the Lord. I didn't say you had a thrilling time, but you did recover where so many never do. Isn't that something to be thankful for?"

"I slaved my guts out to get over that stroke. Brother! What do you mean? I went through therapists weekly. I wore them out I worked them so hard. Why should *I* be thankful?"

"Because all blessings come from God."

"I've always known there was a God."

"Well, at least that's a start. But you have to believe, really believe, before you can expect God's miracles. It helps to listen to someone like Pat Roberston. Then—"

"I did watch that show a few times."

"You have to watch it with the desire to learn, not just be entertained. You also have to read the Bible with a hunger to absorb all that God holds out to you. And—and this is the crux of the whole thing—you have to strive to obey all His rules, to do your best to walk in Jesus' footsteps."

"Except for swearing a little, I do. I always have."

This was where I had to step very carefully, watch every word. Mother's fantasy that she was perfect had come to the fore. I would get nowhere by expounding on sin. When she started reading the Bible, and understanding it, she would learn through God's own words. Mine, here today, would only end the conversation. I tiptoed into it. "Once you begin to learn what God expects of us, and Jesus is the example, you will see for yourself how far off the track we all are, and I assure you, Mother, you aren't an exception. Everyone has much to deal with when that first light starts dawning. But the thing is, we aren't alone in our struggle. Jesus is with us every step of the way. You have to call on Him, though—He will never force Himself on you. You have to ask for His intercession."

"You didn't have anything to apologize for. You were goody-two-shoes, for Christ's sake."

"I most certainly did, and there you go using Christ as a profanity again. If you knew Him, you wouldn't be able to."

We went around and around the subject of sin, without actually tackling it head-on, and back and forth on the subject of the acceptance of Jesus, without Mother ever addressing the point directly. Kathryn tried to ask something once or twice, but Mother shushed her each time. We eventually came to the moment when Mother said, "*My* god understands me. I've always discussed everything with him and he *approves* of everything I've ever done." There was no way of tiptoeing around this particular subject and I did not try to.

"There aren't separate gods, Mother. There's only one God and only one set of rules. Those rules are set forth in the Bible for all to see. They apply to all of us. Why do you keep saying your god and my God?"

"Does your God—"

"Stop calling Him *my* God! God is God. There's only one. If you think you have your own private god who rubber-stamps anything you decide to do, perhaps you ought to stop and think about who your god really is. There is God and there is Satan. Serving Satan is a very dangerous pastime, particularly if you celebrate it with the kind of determination you're showing. That's how Satan was kicked out of heaven in the first place. He thought he knew better than almighty God. He's still trying to prove it by deceiving people in order to hold on to them. Satan is a liar."

"Brother! You're really something."

"Why? Because I would prefer to see my mother in heaven than up to her neck in the fires of hell?"

For a few seconds, such a very few seconds, I thought she had let go. Instead of taking umbrage at my outburst, she asked the most exciting question I could have heard. The answer, unfortunately, hit the old stone wall.

"Okay, B.D.," Mother said, "have it your way. I don't understand you but I'll try to read your Bible." Next came the exciting part. "How do you know if you're born again? What do you have to say to Jesus?" I took out of my pocketbook the three copies of *Voice Magazine* that I had brought for her, handed her two and opened the third to the appropriate page. "I'll tell you what I'll do. I'll read you through the scriptural steps to salvation. They're right there in each of the magazines. Okay? The first is to acknowledge: 'For all have sinned and fallen short of the glory of God.' Accept that—"

"*What?*" she exploded. "Are you *crazy*? *No* one is going to tell *me* that I've sinned. *Jesus! Never!* I have *never* done anything in my entire *life* to apologize for, let alone to have it called *sin*. No, sirreee Bob!" The fury was gone as quickly as it came. It was replaced by an alarming impression of Shirley Temple at her cutesiest. "I'm a good girl. I always have been."

I ignored both extremes of Bette and went on talking to Ruth Elizabeth. It was the only way I could keep my own thoughts straight. Hers were beyond my comprehension. "Mother, slow down," I said. "Perhaps you don't understand what God means by sin. It's not just the obvious, like murder or robbery or rape or adultery; it's abortion," she winced slightly, "drunkenness, unkindness, lying—"

"Let's just drop it, shall we? *I'm* in charge, and I'll tell you something else: I've been very close to god all my life. I don't know about *your* God, but *mine* understands me. He *approved* of all the things I've had to do in my life, like divorces and abortions and such. I talked it over with him each time I had to make one of those decisions and he *approved*. *My* god loves me, so let's just drop it. I'm a very good girl and my god knows all about it."

And that was that. I was there for another couple of hours but there were no more openings. To try to force the matter would only lead to confrontation. I felt that I had failed as a person and as a witness for the Lord. I was terribly disappointed . . . but what else could I have said? Or had I said too much? Had I mistakenly—because it was my last chance—tried not only to sow the seed, but also to fertilize and water it? Had I been wrong to beard Mother with Satan?

It seemed like the right thing to do at the time—but had I truly been led by the Spirit, or was it simply a selfish reaction to Mother's persistent, and mightily offensive, references to her personal god?

For a little while, at least, Mother had been sensitive to Jesus' light shining through me—but then it had all gone wrong. Was it my fault, or was it the inevitable route that any attempt to witness to my mother was doomed to follow? Was her sense of right and wrong, good and evil, perfection and imperfection, so ingrained in her—with herself perfect and beyond reproach—that no mere human could ever convey to her that simplest of ideas: For all have sinned and fallen short of the glory of God?

There was really no point or purpose in tormenting myself. What was done was done, and there was always the possibility that I had done no more and no less than God wanted of me. He knew what tomorrow would bring and I had to be firm in my faith that I was acting within His will.

I had tried to stay the course, but I was out of time. Mother was leaving for London and I was moving to the Bahamas. *My Mother's Keeper* would have to go on the presses as written. It would be the two-by-four wherewith, God willing, I would be able to break through the obsessive presence that was Bette and reach out to grasp the hand of my real mother— Ruth Elizabeth.

CHAPTER

13

THE WEEKS OF PACKING UP THE FARM TO MOVE WERE FILLED WITH mixed emotions. We were about to undergo such a radical change of life-style that at times it seemed unreal. The most difficult part was deciding what we wanted and could use in the Bahamas, and what we didn't or couldn't, then selling or giving away the latter. Despite my best efforts not to let myself get bogged down in attachment to material things, there was so much that held sentimental value. None of our dark wood antique furniture, or cowhide armchairs, or suede couches would be suitable in the tropics, and I knew it as well as the next person. To pay vast sums to ship it, then pay duty on top of that, would be the height of absurdity, but it made the parting no less wrenching.

All of our artwork, bronzes, silver, crystal, china and personal things would be going with us and, although I thought I had virtually stripped us to the bone, possession wise, would end up weighing four thousand pounds. I fought back many tears as our picture-perfect little farm house was reduced to stacks of cartons and the odd chair and bed. Together with my husband, I had created and loved every old-fashioned inch of it and, even near empty, it still had personality.

The kitty-cornered stone fireplace with the old barn-beam mantel that I had lovingly labored over for days before it was set into the stone. The huge country kitchen with the open-raftered ceiling and brick floor. I thought of the puppies we had whelped there over the years and the vegetables that were canned every summer and fall to fill the larder cupboards.

Justin had been conceived and born here. The one piece of furniture we were keeping, at the request of both boys, was the Amish cradle that Justin had slept in for the first few months of his life at Ashdown.

I was filled with such conflicting feelings. Memories of my childhood and early marriage filtering through certain pieces of furniture. Inanimate objects that were more, and yet not. Then there were the animals, particularly the horses. It was completely impractical to take them, the climate alone being a terrible adjustment. There were moments, silly as it sounds, when I doubted that I would be able to enjoy life without Pasha, my Arabian. We had to find good homes for all of them and yet, in my heart, Pasha would be mine forever. I fully intend to find him again when we are both together in heaven one day.

God was good and each of the four horses went to the perfect owner. Chocolate, the twenty-three-year-old pony who had been a part of our family for ten years and on whom both Ashley and Justin had learned to ride, went to our blacksmith to teach what would probably be her last child, his grandson, the art of horsemanship. The three big ones went to 4-H kids; Pasha to a boy who wanted to compete in horsemanship classes; Dolly, Jeremy's horse, to a girl who wanted to compete in jumping; and April, Ashley's paint, to a girl who wanted to compete in trail classes and pole bending. We either knew personally, or knew of, each of the families taking our babies and were thrilled. As an added bonus, the family who took Pasha also took Scooby, the Great Dane. I could not have asked for more.

For the week or so after they were gone I could not bear it. Whenever I looked out across the empty pastures, or walked into the barn without hearing their friendly nickers, my eyes filled. I steeled myself one day, cleaned out the stables, and never set foot in them again. I could not avoid looking at the empty pastures, though. I was so used to seeing the horses from so many windows of the house that my gaze went automatically to the fields countless times every day. There were still a few cats, the ones too wild to be caught and relocated, but all was otherwise unnaturally quiet and still. Empty is empty.

As excited as I truly was about the Bahamas, and all the discoveries and adventures that awaited us, my heart ached as never before. That I was exhausted from the last-minute scramble to pack, ship and clean up only made things worse. Some dear friends, the Carmichaels, helped us with the loading of the truck on which the sea shipment went. Other good friends, the Keelers, insisted we stay with them the last few days while we tidied up loose ends and said our good-byes.

As we drove down the hill past the Sharers' for the last time, I wondered strange things: would the new owners plant my beautiful vegetable garden? Would they mow around the lake and keep the fields as clean as Jeremy did? Would horses again fill the stables and pastures? Would the banks of day-lilies I planted be visible if the grass weren't pulled from between them? So many little things that seemed to matter so much. Take a deep breath. Try to focus on the frozen water troughs—having to carry so many buckets of water every day when the lines to the barns were frozen for weeks at a time—worrying about frostbite on Justin's face while he waited for the school bus—the ice-rutted, treacherous roads that were with us for most of every winter.

It all seemed so remote.

Good-bye, Ashdown Farm. I loved you very much.

Part Two

CHAPTER

1

I RAINED ALL OVER JEREMY'S PARADE WHEN WE ARRIVED AT Newark Airport. He wanted to play "Betcha can't find Bahamasair" but, fraught with anxiety, grossly overtired, and trying to keep track of twelve pieces of luggage weighing several hundred pounds—they contained everything we would need until our air shipment arrived in a few weeks—I was in no mood for levity. The plane, fortunately, was only half booked and no one cared how many bags we had or what they weighed.

The flight was on time and, as we neared Grand Bahama, the two boys and I peered out of the windows, anxious for a first peek at our new home. All we could see were clouds—there had not been any all the way down, nothing but clear skies. And the clouds were not horizon-to-horizon or anything like that either. They were over Grand Bahama and nowhere else. I voiced my conjecture that this must be why there was no water problem on the island—a permanent supply was parked overhead.

Jeremy hastened to point out that the water supply had to do with a forty-foot aquifer beneath the island, not the clouds over it. He also tried to convince me that the rainy season had ended. As the plane descended through the clouds into a tropical monsoon, I was given pause to wonder what it was like during the rainy season.

"It's raining, Dad," Justin complained. "I thought you said it was sunny all the time."

"Yeah, Dad," Ashley put in his two cents. "You just told Mom the rainy season was over."

"Quiet!" I told them both. "It's not your father's fault it's raining." They muttered to each other softly, obviously feeling that they had been brought all this way under false pretenses.

The plane rolled to a stop and we alit into torrential rain and a puddle about an inch deep that stretched all the way to the terminal buildings. A sign greeted us: IT'S BETTER IN THE BAHAMAS. I had my doubts but was reassured by the thought that we would be rushed to our apartment, and dry clothes, by the real estate lady, Louise, while Jeremy brought the rest of the luggage in the car he had bought from the dealer. We had, of course, both cabled and phoned each of them to make sure there were no slipups. Louise had even been kind enough to volunteer to put a few necessities into the apartment for us: coffee, milk, eggs, bread and so forth.

We cleared Customs and Immigration and exited the building to look for our welcoming committee. The rain continued to pour down while Jeremy doggedly refused to accept that neither of our greeters was at hand. Finally admitting defeat, after coursing the entire terminal several times over like a foxhound searching for a scent, he went to the pay phone and called Louise's office. Even though we were all sheltered from the rain for the time being, the heat and humidity were such that we were getting wetter, not drier.

"Where's Dad gone?" Ashley had become the archetypical teenager. He could tell you the color of a girl's eyes, and the make of her sneakers, at a hundred yards, but would not notice if terrorists blew up the car next to him in a parking lot. His inattentiveness was the bane of his younger brother's existence. "To call the real estate agent, you dummy."

"Shut up, you little twirp!"

"Stop calling each other names! One more time and I'll

leave you both here—your father and I will live happily ever after."

"Justin started it. The little twirp called me a dummy."

"I'm not a little twirp, you dummy, and you are a dummy. You never know what's going on."

"I know what's going on when it's something I care about, so don't call me a dummy."

Ashley had goofed; he had given Justin a point of logic to debate. "If you know what's going on when it's something you care about, how come you asked where Dad's gone? If you cared, you would know where he's gone, and if you don't care, why ask?"

I felt that Ashley deserved one more turn before I put a stop to this enlightening discussion. "Because I didn't care before but now I do."

"Alright, gentlemen," I said. "That's enough." I then added, more for appearances than anything else, for I had said the same thing a few thousand times before without beneficial effect, "If you can't speak nicely to each other, don't speak at all."

We were spared further ado by Jeremy's return. I would like to hear Gloria Steinem address this particular aspect of equal rights one day. All Jeremy had to do was heave over the horizon and the boys all but snapped to attention and saluted. It has always been a puzzlement to me.

"What's going on?" I asked.

"I called Louise's office. The girl says she doesn't have any idea where Louise is, but she's certain she's not on her way to the airport. She promised to try to track her down and get her over to the apartment with the keys."

"Thrilling," I said, envisioning us moving into a hotel, lock, stock and hundreds of pounds of baggage, until the marvelous Louise could be located. "What about the car? Did you try calling the dealer?"

"Sure did."

"Well, what did he say? Stop being mysterious."

"He couldn't even remember my name."

"What about the car he agreed to hold for you?"

"He sold it a couple of weeks ago."

The only consolation was that my husband did not seem

terribly put out. Perhaps his earlier few days on the island had given him a better understanding of IT'S BETTER IN THE BAHAMAS.

"What do we do now?" I asked, trying my best not to scream, cry or do both at once.

"Stay where you are. I'll be right back." Jeremy dashed across the road in the direction of car rental offices.

"Oh, great," said Ashley, probably to prove to Justin that he cared, "Dad's gone again."

"I want a soda," said Justin.

The rain continued to pour down and everywhere I looked there were puddles resembling lakes. I was to learn that there is no drainage to speak of on the island. Since it is so flat, I guess the powers-that-be felt that sooner or later the rainwater would inevitably find its own level—the ocean. While it is searching for its own level, however, the whole island is a mess. Jeremy returned in ten minutes driving a huge van. The kids were thrilled since it had all sorts of rotating armchairs. I was relieved, at first—because there was room for all the luggage—but then the ominous portent of the size of the thing dawned on me: perhaps we were going to have to live in it until we found Louise. Notwithstanding the fact that it was air-conditioned, it was a possibility I chose not to dwell upon.

With the van loaded and ourselves dripping wet, we rolled through a few formidable lakes and out onto a divided highway where we turned left. Along both sides of the highway, and up the grassy divider, stretched lines of palms and bottlebrush trees. We came to a beautiful roundabout, planted with more palms, casuarina pines and assorted other flora, and also sporting a sign saying IT'S BETTER IN THE BAHAMAS. The Board of Tourism seemed convinced even if I remained more than a little dubious. We went south on another divided highway, East Mall, which was lined with huge rubber trees. We passed intersecting roads with names like Adventurers Way, Pioneers Way, Settlers Way and, as we passed the Town Center, Ashley made his first approving noise. "Hey, great, Dad! There's a Colonel Sanders."

We came to another roundabout, this one with a fountain in the middle and called Ranfurly Circus, and turned left onto yet another divided highway with palms along the divider and

Caribbean pines—which cover all undeveloped land—crowding in on either side.

"Wow!" said Justin. "There's a Burger King, Dad." Apparently Jeremy was now forgiven for the weather.

"Are all the roads here divided highways?" I asked, finding it a bit odd.

"Not on your life," Jeremy replied. "They're for the tourists. The minute you're out of the areas normally seen by tourists, the roads are regular two-laners. Some are still dirt."

At a traffic light we turned right on Coral Road and things became normal. It was a two-lane road with houses scattered along either side. Where there were no houses, there were the omnipresent Caribbean pines and thatch palms. The houses all appeared to be built out of block and stucco with tile roofs of assorted colors. Halfway down Coral Road the rain stopped and we were in brilliant sunshine. The kids were thrilled but, as I had been paying only nominal attention to the landscape, the sun did not impress me much either. I was too busy praying that we would be able to get into our apartment. Jeremy was too preoccupied to notice my distraction.

We bore left at Bahama Reef Boulevard and, a quarter of a mile farther along, turned right into a little lane leading to a white, two-storey apartment building. It was not unattractive and did enjoy privacy and a canal. Could we get in, though? Jeremy jumped out of the van and ran up the staircase on the right. All was not lost—the keys were in the door with a note from Louise's husband apologizing for her not having been able to meet us. It said that she would stop by later.

In case it started to rain again, we dragged all the bags up the stairs before I even inspected my new home. The first thing I noticed was an air conditioner. I tried to turn it on but no luck. Jeremy, seeing my lack of success, tried a light switch—nothing. Justin helped a lot. "The power's not on, Dad." He was very accusing.

"Oh, great!" said Ashley. "What do we do now?"

"Maintain our poise and call the power company," said Jeremy. He did not look as poised as he would have us believe. He picked up the phone—no dial tone.

Ashley watched the look of annoyance that crossed his father's face. "The phone doesn't work either, right?"

"Terrific!" said Justin. "Now we can't even call anyone to tell them the power doesn't work."

I wandered off to look around, hoping that Jeremy would have a brainstorm by the time I got back. The door by which we had entered led to a dining room/living room, an adequate kitchen off one end, the master bedroom/bathroom down a hall, and a guest bathroom and den at the other end of the hall. There was an archway at the far side of the den which led into another hall, giving access to another bathroom and two bedrooms. There was a utility room which had obviously been a kitchen before the two apartments had been made into one. Justin came scampering after me and threw a light switch. The light went on.

Justin and I rushed to tell Jeremy the good news. A little experimentation revealed that the power was on in what had been Apartment 205, but off in 206. We were puzzling about this when there came a knock at the front door. Jeremy opened it and led in a very nervous little lady whom he introduced as the elusive Louise. She was all smiles and effusiveness.

"The power's not on in two-oh-six," said Ashley.

"The phone isn't, either," said Justin.

"I'm sorry to hear that," said Louise, "but your father was supposed to take care of those things. It's not—"

"How *dare* you be so rude?" I blared at the children. My pent-up anxiety had found a target for its release. "I'm sorry that you two are so discommoded, but it's not Louise's problem—it's ours."

"Thank you," said Louise. I was not sure what she was thanking me for and was thrown completely off-stride. Jeremy later explained that "thank you" was an island expression indicating agreement, rather like the American "You bet."

I finished rather lamely. "So, say you're sorry to Louise and remember your manners from now on."

"I'm sorry," said Ashley, superfluously offering to shake hands again.

"I'm sorry," said Justin, who then added, "it's a good thing you didn't bring eggs and milk and things like you said you would—the refrigerator isn't working." I was about to jump on Justin about his manners again when I realized that he had only voiced something running through my own mind.

"That's alright, sweetheart," I said. "Your father will pick up some things when he goes out about the phone and the power."

"But where will we keep it?" asked Justin, afraid that I might have forgotten the kitchen had no electricity.

"Do us a favor," Jeremy snapped. "Go and unpack a bag or something while your mother and I talk to Louise. We have a lot to do and not much of the day left to do it in."

"I'm thirsty," said Justin.

"There's water coming out of your bathroom faucet," Jeremy growled. "Drink some of it."

Having sufficient common sense to know when their father had had enough, the boys retreated to their end of the apartment.

Louise made a suggestion: "Why don't you buy or borrow some extension cords and hook up some lights and the refrigerator until the power company comes? You could run the cords from two-oh-five."

"Now, that makes sense," Jeremy said.

He left me with Louise and her part-French, part-Bahamian rendition of the English language. My ill humor must have been showing badly, for Louise took it upon herself to launch into what I needed least at that moment, a lecture on keeping one's cool and coping with Bahamian customs. With great effort, I reminded myself that I was a Christian and permitted her to finish her lecture uninterrupted. With even more effort, I thanked her for her advice.

"That's quite alright, dear," she said patronizingly. "I know how difficult it can be for newcomers to the island and I like to help as much as I can."

Louise left a few minutes before Jeremy returned with a bundle of assorted extension cords which various of the apartment owners had been kind enough to throw into the pot for us until we got organized.

"The nerve of that woman," I spluttered. "Giving me a lecture on how to cope with Bahamian unreliability when *she's* the one who caused me to worry all the way from the airport. I wanted to strangle her."

"It wouldn't help," Jeremy said, "and anyway, she's not all that bad. She may be a bit dippy, but she means well. We talked in the parking lot before she left and she's bringing a television over tomorrow. We can keep it until our air shipment gets here."

"That is kind of her. Maybe she's right," I conceded reluctantly, "maybe I have to learn to cope. But it's certainly difficult when the person lecturing you is the one who caused you to come unglued in the first place."

"You'll get used to it," Jeremy said reassuringly.

"Don't waste your time trying to convince me that you're all calm and unruffled," I challenged. "You're ready to kill someone and we both know it."

"Be that as it may," he said, heading for the door again, "I have about two hours of working day left to pick up a few supplies, buy a car and convince the telephone and power companies to be nice to us. If I don't keep smiling and waving, we'll wind up sitting in the dark, incommunicado, and walking five miles each way to restaurants for meals."

The apartment had just been painted and cleaned and there was not much I had to do before I could start unpacking. I dug the kids' bathing trunks out of the bags and dispatched them to the pool behind the building with instructions not to return until called. Then, housewives being what we are, I found all the nooks and crannies missed by the cleaners and scoured them before running the vacuum over the whole place just for luck.

By the time Jeremy returned I had everything tidied up, the bags unpacked and the refrigerator clean and hooked up to a long extension cord running to an outlet in the hall of 205. I had more cords arranged so that we had light in the living room and in our bedroom. "How did it go?" I asked, helping him through the door with his armful of grocery bags.

"Not too bad, all things considered. The power company says it will have a man here first thing in the morning. The—"

"But how did they get so messed up in the first place?"

"No one could account for it. The computer showed that the service man turned on two-oh-five and one-oh-six. Since the man had to pass through two-oh-six to get to the meter in two-oh-five, even the girl in the office thought it to be rather dumb. Her exact words were, 'Dat don't make sense.' I got the groceries, as you can see, and I bought a Honda Civic that will be ready in the morning. It's secondhand and rather small but it will do until we know exactly what we need. The phone company doesn't sound too promising, though. Their computer shows that we're scheduled for hookup in three weeks."

I contemplated the bleak outlook of a few hours earlier and felt much better. "Well, praise the Lord," I sighed. "If we have to do without something, I'm glad it's only the phone."

I realized that Mother might be dismayed at her inability to phone me for a while, but consoled myself with the knowledge that my letter to her telling her of our move to the Bahamas—I'd had to write her a letter since she had not, as she usually did, called me upon her arrival in London to give me her phone number—had also warned that it might be a few days before I could let her know *my* new phone number. As it turned out, Louise's husband had a friend at the phone company and we were hooked up in a week.

Mother, when I finally spoke to her, was far less disturbed at our move than I had expected, and even expressed appreciation of my not telling her of it prior to her departure, agreeing that my reasons were well founded. She would not, she admitted, have left to do her movie had she known what I was undertaking. No more than a day or two passed before I heard from her again. She called to let me know that she was coming to spend Christmas in the Bahamas and that she would look for a house to buy while she was here.

Instead of panicking and going into a depression, I was delighted to discover that my faith in God's perfect plan was growing. I had no doubt that either something would occur to prevent Mother from going through with her plans, or—and this is what really amazed me—that if she did come, it would be to fulfill God's purpose. I was convinced that I would never again be subjected to her nastiness and ill behavior in my own home.

I would never have guessed that Harold Schiff would do the deed that would change Mother's plans.

CHAPTER

OUR FIRST FEW DAYS WERE FRENETIC BUT ENJOYABLE. THE weather was outstandingly beautiful—cool nights and hot sunny days—and such spare time as we had was spent investigating the beaches. The boys passed their entrance exams without trouble, although, due to the English-style curriculum, Justin had to take a crash math course to catch up with his peers. They began school the following Monday. Jeremy took the first steps toward buying a boat and we did our homework regarding where to shop and where not to.

From the first moment of entering our new church, Calvary Temple, the feeling of belonging was overwhelming. I could not help but think back to all those moves I had undergone during my early years and my constant struggle to find acceptance. The cliques and snobberies, the concern with social standing, the determination to preserve it. Every time we moved I had to go through the same ritual: the doubly cold shoulder because I was not only an outsider but also a star's daughter; the painful awareness that, even though I was the same as everyone else, they were determined to make me out as different and keep me at bay; the eventual acceptance of me by some brave soul, usually an outcast like myself, and a resulting friendship. It had always been that way.

When I got married I naturally became part of my husband's circle of friends and acquaintances; when we moved to Pennsylvania I was too busy helping with the renovation of our farm to notice how long it took for me to find women friends; but now, in this church in Freeport, it seemed as if the entire congregation went out of its way to welcome me and my family. Nobody asked about our work or where we had come from; they just welcomed us and expressed delight that we had moved to the island permanently and had joined them as members of God's family.

I met Pastor Ernie DeLoach for the first time. He was all that Jeremy had said and more: effervescent, ebullient, deeply dedicated to his calling, full of humor, and with a love as great as all outdoors. I recognized in him that same elusive aura that had first drawn me to Serafino Fazio: that presence that is known as Jesus' light shining through someone. He was about five feet eight inches tall and slightly rotund, had a great booming voice that shook the rafters of the church—although his singing voice was atrocious—and an ever-present grin that broke into laughter at the slightest provocation. His greeting was such that I felt I had known him all my life. His wife, Kay, an attractive and petite lady, was just as warm and equally without pretense or guile.

As we attended church each week the feeling of belonging grew, the faces became names and the handshakes became hugs. The sanctuary seated about three hundred people, but had almost as many leaks as pews. On rainy mornings the drips and puddles were disconcerting, but were more so if the rain hit during the middle of a service. The leaks never seemed to be in the same place. If it was raining when we arrived at church we could sit where it was dry; an onslaught during the service, however, necessitated a good deal of shuffling from one pew to another.

It seemed odd to us that no effort was being made to repair the roof; but apparently all available funds were going toward the construction of a new and bigger sanctuary next-door and no one cared about their current discomfort. It didn't take many leaky roof services before my family and I were praying for the early completion of the new building.

A wholly new area of interest opened up for us one day when Jeremy discovered, quite by accident, that there was on the island an amateur theatrical group—complete with a lovely theater that had been built some years earlier—that was looking for new members.

My husband had taken to dropping by a coin shop to discuss with its English owner his interest in British historical medallions. It was there that he heard about the Freeport Players Guild, the upcoming Christmas pantomime, and the shortage of people for the chorus.

Neither Jeremy nor I were interested in appearing on stage, but Ashley loved the idea. We went to the next rehearsal of *Sinbad* and Ashley was quickly assimilated into the chorus. The next thing we knew, we had paid our annual dues and were involved in set decoration, painting and odd jobs.

Unlike the church, which consisted mostly of Bahamians with very few expatriates, the Guild membership was mostly ex-pats with only a smattering of Bahamians. We quickly became acquainted with some very nice people and our social life took on a broader dimension. My husband had always taken the making of new friends for granted—I suspect that all Englishmen do—but I was enormously pleased at the short time it had taken for me to feel at home.

We settled on a boat that would suit our purposes, and shortly thereafter there was fishing and snorkeling gear for each of us. Fishing was fun but nothing compared to snorkeling. Jeremy tried constantly to arouse in the boys and me an interest in trolling, but it was no use. A few minutes in the hot sun and all we wanted was to get into the water. We quickly became acquainted with the reefs around the island and the most likely places to find lobster. They are actually crawfish but lobster is less of a mouthful and islanders generally refer to them as such.

Jeremy's first success at spearing lobster fired in him a passion which has done wonders for our diet. I now have more recipes for lobster than I would ever have dreamed existed. Our most memorable day was to occur the following March when we set out to search coral heads some ten miles off the north shore. The season would be closing for four months commencing April 1, and Jeremy was determined to harvest enough to last us through the summer. In that one day we brought back 202 lobsters, enough for ourselves with plenty left to share.

As Thanksgiving neared I felt my first real pangs of dislocation and loss. I missed the friends with whom we had shared the holiday the previous year, the comfort and laughter of tried and tested companionship. I missed my lovely old farmhouse and, perhaps most of all, my wonderful great kitchen with its cathedral ceiling, exposed rafters and brick floor. I loved cooking for Thanksgiving, but I did not have any pots wherewith to do so. Our airfreight shipment was still in the air somewhere and so was everything I needed—beyond the bare essentials we had carried with us, that is.

I was feeling a bad case of the blues—not being able to prepare a holiday feast for lack of tools, having no one close outside of the four of us even if I could, and facing the prospect of eating out yet again—when Kay DeLoach invited us for Thanksgiving dinner. I was as excited as a child on Christmas Eve and my glums evaporated into thin air. They were soon to return, however.

On November 24, Kathryn called. "Mr. Schiff has told your mother that you've written a book. She's under sedation, but she instructed me to tell you to call her right away."

"Why didn't she just call me herself? Why don't you just tell her I'm on the phone?"

"She wants *you* to call *her*. She's terribly upset. Please do as she asks—it'll make life much simpler."

"Has she finished the picture?"

"No. She still has two scenes to do. It'll take one more day . . . two at the most."

"O.K., I'll call back in a few minutes."

Why on earth had Harold played it this way? Why had he waited until Mother had one more day of shooting, and then told her the one thing in the world that would guarantee her taking to her sickbed? Did he think that I would fall for a "Your mother's on her deathbed" routine? Did he think that threats of lawsuits by insurance companies covering the production would move me? What did he think? Why had he done it? I had no doubt that he had chosen this moment with precise forethought, but it did not seem to make any sense.

That Harold wanted a copy of my manuscript prior to publication went without saying. It would be much easier for him to claim libel and get an injunction against publication pending a hearing—which hearing might be manuevered into taking forever—than to prove libel where none existed. But he would have to consider me either inordinately stupid or ultimately naive if he believed that Mother throwing a tantrum and refusing to go to work—for the umpteenth time in her life—could persuade me to change my mind and let her, and thus him, get what they wanted.

There was no point in wasting time trying to figure it out. I might guess rightly, and I might guess wrongly, but neither event would make any difference. Harold had done what he had done and everyone, including his client, would have to live with the consequences.

I dialed Mother's number in London. As I waited for the call to go through I contemplated what was about to transpire and steeled myself for the impending drama.

"Hel-lo." A very, very frail voice. The word broken in the middle by a slight choke. Near death's doorstep.

"Hello, Mother." Normal, chirpy tone.

"Who's this?" Very weakly. I wonder how many people, with female voices, call her Mother.

"It's B.D."

"Oh." Voice almost normal strength.

"I hear that Harold's told you about my book."

"I have one question. Why?" Mother's voice now quite normal and filled with anger.

"Because I believed, and still do, that—"

"Just tell me why! Was it for money?" Death's doorstep completely forgotten. Each word clipped short in fury.

"I wrote it be—"

"Why won't you answer me?" Shouting.

"I'm trying but you won't let me finish." Keep your cool, B.D. You knew this was exactly how it would go. And she does not know, nor has she even asked, what the book is about. Or does she know? Is it possible that she is as aware of her behavior as are those upon whom she inflicts it?

"Don't you dare fight with me! I'm a very famous woman.

166

You had no right . . . no right at all. It's sinful. Brother! Why?"

"It certainly isn't sinful to write a good book, and I think I have. But I didn't want you to know about it until I was in a position to hand you a bound copy. I'm not—"

"I'll bet! You always lie to me—for twenty years you've lied."

"Ever since I got married, you mean? What about? When did I lie? Give me one example!" I was losing control. "And where's the lie now? I didn't tell you about my book, but I did *not* tell you a lie." I was shaking with anger and all but shouting.

"I suppose you wrote a book about how much you love your mother?"

"I wrote it because I *do* love you."

"Well . . . you've finished me off. That's all I want you to know." She had sounded almost calm for a moment, but she was quickly back to shrieking. "I'm a very famous woman and you had no right! *Why?*"

"It was very important to me to write our story. You'll understand when you read it."

"Read it? *Ha!*"

"Harold's known about it for months. Why he decided to tell you about it *now* I don't know, but—" I was talking to a dial tone.

Well—that was that. One problem was solved, but a far more important one remained. Mother would not be coming to the Bahamas for Christmas, let alone be looking for a house to buy in my backyard. But what about my anger? I had really thought that I was making progress, growing in the Lord; that I was becoming tolerant, understanding, forgiving.

I had not made any progress at all. I had been kidding myself. The minute my mother started up, I lost it. I was just as full of resentment and anger as ever. It was a conditioned reflex. It did not even make any difference who was at fault. She started shouting and I became angry. All my praying and self-examination had been for naught. One phone call, and I was right back where I had always been.

Jeremy and I talked a great deal over the next couple of days. We eventually decided that it was the unexpectedness of the whole thing that had so upset me. I had expected to be left in peace for at least another few months before having to gird up my mental and emotional loins to face the furor that actual publication of *MMK* would create. I had not been prepared for Harold's ploy and my guard had been down. Talking about it did help a little. At least I was able to sound civil and composed when the next phone call from London came in.

It was a Dr. Greenborough who wanted to talk to me about my mother. He was charming and polite. He informed me that Mother was very ill due to her inability to read my book, so much so that she had, for the past two days, been unable to report for work to finish her last two scenes. He wondered whether I would be kind enough to send a copy of the manuscript over right away.

I tried to determine his precise relationship, medically speaking, to my mother, but his responses were a bit vague. I induced that he was actually representing an insurance company; that a claim had been made under the production's cast insurance policy. I sought clarification of the nature of her illness but it seemed that the only definable symptom was higher than desirable blood pressure. The doctor did admit that Mother had told him to call me and let me know how sick she was.

I explained to him that Mother was perfectly welcome to call me herself if she wanted to, but that I would not call her. I'd had enough of being hung up on. I also explained that Mother had a lifelong history of throwing tantrums in order to get what she wanted and that she would persist with the tantrum for so long as she had an audience. I likened it to a spoiled child which holds its breath—and hopefully turns blue in the process—until its parents become frightened and give in.

The doctor said it sounded as though I was determined not to show my mother my manuscript. I said that he was absolutely correct. He was silent for a while, obviously pondering his dilemma. Then he asked whether Mother would see the book prior to publication. I said that she would, but hastened to point out that it would be several months until publication. He thanked me for my help and sounded so polished that I gained the distinct impression that the quaint behavior of movie stars was nothing new to him.

Yet another two days passed and then, on November 28, Kathryn called to tell me that Mother had finished the movie but had not yet received the copy of the manuscript I had promised to send by overnight delivery. It seemed that the good doctor had indeed had prior experience and had not been caustic in his thanks for my help. He had told Mother the manuscript was on the way and she had promptly recovered from her illness, high blood pressure and all. What would happen when the truth came out was not the doctor's problem—the movie would be finished. Kathryn was not at all happy about being the one to break the news to Mother. She asked if I would do it. I declined but suggested that Kathryn call Harold and hand the problem over to him. "What the heck," I said, "he started it—let him finish it."

My closing quip about telling it to Harold buoyed my spirits for a short time, but then the glums returned. I was still angry, despite my best efforts to put the matter out of mind. It seemed that thirty years of being shouted at by one person was too long a history to be overcome simply by willing it away. I did feel sorry for my mother, in her self-imposed loneliness, but only when I consciously focused my attention on her in the attempt to eradicate the resentment within me.

I tried it now. I thought about her age and the illnesses she had overcome a couple of years ago. I tried for the thousandth time to accept her own rationale—that you have to be tough to succeed in life—as a rationale for her behavior in general. I thought about the good times and her love for me. I thought about the two realities which were the cause of most of the trouble that seethed around my mother.

The first was *her* reality, one born in her imagination and refined into a shooting script. Her role was clearly defined as center of her personal universe, and all about her joyfully worshipped and danced attendance. Only the good qualities—that is to say, qualities acceptable to Mother—were evident in those around her. No character or personality traits in others which Mother did not like were permitted in her reality. *She* was perfect, and everyone around her was perfect.

Then came the real reality. As soon as the first flaw forced its ugly head into Mother's fantasy, she reacted quickly and with passion. The offending person had to be bludgeoned into line or cast out. And that was the trouble where I was concerned: she never stopped trying to bludgeon me into line because she was unwilling to cast me out. My offense, the flaw that kept rearing its head in Mother's reality, was that I loved my husband and children. No one in Mother's reality is allowed to love anyone but Mother.

It is so very sad that a person who means nothing but well for those she loves, who truly cares, can wander so far off the track and create so much misery.

I had often wondered whether Mother made herself miserable as well as those around her, or whether she simply thrived on high drama for its own sake. Did she view life as a constant struggle to win Academy Awards? Everyone knows that awards are most often given for thundering emotional performances, hardly ever for lovey-dovey relationships. Was this so deeply ingrained in her that it had spilled over to become part of her philosophy as a whole?

But that course of thinking was a waste of time too. She had always been this way. Aunt Bobby, her only sister, had said she was this way as a child. Jack Warner said, when Mother was nominated for best actress in *Of Human Bondage*, that he did not know why she should receive an award for playing herself. So, why are you trying to figure out what she is all about all over again? You satisfied yourself that the problems all derive from her determination to fight for supremacy in everything—to keep the Lilliputians at bay—and the confusion wrought within her when the two realities clash.

You wrote a book about the whole thing. You know she has never known true happiness—she has said so herself often enough, even seeming proud of the fact, as though misery is a merit badge for hard work—and you are hoping that the book will shake her to the very core of her being. You are hoping that it will force her to pay attention, that the very publicity of it will deny her the ability to pretend that you have not spoken. You are hoping that she will first hear the words and then, ultimately, accept the concept: the concept, so alien to her lifelong patterns of thought and behavior, that happiness is available to all who seek it and that love means letting down one's guard and giving of oneself; that love does not mean the acceptance of mindless idolatry, and purchased obligation, in exchange for empty lines from an overworked script.

You figured that all out long ago. You also realized, once you accepted Jesus, that it would take one of God's miracles to bring your mother around, that she would have to accept salvation before she could have any chance of accepting you as you are.

Using an empty soda bottle as a rolling pin, I set about the attempt to distract myself by baking some pies to take to Pastor's house the following evening. It helped, but not completely. Mother's automatic assumption that I had nothing good to say about her kept coming back to me. She did not even know the title, let alone the contents, of my book, yet she assumed the worst. "I suppose you wrote a book about how much you love your mother?" had been uttered with oozing sarcasm, and said it all.

So here I was again—full circle. She meant well, yet she destroyed. Ruth Elizabeth and Bette. The former wanting to be a loving wife and mother, the latter always getting in the way. And all the statements over the years that were both challenge and confession—challenge by Bette and confession by Ruth Elizabeth: "I sure am a gutsy dame to let you talk to the press without my being there," "You think I'm a monster woman—you always have," and, perhaps the most significant of all because it followed discussion of *Mommy Dearest* one day, "Brother! Could *you* write a book."

Bette knows what is in *My Mother's Keeper* because she knows it cannot be anything else. She knows how she has treated everybody through all the years because she deems it her right, as a famous actress, to have done so, just as she considers it the obligation of all of us to tolerate that treatment. She knows that I love her and resent her, just as she loves and resents me. I love Ruth Elizabeth and resent Bette— she loves B.D. and resents the married daughter.

But, if you understand all this, why do you permit yourself to get so upset? Because I am human and I am always having to deal with Bette; because every time Bette does a number on me, an underlying bitterness rises up in me and overwhelms all other emotion.

And now I have written a book to cure it all, and I have to

live with the knowledge that it may not work—that it may be the same as announcing that I no longer have a mother and slamming the door in her face.

Put the pies in the oven and stop driving yourself crazy. It will only be a few more months before the course of events will change forever. And not only that, Harold has done you a favor: he's told her. You don't have to worry about Christmas anymore.

CHAPTER

3

ONE TENDS TO THINK OF MIRACLES AS EVENTS IMMEDIATELY OB-
servable, preferably even provable: the healing of my back and
Howard Roediger's emphysema; the disappearance, at a later
date, of a tumor from the abdomen of Pastor DeLoach's sister
Sue—the tumor was clearly visible on the X rays but completely gone when the surgeon made the incision. These were
miracles indeed, and nice dramatic ones, with doctors to bear
witness.

But as I was learning, perhaps too slowly, God does what
He does according to His own timetable, not ours. God does
not simply invest in His children the fruits of the Spirit—we
have to grow into them, strive for them and earn them.

So it was with my resentment of my mother. My family
and I arrived at the DeLoach's that Thanksgiving evening with
me very heavy of heart and down on myself because of my
failure. Nothing out of the ordinary occurred and yet, mirac-
ulously as far as I am concerned, I left feeling a bit better and
continued upward from then on. It was weeks before I realized that a change had taken place and more weeks before I
was able to define the nature of that change.

The essence of the matter was that a soothing balm had been applied to my spirit. The anger and resentment—never, it seemed, far below the surface of my consciousness—were gone, replaced by a deep and abiding sadness for my mother. My problems were solved, but hers would continue for a long time and there was nothing I could do for her but pray. I was confident that God would work His miracle, that He would take Mother's hand and guide her first, tentative steps along the narrow way that leads to salvation—and also to reconciliation with me and my family—but when? That was the cause of my sadness. I felt that it might be a very long time before Mother would actually bring herself to read what I had said; and would, thereby, be given pause to contemplate. In the meantime, I would be happy in the bosom of my family—enjoying everything that God has to offer—and Mother would be alone.

Her loneliness would be of her own making, certainly, but that did not change the fact. It would be so simple for me to pick up the phone and ease the burden on both of us—but that would defeat the purpose. The greatest part of my miracle was that my sadness never turned to guilt. I did not waver in my judgment that publishing my book was the only thing I could do.

Little did I know—for it was entirely without my perspective—that my vindication would come a few months hence when God would speak, not just to me but to almost four thousand people in my presence.

There were a dozen people there for Thanksgiving dinner, apart from Pastor and his family, and Jeremy had the chance to learn about hotel management from a charming gentleman who managed one of the largest hotels on the island. He also learned something of the construction of the new sanctuary—begun by Pastor a couple of years earlier—from the consulting engineer who was visiting from Canada. He would learn much more than he expected in the very near future.

In addition, prompted by more questions from my husband, we learned that Pastor had been born and raised in Key West, Florida. His father had, tragically, died in a boating accident when Ernie was four, and the pastor of the local church, a kindly and loving man by the name of Wayne Pitts, had seen him on the street with his bicycle one day and stopped to talk to him. Pastor Pitts talked Ernie into attending Sunday school and developed a special liking for him.

In time the pastor became the little boy's adoptive father in all but the legal sense—they still call each other Dad and Son—but then baseball reared its head. By the time Ernie was ten it was quite apparent that he was extremely gifted at the game and the ballpark became the focal point of his life, to the exclusion of all else.

He drifted away from the church and his "dad," and becoming a professional ballplayer was the only thing to occupy his mind. But that was not what occupied God's mind. In the middle of a City League game one Sunday—when Ernie was sixteen—he was playing left field when he received a call from the Lord. One minute Ernie was playing his position in the full belief that fame and fortune were just around the corner—the next minute he felt God's presence in his heart and was standing there in tears.

His "dad" was delighted to welcome Ernie back into the fold. He found odd jobs for him so that he could help out at home, then made it possible for him to go to Bible school "on faith." (Doing things "on faith," Jeremy and I learned, means committing to a course of action without the least notion of how one is going to accomplish it. The faith is that God will provide the means. It can encompass anything from agreeing to go somewhere when there is no means of transportation to starting the construction of a church when there is no money.)

Ernie met Kay at Bible school and they were married when he graduated. Still on faith, and with Kay at his side, he sallied forth to evangelize the Bahamas. During the fourteen years that preceded his coming to Freeport he made his mark on two big islands and an assortment of cays. He resurrected a few defunct churches, built—or facilitated the building of— several new ones, established and built a youth camp for all the Bahamas, and brought uncountable numbers of people to the Lord.

He had been in Freeport for six years and was engaged in his biggest construction project yet—still on faith.

The Thanksgiving feast was long since finished and it was getting late. The kids had to go to school the next day and I nudged Jeremy out of his absorption with Pastor's story. As we were leaving, Pastor said to my husband, "By the way, Jeremy, how would you like to come over to the church tomorrow and lend a hand unloading a couple of trailers? The steel for the balcony has arrived and we have to get it off the trailers ourselves. It shouldn't take very long if a bunch of men lend a hand."

Jeremy agreed, a bit too quickly I felt, for I had the firm conviction that there was more to this than met the eye. It smelled like a classic example of Pastor bashing ahead on faith. Nonetheless, my husband promised to be in the church parking lot at eight the next morning.

With a month of island life under his belt Jeremy was far too experienced to make any unusual arrangements in order to be at the church parking lot by eight o'clock. He dropped the boys at school at 8:25, as usual, and went to the church. Not entirely unexpectedly, he found himself alone. Pastor cheerfully hove over the horizon at nine and said, "We seem to be the only ones here." Jeremy refrained from comment and inquired about the trailer loads of steel. "Oh, they'll be here soon. Come and look at the new sanctuary. I'll show you what we're doing."

The two men walked over to the area of new construction alongside the existing church. Jeremy gleaned that actual construction had started and stopped many times over the preceding two years. When there was money for materials, construction commenced; when money ran out, construction ground to a halt. Pastor was reluctant to borrow and was building a million-dollar sanctuary on faith.

He led Jeremy through a great encircling corridor, roofed and with partitioned areas for offices, into the wide-open space of the sanctuary itself. There were two partially completed block walls, about fifteen or eighteen feet high, which ran from an apex at about ninety degrees to each other. At the far end, some ninety feet away, was a third wall which described an arc from the apex. It was considerably higher than the side walls which it connected.

"How many people will this accommodate when it's finished?" Jeremy asked.

"About twelve hundred, including the balcony."

"Good grief! The church only has five hundred members. Why so much space?"

"There were only a hundred and fifty when we started building. By the time it's finished we'll need every inch of it. God's going to do a mighty work here."

Jeremy gazed about him in silence for a few moments, contemplating Pastor's conviction. His reverie was broken when Pastor said, "The pulpit goes here." He was standing twenty feet forward of the apex. "The choir stalls will be behind the pulpit with a baptismal tank over there."

"Why the odd shape?" Jeremy asked. It felt familiar, somehow, but he could not put his finger on it.

"It's a ballpark," said Pastor with a big grin. "The pulpit's at home plate."

Pastor described to Jeremy how the balcony would start at the present height of the two side walls and step, tier by tier, upwards to the height of the far wall. One or two would-be helpers stopped by and left again when they found no trailers to be unloaded. Pastor phoned the trucking company, which uttered reassuring but noncommittal words regarding delivery. At 2:25 Jeremy left to pick up the boys from school and bring them home. Pastor seemed not at all dismayed by the turn of events and made Jeremy promise to come again the next morning.

When my husband arrived at the church, again at 8:30, it was to find an intimidating sight. His better judgment told him to head for the hills and stay there until further notice. His curiosity, however, if not his sense of obligation, got the better of him. The trailers, loaded with steel, were parked side by side—the tractors which brought them had dropped the dollies and left—and Pastor and two other men were staring at them.

It was easy to see that any number of items on the trailers could be moved by hand, but by far the bulk of the fifty tons of steel that Jeremy was supposed to "lend a hand" getting off the trailers consisted of immense steel girders, none of which could possibly weigh less than half a ton, and several of which must weigh well over a ton.

Pastor was beaming with delight at the formidable sight, seemingly unaware that there was a problem. Jeremy joined the assembled group of three and, for once in his life, kept quiet to await developments. As one of the other volunteers began to release the tie-downs on the nearest trailer Pastor said, "We'll put the big stuff right next to the trailers and take the small stuff inside where it won't get stolen." Still Jeremy held his tongue. Someone climbed up on the trailer and heaved at a mighty piece of steel. "This is pretty heavy, Pastor."

It was at this point that Jeremy, who had been nursing serious doubts about Pastor's intelligence and/or sanity, became convinced that he was neither dumb nor disingenuous—simply an indefatigable optimist. The spiritual leader of the group, looking honestly surprised and more than a little dejected, said, "I guess we need a crane. I'll have to make a couple of calls."

Percy went for coffee, Geoffrey gave Jeremy a capsulated history of the Bahamas, and Pastor repaired to his office to materialize a crane—preferably one that would do the job on faith rather than for pay.

Fifteen minutes later Pastor rejoined the others, once again beaming. "Mario's on his way over. He's free till lunchtime but has to be on a job by two o'clock. He's doing us a favor so we'll have to work fast."

The four of them busied themselves moving all the small stuff out of the way so that the crane could do its thing unobstructed in the short time available. During the course of the frenzy of activity, Jeremy jumped down from a trailer and twisted his ankle. He hobbled around for the rest of the day, hoping that it was only a strain.

Mario arrived and positioned the crane. The topography was such that, from the cab of the machine, he was able to see the trailer beds and the men fastening the hoist hitches but not the ground beyond the trailers where the beams were being stacked. This meant that he had to operate on signals from someone. After ten or fifteen minutes of utter confusion, during which Percy, Geoffrey, Pastor and Jeremy all signaled, waved and shouted totally unintelligible—not to mention conflicting—instructions to Mario, Mario beckoned Jeremy to come over to the machine.

"Listen," Mario said, "I've only got two hours for this and if I leave without finishing, the pastor's going to kill me. I'll show you the signals to use and then ignore everyone but you. Stand on the trailer where I can see you; figure out what you want me to do and then give me the right signals. If we go on like this we'll be here all year."

So Jeremy learned the sign language of crane operators, and things proceeded more quickly and efficiently. The others kept right on waving and shouting—as did a number of casual bystanders who had by this time gathered round—but Mario ignored them, and Jeremy got the hang not only of the signals but also of the most beneficial instructions to give. Mario managed to leave on time to be punctual, at least by Bahamian standards, for his next appointment.

Pastor and the others continued to work, carrying the smaller pieces of steel, boxes of huge nuts and bolts, and bundles of corrugated steel that would support the pouring of the concrete floors, but Jeremy was out of action. He tried to go on, but walking back and forth proved too much for his ankle as the swelling increased and the pain became severe. He sat down and waited until it was time to fetch the boys and bring them home.

Even pressing the accelerator, and more so the brake, was excruciating and by the time he got home he was convinced it was a sprain. I was torn between anger at his carelessness and sympathy for his plight. The last time he had sprained an ankle, twelve years earlier, it had taken the better part of six months to heal. I made him soak his foot in steaming hot Epsom salts for an hour before he lay down on the sofa.

By evening the ankle was twice its normal size and still swelling. Even with an Ace bandage it was all he could do to hobble about the apartment. I do not know whether he was more concerned about his inability to continue helping Pastor or the fact that boating and snorkeling were out of the question for several months.

When I said my prayers that night—without mentioning anything about it to Jeremy because, I suppose, my faith was not that great yet—I asked God to heal his ankle. When we woke up in the morning the ankle was enormous. Jeremy put his feet on the floor, bracing himself with one hand on the bedside table and the other against the wall, to see whether he could walk at all. He put a little weight on the injured ankle; then more; then all his weight. There was no pain. It looked terrible but felt perfectly normal.

I told him about my prayer and he shook his head in amazement. "I didn't even think of asking for a healing," he said. "Thank you, Sweetie; and thank *you*, Lord." Several months went by before the swelling completely disappeared The pain never returned.

I suggested to my husband that he take it easy for the day and not push his luck but he insisted on going to the church in case there was any more work to be done. There was, and after everything was piled in its appointed place, Jeremy said to Pastor, "What's the next step?" He regretted the question as soon as he asked it.

"We're going to put the balcony up," Pastor replied airily.

"Put it up how?" Jeremy asked in fear and trepidation. "We need steel riggers, people who can walk beams in mid-air. And not only that, but who the heck knows how all this goes together?"

"Oh, that's no problem," Pastor replied, waving confidently at the piles of steel. "There are all sorts of men in the church who'll help, and we have the drawings to work from. Come inside and I'll show you."

They went to the office, where Pastor rummaged about and produced several huge rolls of drawings and blueprints. Finding the page he was looking for, he pointed here and there on it. "See . . . each piece of steel is numbered. All we have to do is put the right thing in the right place and it will all fit together like a jigsaw puzzle. We'll have it up in no time."

Although Jeremy's common sense dictated that there had to be something missing in Pastor's simplistic view of what was obviously a gargantuan task, the man's enduring faith and enthusiasm were beginning to infect him. It finally dawned on my husband that Pastor went about everything with an equal disregard for the exigencies of reality and, notwithstanding the seeming impossibility of the tasks he so blithely undertook, he always managed somehow to get them accomplished. It was not many days before Jeremy was once again dragooned into service.

A steel spike had been left firmly implanted in the ground to mark the apex from which all measurements should be taken.

Pastor had determined that the first thing to do was dig six holes and fill them with concrete as footings for the six steel columns that would support the front of the balcony. By the time Jeremy arrived the holes had been dug by hand and a small concrete mixer was doing its *gloppada-gloppada* number off to one side. Pastor had hustled someone somewhere into lending it to him free of charge. "We're going to set the anchor bolts in the wet concrete but make the pads nice and big in case we don't have the measurements quite right." Jeremy agreed with Pastor that that was a wise decision and took it upon himself to set up the transit.

The columns were heavy but, once the concrete was poured and had hardened sufficiently, there were enough volunteers on hand to get them upright and in position. Pastor stared at the accomplishment with satisfaction. "I guess we'll need Mario again to get the beams into place," he said musingly. "We'll have to pray some money in before I call him. His partner's the local rabbi. I don't think the promise of a blessing's going to work again."

Thus it was that Jeremy had time on his hands and we decided to start writing our second book. We worked together for a few weeks and had the book well under way before Pastor announced that the church had accumulated sufficient funds to begin construction once more. Mario and the rabbi had given him a very good deal on the crane and a welding crew—which he had not realized he needed until Mario mentioned it—and the man who had drawn the specs for the company that had fabricated the steel was coming to the island for a few days to act as consultant on how to put all the pieces together. Pastor was in great fettle and raring to go.

The shape-up on the first day was impressive, though not particularly productive. There were Mario and his crane, the welding generator and its attendant crew, all sorts of volunteers from the church, Pastor bustling about and bursting with excitement, and Vernon, the consultant from the steel company. Even the rabbi, who to Jeremy's utter astonishment actually was a rabbi, stopped by from time to time to make sure that his partner had not been killed through the bumbling of all the amateurs.

That there was no progress the first day—or the next one—

was the fault of no one present. The cause, when ultimately isolated by Vernon, was unattributable. The simple fact was that when the first beam was lifted by the crane—with Jeremy positioned as the resident expert on passing hand signals to Mario—and then swung across the wall and lowered into its position between the west side wall and the first steel column, it did not fit. It projected beyond the column and could not be bolted fast.

Vernon pored over the diagrams, checked and rechecked all the measurements, and came up empty. The walls were at the proper angle to each other; they were the right height; the distances from the center point along the wall and from the center point to the column were correct; the distances between columns were correct; the column was plumb and its elevation was correct; the beam was the right length according to the drawings that Vernon himself had prepared for the steel company. It was impossible that the beam should not fit, yet it didn't.

Mario studied the drawings and the layout. Vernon measured other beams to see if somehow they had been numbered wrongly. Pastor grew increasingly anxious as the minute hand inexorably wound its way round and round the face of his watch. The crane and the welding crew were being paid by the hour, working or not. It was Mario who suggested that the welders could go to another job until the riddle had been solved. He also voluntarily stopped the clock as far as the crane was concerned.

After hours of fruitless endeavor, and with the pressure off, it was decided that Vernon, the only person present deemed to stand the remotest chance of finding the solution to the problem, be left in peace to do just that. As Jeremy was leaving he heard Vernon asking Pastor whether there were any more drawings lying around.

The following evening Pastor called Jeremy. "You're not going to believe it but Vernon stayed up almost all night and he's only just figured out what happened." The explanation was almost as paradoxical as the question.

Over the two years that had passed since work was first begun there had been two architects and an engineer who had prepared different versions of the drawings. Pastor and the

Canadian engineer had been working from a set of drawings which required a center point on true center—precisely where the steel spike was placed and from which all the current measurements were being taken—while Vernon and the steel company had somehow been provided with a different set in which, for reasons unfathomable by anyone, a different center point, thirty-three inches off to one side, had been used. Vernon had finally solved the mystery when it occurred to him to work backwards from his own drawings rather than forwards from anyone else's.

With a new spike driven into the ground thirty-three inches west of true center, Vernon had taken test measurements and satisfied himself that everything would now fit together.

"There's only one problem," Pastor added. "All the columns have to be moved. We have to drill holes into the concrete and sink new anchors."

It took almost all of the next day to accomplish the replacement of the columns. The concrete was extremely hard and difficult to drill. In addition, it had not been leveled properly. Some pads had to be chiseled down to get the right elevations, while steel shims had to be placed on others to raise the columns. Eventually, though, Vernon was satisfied. Pastor repaired to his office to phone Mario, hoping that he and his welders could come the next day. The elation was back in his voice when he returned and said that all was well.

The next morning Jeremy situated himself in the opening for a doorway where he was clearly visible to Mario in the cab of the crane, and from whence he had a clear view of the interior work area. The first steel girder was once again raised and maneuvered into position. It fit. The welders secured the end resting on the wall to its plate while the end resting on the column was bolted fast.

"If the next one fits too, we're in business," Vernon said as he and a helper went outside to pick out the beam to go next in line in the front row.

The next girder was hoisted, swung across the wall, lowered and found to fit. A great cheer went up and Pastor said a prayer of thanks.

That first day went swimmingly. The beams took longer to secure than had been expected, but no one, including Vernon, had done anything like this before. Except for a few grazed knuckles, no one was hurt and by the end of the day everyone was in high good spirits, even believing, as Pastor did, that the whole thing was going to fit together like a jigsaw puzzle and take but a few days to accomplish.

On the second day the problems began. The biggest of all the beams were those that would be bolted to the steel erected the previous day and that would reach upwards, via six stepped tiers, to the curved end wall. The first of these monsters now had to be put into place. It was quickly learned that it was all but impossible to move it more than a hair's breadth in any direction once its full weight was lowered. Thus, it had to be raised at the precise angle at which it would ultimately rest. It took many tries before the right positions were located for the hoisting cables.

Hours were spent on the one beam and Vernon, who had been a draftsman working in an office all his life, assumed the role of foreman. Everyone was happy to let him be the boss but, although he at least knew one piece of steel from another, he had no more on-site experience than anyone else. Mario tried running back and forth between the crane and the work area with good advice, but he could not be in two places at once and finally gave up. The amateurs would have to learn the hard way.

And so it went. Each piece of steel seemed to have a mind of its own. A few pieces fell right into place, but the majority required pushing, pulling, bashing with sledgehammers and much blood, sweat and tears. Vernon became manic in his determination to see the job finished before he returned to the States. He got permission to stay for a second week.

He was a changed man. He had arrived a quiet, sensible and competent draftsman. As the days passed he took more and more upon himself as he despaired of the insufficiency of tools and the lack of comprehension when he shouted orders at people. He was up and down the ladders, walking on the beams, bullying the welders to work faster, running hither and thither, fastening nuts and bolts himself because he thought he could do it quicker than anyone else, bashing his head on things, killing his knuckles, and getting more and more ill-tempered. He was a blur of motion, and even accomplishment, but the volunteers began to evaporate from the job.

As Vernon became more and more obsessive some, including Jeremy, contemplated strangling him. Mario pointed out that this would not be necessary since Vernon, jumping about in midair like a jack-in-the-box, was about to kill himself. Pastor, fully aware of the mounting tension, found people to fill in for him in his other work and never left the job site. Geoffrey, who would in any event rather talk than work, took to doing the rounds preaching on tribulation and patience. The whole scene would have been hilariously entertaining had it not been for the very real presence of danger. Everyone lacked expertise, no one had a hard hat, and Vernon seemed to have developed a death wish.

As the second week neared its close, those who had stayed the course from the beginning achieved a fair level of competence, not only in rigging steel but also in coexisting with Vernon. The only things that had kept the work progressing—if not in peace and harmony, at least in nonobstructive cooperation—had been everyone's awareness of Vernon's virtual indispensability, coupled with Geoffrey's constant reminders regarding Christian attitude.

There was no great celebration when the last steel girder was in place, just a sigh of relief. There was still much work to be done, but by the welders, who would need another week or so to complete their part of the task. The volunteers, and Vernon too, were free to return to their normal duties.

It fell to Jeremy to give Vernon a ride to the airport. He frankly admitted that he dreaded doing it but was, after the fact, glad that the task had been his. Vernon had reverted to his normal self. Except for the sticking plaster covering the wounds on his head, one could never have discerned the wars of the past two weeks. As Jeremy shook hands with "the consultant from the steel company" without whose dedicated frenzy—though it bordered at times on Hitlerism—the balcony could not have been erected, Geoffrey's preachments on Christian attitude returned clearly to his mind. Compassion for Vernon's overwrought state, self-generated though it may have been, would have served far better than had giving in to anger. My husband resolved to remember the lesson.

CHAPTER

JEREMY AND I CONTINUED TO WRITE—WE HAD NOW SETTLED ON a title for our second book—and the block walls of the sanctuary continued their relentless climb upwards. Pastor phoned from time to time to talk about progress and Jeremy occasionally stopped at the church, after dropping the boys at school, to see for himself how things were going. It was on one such morning that he found disaster awaiting him.

Pastor had learned much about construction over the years, but there was also much that he did not know. Being his own contractor meant that he was constantly at the mercy of the workmen themselves; if the workmen erred, everyone was in trouble. Added to this was the fact that Pastor had many other duties and obligations. He got very little sleep, four or five hours a night was the most he could hope for and he frequently got far less than that.

His phone was never off the hook and his door was never closed to anyone. Drug addicts woke him in the small hours begging for help; people with marital problems turned to him as their first course of action; kids with drunken parents were constantly on his doorstep; every conceivable human problem was brought to him daily; even the biggest drug dealer on the island—not a member of Calvary Temple, I hasten to add—had Pastor called to the hospital to pray for him after he had been gravely wounded in a machine-gun battle. Pastor gave of himself until he dropped—he never said no.

The occasion of the disaster was simple: the block layer, finding that he had time for a few more courses of block on the area of wall where he was working before quitting time the previous day, but not enough time to pour supporting columns, had gone ahead with the block. He had far exceeded the number of courses that may prudently be erected without support in the belief that nothing could go amiss during one short night.

Pastor, as contractor, had not been present to proffer an opinion and the deed had been done. That night a squall line came through; not a hurricane, just an unpredicted squall line. The winds had been very fierce, albeit briefly, and the wall had gone down. It was not the loss of the blockwork that was the disaster—it was that most of the falling block had landed on the roof of the lower, circular area containing the offices and other rooms. An entire section of roof and rafters had been wiped out.

Several men from the church were talking in hushed tones. The block layer was in a state of shock and full of self-recrimination. Pastor was in tears. Jeremy spoke to a member of the church board who was standing nearby and then went to survey the damage. He knew almost as little about block laying as he had about steelwork, but he did understand carpentry and was good at it.

The damage, he found, looked more devastating than it actually was. There was considerable material to be replaced, to be sure, but the repairs would be more a question of know-how than of dollars and cents. He made up a mental lumber list, returned to the parking lot, and said to Pastor, "If you'll get me eighteen twelve-foot two-by-tens to replace the broken rafters, and let me help myself to the stockpiles of plywood and two-by-fours, I'll have it repaired in a few days."

Pastor brightened in an instant. "I'll get some men to help you."

"No," my husband said. "Thanks for the offer but it will take as much thinking as working. I'd rather do it alone. Just find me a ten- or twenty-ton house jack and I'll be fine." Pastor went to the phone, as usual, and Jeremy came home to get some tools and change into work clothes.

When I heard the story I bled for Pastor but was also a bit miffed with Jeremy for volunteering so quickly when we were in the middle of our own work. Jeremy explained why he had done it. "It just seemed to be one of those times when somebody had to do something other than rend his garments in anguish and stand around and talk. Pastor was so down in the dumps, I figured that someone both making light of it and undertaking to fix it would buck him up."

My husband was right, of course, and even though it took him almost a full week to finish all the repairs, Pastor's despair was much mitigated by his immediate undertaking of the task. Jeremy was convinced that—as we often tend to overlook—it is the spirit of the act, rather than the act itself, that is the most important.

It was only a few weeks before my husband had to desert the typewriter again.

The roof was arriving the next day and, once again, it was up to the men of the church to unload the trailers. Jeremy was most relieved to hear that Pastor had laid on Mario and his crane to do the lifting since the center beam alone weighed fifty-four hundred pounds.

When my husband reported for work the next morning it was to be greeted by a sight even more imposing than the trailer loads of steel had been. Not only were there close to seven thousand square feet of pine roof decking to be dealt with, but the beams were overwhelming: great forty-eight-by-eight-inch laminated rafters, the one for the center—the fifty-four-hundred-pounder—being ninety feet long.

Two-by-fours were laid out on the ground to rest everything on as it came off the trailers and the unloading process began. With everyone having achieved a degree of professionalism since the unloading of the steel, the job was finished by midafternoon. Pastor, Jeremy and the other helpers stood back to survey the mountains of wood now occupying a significant portion of the parking lot.

"What do we do now?" my husband asked, fearful of the answer.

"Put it up," Pastor replied confidently. "it shouldn't take long."

Jeremy shook his head and sighed . . . but he did not dispute Pastor's contention. He had come to accept that, somehow, God would provide a means for Pastor to go on doing the impossible.

It was not long before Pastor told us that a team of a dozen men was coming from Illinois to help with the erection of the roof; one of them had even been a carpenter at one time in his life. Several of them were pastors who had helped build their own churches. "It'll go up in no time!" Pastor crowed.

And so it did. The men arrived and, together with my husband and many other volunteers from our church, worked twelve- and fourteen-hour days until the job was finished. Kay, myself and a couple of other wives reported to the church every morning to cook a big lunch for the construction crew.

The only tense moment occurred when Pastor discovered that there were no cranes for rent on the island big enough to lift sky-high the big beams. He quickly solved that problem, though, by cajoling the Bahamas Oil Refining Company into lending him—free of charge, of course—their eighty-foot crane and an operator.

It was a fantastic sight at the church every day and one I shall never forget. All those men working and not one, save the crane operator, in the construction business. The seven-thousand-square-foot roof, supported by those huge laminated beams, was up and finished in eight days, every surface and every cut end having been treated with preservative before being set in place. It was much more than a case of "Where there's a will there's a way." It was a clear example of God at work through His children.

CHAPTER

5

LATE IN FEBRUARY I WAS STILL ENGAGED IN THE SELECTION OF the photographs to be included in *My Mother's Keeper* and obtaining clearances for their use. The book, however, had long since been listed in Morrow's catalogue of upcoming publications and the calls and letters to the publisher from magazines, newspapers and television stations—all requesting interviews—were pouring in.

Morrow's publicity department called one day to ask whether I might be willing to make an exception to my previously stated rule that I would do a publicity tour but no random interviews. I had insisted that my family would have nothing to do with any of the press. I was informed that *People* magazine wanted to send a crew to the Bahamas to do a cover story and that it would be a shame to pass up such an advantageous way of launching the publicity campaign. The timing would be such that the *People* interview, if I agreed to it, would appear in the issue immediately preceding our publication date.

I discussed the matter with Jeremy and we decided that since I had to start somewhere, it might as well be *People* as anywhere else. At least by doing this one interview ahead of the tour, I would get a little practice. We did set a few conditions, foremost among them being that the interview—which would take at least two days—be conducted anywhere except in my home. It was scheduled for a few weeks later.

The publicity aspect of publishing my book had always been the part I most dreaded. It was not the thought of appearing on television, or talking to newspapers, that bothered me; it was the simple fact of appearing publicly to discuss my personal life. Writing a book was one thing; but talking about it, being challenged as to its integrity, and responding without becoming hostile in the face of the inevitable hostility, were not things to which I looked forward with anything but dread. I had always known I would have to do it but it had seemed so far off. Now, it was upon me.

I am afraid that I bored many friends—not to mention my family—by constantly raising the subject of my forthcoming ordeal, but some good did come of all that talk. Pastor Wayne Pitts—Ernie's "dad"—came to visit Ernie for a few days. We were invited for dinner at the DeLoaches' and, as usual, I started to talk about the upcoming *People* interview and the publicity tour that would follow hard upon its heels. Pastor Pitts, a warm and wonderful man, talked with me for much of the evening and drew out of me my testimony—the story of how my family and I came to accept Jesus.

We prayed together and he asked God to cloak me in His armor and to let Jesus' light shine through me, no matter the hostility of those with whom I might be confronted. As we were leaving, Pastor Pitts asked whether I could stop by Louisville, Kentucky, during the tour, since he would like me to give my testimony at Evangel Tabernacle. He ended with, "I feel God has something special for you in Louisville."

I felt very dubious about the request—both personally and from the standpoint of asking Morrow to add to an already overcrowded tour—but agreed to discuss it with the appropriate people and get back to him at a later date. When Pastor DeLoach, a few days later, told me that Evangel Tabernacle accommodated four thousand people it did nothing to bolster my confidence. I was perfectly happy writing my testimony in our second book; I was perfectly happy telling it to friends, and even strangers, who might be interested; but telling it from a pulpit to four thousand people was another thing altogether. I had been interviewed many times during my life, both by reporters and on television, but had never before been asked to stand up and deliver a speech to a live audience.

At first both Jeremy and I were against the idea of my being sidetracked to Kentucky when I was already facing a sufficiently grueling schedule. Slowly, though, and with increasing intensity, Jeremy began to get the feeling that his initial reaction had been wrong and that I ought to go. He could offer no tangible reasoning and I was reluctant to listen; but then I, too, began to feel the same urging.

When I finally called Morrow to discuss the matter I was half hoping that they would object. It turned out that they were more than happy to route me through Louisville on my return trip to the Bahamas at the end of the tour. Thus it was arranged and Pastor Pitts, sounding positively elated at the news, said, but more strongly this time, "I know God has something special for you in Louisville."

The group that arrived from *People* magazine consisted of the interviewer—a very pregnant Andrea Chambers, who had to get back to New York quickly in order to comply with an injunction imposed by her doctor against further travel—her husband, who had come along for the ride, and a photographer. By the time it was all finished, we had spent a day and a half talking and another day and a half taking pictures.

Mrs. Chambers was a very pleasant person by whom to be interviewed and, from the way she spoke and the way she described the thrust of the article she intended to write, I permitted myself the luxury of looking forward to an even-handed, unprejudiced—perhaps even accurate—story in *People* magazine.

A pleasant surprise came on April 2 in the form of an Easter lily from my mother. It was accompanied by a card which said, "I can't get over the habit of sending an Easter lily to each one of my children each year. Mother." It was not exactly a warm greeting but it was welcome because it indicated that, at least thus far, my mother had not been able to put my existence out of mind. I said a prayer of thanks and asked God to put a burden on her heart that she keep on seeking the answer to why I was doing what I was doing.

The next call from Morrow's publicity department was to gain my consent to their giving Mike Wallace my phone number so that he could ring me for a telephone interview. It was a good thing that I was unaware that Mr. Wallace had already chosen a title for his "exposé" on *60 Minutes*—"How Sharper than a Serpent's Tooth It Is to Have a Thankless Child"—and was only interested in finding some facts, if available, that would support his preconceived notion. Had I known this I would undoubtedly have refused to talk to him and might, thereby, have deprived myself and, perhaps, others—certainly everyone at Morrow—of a good laugh at Mr. Wallace's expense.

He called but a few minutes later and we talked for about ten minutes. The thrust of his questioning was how, since I had said nothing unkind about my mother when he had interviewed me a few years earlier in connection with a segment he was doing on Bette Davis, I could now be saying unkind things. Mr. Wallace's contention was that I was now contradicting myself and that my reasons could be nothing but nefarious. He left no doubt in my mind that he was looking forward with relish to exposing my hypocrisy on the air.

I explained several times that at the time of the interview I had not yet come to the end of my tether with my mother; that I did not then lie, but simply answered his questions superficially and under the maxim "If you can't say anything nice, don't say anything at all"; and that he should take my book—of which he had been given an advance copy—and his interview and lay them side by side. I challenged him to show me a single contradiction. He patently was not thrilled with our phone conversation and asked few, if any, pertinent questions about the book itself.

Although the official publication date of *My Mother's Keeper* was still a few weeks away Morrow had begun shipping and, by the time the *People* article appeared late in April, books were showing up in stores. I cannot readily describe my emotions when I first saw the "Bette Dearest" headline on the cover of the magazine. They were somewhere between fury, indignation, horror, and just plain disappointment; probably a combination of all of the above. It took a few days, and my husband's reminder of the facts of life, before I was able to accept the situation with the equanimity it deserved.

First of all, Jeremy pointed out, it made no difference what Andrea Chambers had led me to believe—design of the cover was almost certainly the province of another department of the magazine. Second, and perhaps the only truly operative consideration of the exercise, came a simple fact: the relationship between, in my case, an author and the press is symbiotic. The author and his publisher need the press for the publicizing of their wares—the press needs the author as subject matter for the purpose of selling *its* wares. We had been naive, Jeremy contended, to believe that a cover story would carry anything less than the most scandalous, or at least sensational, headline available for that purpose.

The article itself proved to be accurate—give or take a few minor inconsistencies—and, on the whole, I felt that Mrs. Chambers had been faithful. Since it is again my turn at the typewriter, however, I feel constrained to say something about my ex-stepfather, Gary Merrill, who was also interviewed by *People*. Gary, reportedly, claimed that he never started a fight in our household when I was a child, and that my representation of his dialogue was a figment of my imagination. Then— thanks to *People*'s integrity—he is quoted as sounding exactly as I had done my best to portray him in my book.

His reference to my actual father, William Sherry, was so vulgar that I cannot quote it, but my favorite quote of Gary by *People* was, "Bette and I were both big drinkers, and sure I slapped her and B.D. We had physical fights, but not much more than the average family."

Well now . . . that about says it all, doesn't it? I was three years old when Gary married my mother and twelve when Mother divorced him. He victimized and terrorized the child— now, I could feel in my bones, he was going to attempt the same thing with the woman. Forgive me, Lord, but the disgust and loathing I felt for him then I still feel now.

My last comment with respect to the *People* article relates to the results of it. It was reported in the next issue of the magazine, with enormous relish, that the write-in response had been the heaviest in the history of the publication, and had been some thirty or so to one against me. This disturbed me at first—for I had always expected about a fifty-fifty division of opinion—but then I realized that hardly any, if any at all, of those writing in could have read the book. Their reactions were strictly to the magazine article.

Once the book was fully in circulation, and letters to me began to pour in via the publisher, I was gratified to find that my fifty-fifty expectation had been pessimistic. My mail turned out to be three to one in favor of what I had done. Interestingly, a great deal of the positive mail was from people who had suffered, or were still suffering, experiences similar to mine and who were happy to find they were not alone. Some were extremely touching and the circumstances of the writers were worse than anything I had ever endured.

One such letter was from a woman whose mother had managed to destroy three marriages for her. Finally the woman banned her mother from her house and refused to ever speak to her again. She thereupon remarried her first husband—who had always been the right choice—and they had been happy ever since. This sounds very simplistic without the surrounding details, which occupied many, many pages, and one can easily question the woman's judgment in getting married so many times, but—and this is the point of relating this story— only those of us who have been subjected to certain kinds of selfishly domineering parents, particularly mothers, can comprehend the emotional havoc those parents can wreak in their children.

Just as interestingly, a large percentage of the negative mail went something like, "I haven't read your book and don't intend to, but wanted to tell you you stink." Those, together with the ones that implied that my weight problem excluded my personal rights, were much easier to put out of mind than the ones from people who were genuinely, and coherently, upset over what I had done.

There was one writer, a lady in Georgia, who, it seemed, reread the book every time she wrote to me. By the time of her third letter she had come to accept, albeit reluctantly, my position as being justified. It would be nice if everyone did that but, as my husband pointed out to me, not even Jesus managed to convince *all* the people.

I have mentioned that I thought my book might be a comfort to people who shared my problems, if only to assure them that they were not alone, but Jeremy and I had gone much further than that in our private musings. We had often discussed the possibility that *My Mother's Keeper* might serve as an actual help to others. My husband had relished the thought: "Wouldn't it be wonderful if people were able to send a copy of your book to their pain-in-the-neck relatives with a note saying, 'Read this and let me know if you recognize anyone in it.' " We had, however, mostly kept such sentiments to ourselves for fear of sounding self-important.

There were many letters resembling it in content, but one in particular—perhaps because of its very simplicity—touched us deeply. It bore out that our hopes had been neither a vanity nor in vain.

> Dear Barbara (B.D.),
>
> Upon completing your book, I felt I had to write to you to express my feelings. Yes, I enjoyed your book, but secondly I realized a few things I was blind to—until I read it.
>
> I have similar problems, and my parents aren't famous—at least not nation wide. I've had problems with my children and them for twelve years. Now I realize I even had these problems before, but didn't realize it until I had my own to protect.
>
> I have been very happily married for fourteen years. Now I know I can handle things—if you can, anyone can. I don't have the press agents, lawyers on me. I know I can try and I'm going to do my best.
>
> Thank you for a truly enlightening story made of facts that, I'm sure, were hard to tell and admit.
>
> You did the right thing and I'm sure you're a happier and better person for it.
>
> I just hope I am.
>
> You would be welcome in my average home anytime. Just write and say when. I'd love to have you.
>
> God bless you for your courage.
>
> Thank you,
>
> (signature)

My family and I awaited the airing of the *60 Minutes* episode dealing with my book with great interest. It came on early in

May and we gathered around the television set. The title, "How Sharper than a Serpent's Tooth It Is to Have a Thankless Child," flashed on the screen. It was followed by Mike Wallace brandishing a copy of *My Mother's Keeper* and announcing that I had written an unkind book about my mother. Mr. Wallace was followed by a rerun of the several-year-old close-up they had done on Bette Davis.

And that was it. No more Mike Wallace; no mention of his having interviewed me on the phone; nothing.

We turned off the television and stared at each other in amazement. Jeremy burst into laughter. "He got caught with his serpent's tooth hanging out."

"What do you mean?" I asked.

"He fell in love with a quote from *King Lear*, or whatever, and decided to make the facts fit the quote. Nothing you said on the phone was any use to him; your mother probably refused to talk to him; nothing anyone else might say would have any import without a comment from at least one of the principals; so there he was, stuck with his serpent's tooth and nothing to sharpen it on."

"I wonder why they aired it at all," I mused.

"Five'll get you ten," Jeremy said, "they were jumping at what looked like a sure ratings attraction and had it advertised before Wallace found he had no show. Whatever the case, I think it's great. Wallace did nothing but give you a free plug and make an ass of himself. Three cheers for investigative reporters!"

Morrow's publicity department was thrilled with the free plug. They were reluctant to comment on my husband's analysis of what had taken place, one way or the other, but I gained the distinct impression they thought he might be right.

My greatest surprise came in the form of a letter from my father, William Grant Sherry, which also arrived early in May. We had exchanged the odd Christmas card over the years and knew the barest details of each other's lives—I knew that he had two children, lived in San Francisco, and was a successful artist—but that was the limit of our relationship. Before I quote my father's letter, I think it best that I quote my own words from my book, for those words reflect what I was brought up by my mother to believe:

During that same year [author's note: 1949 when I was two], Mother's marriage to Sherry came unglued. Sherry, who was fortyish, had fallen in love with my nineteen-year-old nurse, Marion. They ran away together and tried to take me with them but were foiled in the attempt by Dell, the cook, who refused to let me leave since she ". . . didn't have any such instructions from Miss Bette." By such slender threads hang our destinies. Dell phoned Mother at the studio but, by the time she got home, my father and Marion had fled. I was to see them again, still happily married with two children, fourteen years later when we had lunch together in New York. Mother was particularly distressed for, separate and apart from having her third marriage come to an abrupt and inglorious end, she was then involved in making *All About Eve*, the story of a forty-year-old stage actress whose career and husband are usurped by a woman half her age. Mother never again permitted Sherry's name to be mentioned in her presence.

During the making of *All About Eve*, Mother met Gary Merrill and their film relationship spilled over into their personal lives. They were married on the heels of Mother's divorce from Sherry, with Mother paying alimony in exchange for sole custody of me.

That was my mother's story, told many times over the years and embellished in various ways according to whom she was telling it to. As far as I was concerned, my father had deserted me as a baby.

Now to my father's letter. (I have omitted, as irrelevant, a paragraph detailing his impending trip to Europe for a few weeks with Marion.)

Dear, dear B.D.

I'm typing this because I have a lot to write. First I have read most of your book and feel I now know you. Secondly I feel you can understand me a little. I feel that you haven't believed all the things your mother has said about me. I've heard some of the things from other people and felt that time would tell.

Marion and I did not run away nor did we try to take you. I didn't fall in love with Marion until after the divorce. Bette saw Gary in a war film [author's note: the film was *Twelve O'Clock High*] and he was what she wanted. She was bored with me because I didn't let her run me into the ground, although she tried hard. She once told me that she had always been able to put men under her thumb but couldn't me. I asked her why she didn't stop trying so we could have a pleasant life which we did have until after you were born. Then she changed, told me I should get myself a French babe to make love to. I was sentimental, she was hard. Bette was living with Gary in Malibu before the divorce. Marion was still with you. It was on a visit when Marion brought you to Laguna Beach that I asked her if she would consider marrying me after the divorce. Her answer was no, but I persisted. She said she finally consented because I was so loving with you . . . also she felt sorry for me because of the way Bette treated me. So we were married and that was 35 years ago. Bette was so furious I don't think she would have married Gary if I hadn't married such a lovely girl. It made her look foolish because she was throwing me away. I was supposed to go down the tube.

I stopped insisting on my visitation rights with you because it was too upsetting to you. You would cry and cry when it came time for me to take you back. Bette said every time you visited me you broke out in hives when you got home. I figured I was doing you more harm than good and I was being selfish. If I really loved you I should give you up. It was a big hurt and I felt you would feel I had abandoned you. I have always loved you and always felt sad because you didn't know me.

There aren't enough glowing words to express my heart-felt feelings for you and Jeremy after reading what you both have gone thru with Bette. I admire your loyalty as a daughter and Jeremy for his love and understanding. I wish we all could be together for a time. I know we would hit it off.

Marion and I send our deepest love,

Dad.

I'm so proud of you!

So there, after all these years, was the other side of the story. A wise man once said, "There are three sides to every story: yours, mine, and the truth." I am not prepared to say that I accept at face value every detail of my father's side of things. Too much time has passed and time, unless we are extraordinarily careful in our objectivity, tends to bend our recollections to suit our own self-image. I do believe, though, and without a doubt, that my father is telling the truth regarding who abandoned whom. It too clearly reflects my mother's style to be anything but true.

I believe, therefore, that my mother—for nothing but egotistic reasons—forced me to live with the lie that my real father deserted me as a baby. It has been no great tragedy, as things have turned out, but there were times long ago when it would have been nice to have had a daddy to turn to.

Another letter arrived at about that same time, this one from Vik Greenfield. Vik had been Mother's man-Friday for many years during the 1960s and featured quite prominently in *My Mother's Keeper.* I am including the text of his letter for, I admit, entirely selfish reasons. So many people, none of them with firsthand knowledge of anything, saw fit to challenge my veracity that I cannot resist the temptation to include the testimony of a person who was there—right in my mother's house—during many of the events related in my book. Vik's letter was addressed to both Jeremy and me.

Dear Both—

BRAVO-BRAVA-BRAVISSIMO-!!!

I'm very impressed. But what's left for me to tell? Your book is funny—that is to me. It's very straightforward and honest—what memories you have. In fact I think you've been reasonably kind to your mother.

I read the *People* article. You all look so relaxed and healthy and I'm sure happy for the most part. Your boys are really growing up fast. As for Gary's remarks—typical—drunks don't remember anything except where the bottle is! And the so called friends . . . when did they ever see you all as a family? As usual, all playing parts.

Harold rang—had I read the book? Between us, he'd like to know my opinion. Of course I'm not fooled. If indeed they are foolish enough to sue they would only enhance the curiosity value of your book. I'm planning on keeping Harold waiting for an answer and when he next calls—if ever—I'm going to tell him plainly. It's very, very truthful. The part of the chicken carve and clutch had me in tears (naturally with laughter.) Oh God all those massacred dinners!

It is written honor thy father and mother—but they never mention—only if they are honorable. Why do we spend most of our lives shielding the truth of our parents and the truth from them? You have opened a can of worms. But in your case I'm afraid it's too late for your mother to see a true reflection of herself.

Thank you for being so kind to me in your book— when all I was was a dummy. But dull it wasn't.

Good luck with your guest talk spots. Oh—your mother is wrong—talent does not skip a generation—one learns by example.

Best to the boys,

Love, as ever,

Vik.

The next development was reported to me in a phone call from Morrow: Gary Merrill was picketing a bookstore in Portland, Maine. He was walking up and down outside the store carrying a placard, "Please Boycott *My Mother's Keeper*." Shortly thereafter he began to place advertisements in *The New York Times* saying:

No Mother Deserves This

ANYTHING FOR A BUCK . . . Greed was B.D. Hyman's guide when she wrote "My Mother's Keeper", the scurrilous new book about B.D.'s mother, Bette Davis. And anything for a buck is what William Morrow & Co. must have said when they published it.

SUPPORT YOUR LOCAL LIBRARY . . . Don't fork over almost 20 bucks for thi8 book. Visit your library, oj buy one copy and pass it along.

AND SUPPORT BETTE . . . Write her* and wish her well. Tell her you are boycotting the book. You'll both feel better. A message from Gary Merrill, Bette's friend and former husband.

Thornhurst Road
Falmouth Foreside, ME 04105

*Write Bette Davis, c/o Harold Schiff, 455 East 57th. St., N.Y., N.Y. 10022

The typographical errors are exactly as printed in *The New York Times*. Only the *Times* could tell us why they let the ads go to press uncorrected. Even Harold Schiff's address is misprinted.

It was just too marvelous for words—Gary, of all people, as the white knight rushing to Mother's defense. Another publisher, who later bought the paperback rights to my book, called Morrow and said, "Tell the truth—how much did you have to pay Merrill to do this?" Every time his ad ran, sales in New York bookstores shot straight upwards. Between Gary's ads, boycott pictures, and other interviews and pictures—some of which even caught the garlic he wears around his neck to ward off vampires—he probably did as much to launch my book as Morrow and I. To pay the devil his due, though, Gary did persist and did come close to unnerving me while I was on the tour.

On May 10, the day before I was due to set foot into the hornet's nest, I received one more phone call from Morrow. "Listen, B.D., I didn't want you to run into this without fair warning. We've just heard that there's a letter circulating all over New York written by your mother's lawyer, Harold Schiff. Apparently it's addressed to Larry Hughes, the president of Morrow, but Mr. Hughes hasn't even received a copy, let alone the original. I should be able to get hold of it fairly soon, I think, since it seems to have been sent to every network, TV station, magazine and newspaper in town."

"Have you any idea what it says?" I asked.

"Well, don't hold me to this—as I said, none of us has seen it yet—but from what I'm told, Schiff is trying to convince the world that you're a congenital liar and that your book is nothing more than a pack of lies. Evidently he's threatening to sue—or implying that he might sue, or whatever—you, us, or anybody who has anything to do with us."

"Is Morrow worried about it?" I asked with some alarm.

"Good heavens, no! I only called to find out if it was going to worry *you*. And to make sure you didn't get hit with it cold-turkey."

I was relieved to hear that Morrow was unconcerned, but took a moment to contemplate other ramifications. Since some such action on Harold's part had not been entirely unexpected, I was pleased to find myself relatively unruffled. "Well," I said, "it certainly doesn't upset *me*. The truth is the truth and Harold will learn to live with it. Quite honestly, it sounds to me as though he's just doing a bit of saber rattling to appease my mother."

"Okay. We'll leave it at that, then. So long as they can't send you screaming from the room—and it doesn't sound like there's much chance of it—we've nothing to worry about. I'll do my best to have a copy of the letter by the time you get here tomorrow."

When I saw the letter a few days later, I found that my assessment had been pretty accurate—saber rattling. There were carefully contrived insinuations and carefully veiled threats. It was pure poppycock. Nonetheless, it stirred up quite a fuss and, coupled with Gary Merrill's antics, pretty well ensured that *My Mother's Keeper* could escape the attention of no one.

I would be confronted with Harold's letter quite often during my first few days of exposure to the media, but they quickly tired of trying to evoke an hysterical reaction from a nonhysteric. Larry Hughes—who was not to receive the original letter until a week or so after copies had been circulated all over the city—responded to the press, when questioned, "I have not received any letter from Mr. Schiff, and anyway, I do not comment on press releases."

As I finished the last bits and pieces of my packing, and got ready for my departure the next day, I reflected upon the situation to date. I had done what I had done in order that my mother could not pretend that I had not spoken. I had discovered an extension of my second alternative.

The first alternative—that I continue to permit my mother to run roughshod over me and my family—had become intolerable.

The second alternative—that I fight tooth-and-nail with her, shouting, screaming, pulling hair and throwing things, as Mother had done with her mother and her sister, Bobby—had never been acceptable and had not even accomplished anything on the one or two occasions I had been driven to it. Mother loved it . . . . I felt sick.

The third alternative—to lock my door and refuse ever to speak to her again—was something I frequently would have liked to do, but could not. She was my mother and she loved me. She was my mother and, come what may, I loved the person who had suckled me, raised me, spoiled me, and loved me.

The decision to fight with her, but publicly, seemed logical. Mother was at her best in public. All actors thrive on publicity; "bad press is better than no press at all" is an ages-old axiom of the profession. She loved her image as the tough, indomitable woman whom no one could pin for a three-count. No matter what I said, my mother could, and would, not only survive it, but increase her popularity because of it. The fans would flock to her support.

But—and a mighty great but it was—the furor, provided it lasted long enough, would force her to read what I had written. She might throw away the first dozen or so copies of the book which came her way, but, if the pressure were sufficient, she would finally hear me out.

So, all things considered, we were off to a good start. The

scandal sheets were in full cry; reviewers were reviewing, according to their lights; Gary was doing his bit; Harold was adding grist to the mill; magazines were doing articles; gossip columns, even in respectable newspapers, were getting their two cents in; the crowd could be said to be in a frenzy.

There was only one problem: the lions were loose in the arena, and now the Christian had to make her entrance. Before going to bed that night Jeremy and I prayed together. We repeated Pastor Pitts's prayer that God would cloak me in His armor and let Jesus' light shine through me. I also asked for the physical strength not to wilt along the line. More and more interviews had been scheduled as the weeks went by; my schedule was now so tight that meals would frequently have to be eaten in the back of cars, or skipped altogether.

CHAPTER

THE PLANE WAS STILL SITTING ON THE RUNWAY IN FREEPORT. I
had not even left the island yet and I was miserable. I stared
through the window at the glass front of the terminal building. I could not see Jeremy and Justin, nor could they see me,
but I knew they were still there. I fought back another onslaught of tears.

It was so hard for me to be away from my family; three
weeks stretched out before me like a lifetime. We had always
been so close, hardly ever doing anything except together. In
twenty years of marriage we had only four times been apart
for more than a day at a time; and each time both Jeremy and
I had been ridiculously lonely. Knowing that I was going to
spend three weeks trying to hold my own with the press only
made it the more wrenching.

So I stared out the window towards the spot where I knew
my family stood, eyes blurred by the tears I refused to shed.
I tried to focus on what was ahead of me in order to escape
the feeling that I was falling off the edge of the world. Finally,
the plane began to move . . . to rise . . . to turn towards
Miami. The glass front of the terminal got smaller and smaller,

then passed from my sight. Then the island faded into the distance.

I thought of palm trees, turquoise water, and coral reefs. I tried to think of the business ahead of me again. I tried to push my loneliness aside; all I could see was the glass front of the terminal building. I was not even halfway to Miami yet, and I was homesick.

My arrival at Kennedy Airport was an hour late due to a holdup in Miami. I was met by Debra Sherline, who explained that her boss—Lela Rolantz, who was chief publicist at Morrow—would be escorting me on Monday but had a prior commitment tonight. Debra and I had talked on the phone many times and were almost friends before we met.

Once in the car and on the way into Manhattan she handed me a schedule for the tour. It covered nineteen pages. Debra said, "It ought to be accompanied by a drum roll; it's a killer." She grinned to soften the impact. "I hope you're still talking to us at the end of three weeks."

I scanned the list and found that it more or less bore out what Debra had warned me of in advance: large numbers of interviews crammed into each day; meals to be eaten on planes for lack of time between interviews; scheduling so tight that cars would have to be virtually waiting with engines running in order to get me on time from the last interview in one city to my plane to the next city. I was glad that I had insisted on a three-week maximum for the tour.

I checked to be sure that Phil Donahue had not been slipped in while I wasn't looking. He had called Morrow a couple of times and insisted that he would conduct a friendly interview, but I had refused to go on his show. It wasn't whether or not he was friendly that concerned me; it was that I would have to take him on too soon in the tour. I wouldn't have had time to learn the ropes and develop some expertise of my own. I had watched his show many times and was afraid that, between his speed of thought and his amphitheater forum—not to mention his audiences, who always seemed to be spoiling for a fight—I just plain wasn't competent to take him on without some experience in the trenches first.

Debra accompanied me to my suite at the Plaza Hotel and we went through the schedule, day by day and item by item. She handed me my bundle of airline tickets and I thanked her for her care and consideration.

"You'll need all you can get, kiddo," she said with a smile. "Just remember . . . if there's anything you want, even if it's only a warm body to talk to, call me any time." I thanked her again and said I was sure I would still be talking to her in three weeks' time.

When Debra left I went straight to the phone to call Jeremy. It was 10:30 at night and I had only been gone for seven hours, but it felt like a week. It was a great relief to hear his voice and I gave him a capsule version of my schedule. We agreed that the first day would undoubtedly be the worst; sort of like a parachute jumper: once out of the plane the worst was over, there being nothing left to do but flow with it. He confirmed that he would keep the boys home from school on Monday to watch me on the *Today* show—more as a topic to keep the conversation going than anything else—and then we both felt silly, behaving like a couple of adolescents with telephonitis, and said goodnight.

My phone calls to my husband turned out to be my lifeline. Just hearing his voice—and those of the children when I called early enough—buoyed my spirits at the end of each day and made me feel less remote and alone. Jeremy always waited up for my nightly call, frequently until one or two in the morning when I was in the western time zones, and it made my arrival at each new hotel a moment to look forward to. Hanging up was always painful.

On the following day, Sunday, Josie Hamm came in from Connecticut and Dave and Andi Keeler from Pennsylvania. It was lovely to spend the day with old friends and I felt completely relaxed for a while. Unfortunately, the minute they left the nerves returned and caused me to spend a restless night. I woke up and looked at the clock so many times that, when my 4:30 wake-up call finally came, it was a relief to be able to get up and start doing things.

With my toilette completed, and dressed in my most conservative outfit of gray silk, I ordered coffee and fruit and settled down to read Psalms for an hour. Psalms, I had found, were my greatest sedative in times of stress—the beauty of the writing, and the thoughts expressed, never failed to bring me peace—and I had deliberately arisen extra early in order to have time to immerse myself in the Word before setting forth into the world.

At seven o'clock I met Lela in the lobby and we headed for Rockefeller Plaza and NBC's *Today* show. It would have been nice to get even the tiniest bit of practice with live TV "out-of-town," but the networks went first or not at all and I had to live with it. As we ascended in the elevator, fish—they were too big and energetic to be butterflies—started flapping about in my stomach. The doors opened and we were greeted by a sign: WELCOME TO THE DONAHUE SHOW.

"Back! Back!" I cried, holding up my crossed index fingers as though to ward off Count Dracula in a low-budget movie.

"Freudian slip," Lela chuckled as we backed into the elevator again. One floor higher and we were in the right place, and I was ushered into the "green room." All waiting rooms for TV shows are called green rooms—even if they are painted purple—and each one has its own atmosphere. The *Today* show's green room was tense and whispery while *Hour Magazine*'s would be boisterous and partylike.

We were offered coffee and doughnuts. I was asked if I wanted makeup. I looked at Lela. She said that the makeup I had applied looked fine. I put on more lipstick and powder anyway. We watched the ongoing show on the monitor. We watched the hands of the big clock on the wall. We made small talk. Gloria Steinem walked in. She said nothing and looked directly at no one. A staff person entered and addressed her in hushed tones. She shook her head and continued to sit at the far end of the room, staring fixedly at the blank wall opposite her couch.

At 8:05 I was told to stand by. With a reassuring smile from Lela I patted my hair, took a deep breath and followed the staff person through the soundproof door to wait behind the cameras in the studio. Crew members smiled silently and pointed to where I should stand. Jane Pauley and Bryant Gumbel were talking about something on the far side of the stage with all the cameras pointing their way.

I stood there, willing my knees not to buckle and my mouth

not to dry out. The fish had stopped flapping . . . they were now doing spastic darts and belly rolls. Then, an extraordinary thing happened: a cloak of warm, loving peace enveloped me as the Holy Spirit ministered to me. I smiled and thanked Him . . . but silently, for it was live TV.

They cut to a commercial and I was signaled to take my seat. I sat down with absolute assurance; my hands had stopped shaking, my knees were steady, and I felt equal to Jane Pauley or anyone else. The Holy Spirit was with me.

A crew member was pinning the microphone to my blouse and skillfully hiding the wire in the chair when Jane Pauley undid her mike and came from where she had been sitting on the other set at the far side of the stage to take up her position opposite me. She patted my arm and said, "Hello. You must be awfully nervous." Over her shoulder Bryant Gumbel gave me a friendly wink. I smiled back at him and replied to Jane Pauley, who was looking down at her mike as she affixed it, "Hi. No, actually I'm not." Her eyes shot up and she stared at me. After a couple of seconds she said, "You're not, are you!" She almost seemed insulted.

The red light came on and the introduction that would become so familiar after a few days began: photos of Bette Davis in one movie or another, glowing tribute to her brilliant career, introduction of her daughter who has just written a book about their life together . . . a not very complimentary book at all.

The questions were not nearly as tough as I had expected and been prepared to fend off. In fact, they were rather basic: What possible good did I think could come out of this book— that it might eventually bring about understanding between my mother and me. Isn't it just another *Mommie Dearest* (the most frequently asked question of all)—no, I was never physically abused by my mother. And so forth. Not friendly, but not particularly hostile either. A bit of a letdown in fact. When the opportunity afforded itself I pointed out that there was much humor to be found in the book. Jane Pauley looked pained and said that she had trouble seeing anything humorous about it at all. I said that the only thing anyone ever mentioned to me, privately that is, was how funny this or that episode was; I said I was sorry she'd had so much trouble.

The interview lasted about ten minutes, I think. As I headed back to the green room I said a prayer of thanks.

Lela and I threaded our way through the now fully congested New York City streets to be barely in time for my nine o'clock appointment with *Newsday* back at the Plaza. The questions were an abbreviated version of those asked by *People* and I found myself more occupied in observing the antics of the photographer than in my answers to the questions.

I will never understand why professional photographers use so much film—roll after roll, hundreds of photos—when only one or two shots wind up being used each time. The lighting was constantly being adjusted; the photographer seemed as bent on proving he was a contortionist as in taking pictures. Perhaps they are hoping to catch one making a horrible face—they certainly used enough horrible pictures of *me*. The trick, I discovered, was to ignore the photographer; to resist the temptation to ask oneself, "Why is this weirdo sitting on the back of my couch, hanging over sideways?" or, "Why is he pointing the camera into my left ear from three inches away?"

Entertainment Tonight arrived to set up for their 10:30 TV taping and I rushed to freshen up. The moment we started the interview a cacophony of weird sounds beset us from the floor above and blotted out our voices. Power saws, hammers. What sounded like ribbed steel cable being pulled through a wall. The sound man was having a fit and poor Dixie Watley came close to having a nervous breakdown. The cameras started and the cameras stopped. We did everything at least three times and I have no idea what the end product must have looked like for I never did get to see it.

It was because of this that we were very late in leaving the Plaza and only arrived at WOR seconds ahead of airtime. I was ushered straight into the studio, plonked down opposite Joan Hamburg, and supplied with a headset and a glass of water.

Radio is great, much the most relaxing of them all. Your hair can be a mess, your lipstick can be smeared. You can afford the luxury of looking as perplexed as you feel when a member of the audience asks a particularly dumb question. You can scratch your head if it itches and you can drink a glass of water—if you're thirsty—without running the risk that ten million people might think you're doing it because you're nervous. There aren't even any photographers lying upside down at your feet, apparently trying to zoom in on the hairs of your left nostril. Radio is terrific.

While I was still on the air, Lela called the Plaza and arranged for club sandwiches and coffee to be waiting in the suite when we got back there for a 2:30 interview with the *Washington Post*. The *Post*, Lela and I all arrived at the same time and we begged a few minutes to swallow our lunch. In five minutes flat I had eaten and was brushed and lipsticked and ready to go.

The *Washington Post* had flown to New York despite the fact that I would be in D.C. in a couple of weeks. They were not willing to be that far behind New York in reporting a current event. The questions and answers flowed as usual and I began to learn the art of making my answers to familiar questions sound fresh and sharp. It was not the interviewer's fault that much of it was the same thing over and over again.

The *Post* left at 4:00, with Lela and me following them out the door in order to get to West Fifty-seventh Street by 4:30 for a local show, *CBS Five O'Clock News*.

It began tamely enough. I was ushered in to makeup and another layer of goop was applied. As the tour wore on, I became used to having goop piled upon goop until it felt like a mask by nightfall. My interviewer was undergoing makeup in the chair next to mine and he chatted with me in a most friendly fashion. He stayed friendly while our microphones were attached, but then the red light came on.

Film clips (or photos, I forget which); brilliant career; daughter . . . not very nice book.

How can you, in conscience, and we all assume you possess one, defile and smear the name of a great lady like Bette Davis? Don't even *you* find the writing of this book to be despicable and disgraceful? *I* see this book, as do most others I'm sure, as an atrocity. How do *you* categorize your book, B.D.?— I would term it a tragedy; a tragedy of a woman who has attained greatness in her career and thrown away her personal life.

My weeks of concentration on not becoming hostile in the

face of hostility paid off. The interviewer was visibly disconcerted, even dropping his notes. He did a "Yes, but . . ." and
then wandered off into a monologue concerning how obvious
it must be to any thinking person that I could not possibly be
able to reconstruct dialogue from my childhood. How did I
expect people to believe, etc.?—I'm absolutely confident that I
have recaptured the essence of those dialogues because of their
repetition. When something is said to you, or in your presence, time after time and day after day, it sticks . . . no matter how old you were or how long ago you heard it. Not only
that, but many of the situations were traumatic; most people,
particularly children, have total recall in such cases.

Mommie Dearest was brought up again and I gave the same
answer, but then added to it—I've written *my* book while my
mother is still alive. It's a plea for her to hear me before it's
too late. I also believe that it gives an insight into aspects of
her struggles that are of interest.

When the interview was over, an extraordinary thing happened: the crew applauded. Not only that, but a couple of
newscasters came over and said they liked my book and wanted
to congratulate me on the way I had just handled myself. I
might have been quite smug had I not known that it was Jesus' light.

At dinner that night with my publisher, my editor and Lela,
I had my first audience reaction. A man at a table we were
passing jumped up and offered me his hand. "B. D. Hyman,
am I right?" For a second I thought I must know him from
somewhere, but then he said, "I saw you on TV today. We
were just talking about you and I think you're terrific. You
didn't even flinch at those barracudas. Keep up the good work
. . . don't let the bastards wear you down."

I phoned Jeremy as soon as I was back in my suite. He
was elated when I told him about being covered in God's armor just before I set foot onto the *Today* set. He agreed with
my feelings that the Jane Pauley interview had been rather flat
and suggested that I begin concentrating on content and leave
the preservation of my cool in God's capable hands. He told
me that Pastor and Kay had come to our apartment to watch
me on *Today* along with the kids and himself. I asked what
they thought of my first effort. Jeremy said, "Kay seemed to

think you did very well, but Pastor missed the whole interview. He started praying when you were announced and forgot to stop. We had to tell him about it after the fact." I laughed. I could just see Pastor doing it.

As I would from then on, I slept well that night. I finished with *CBS Morning News* and the *New York Daily News* at 10:00 A.M. and rushed to Penn Plaza for a 10:30 to 11:00 taping of a Cable News Network program called *Show Biz*. A great many of their questions had to do with Gary Merrill and his boycotting, ad taking, and general condemnation of me. I said that the absurdity of his behavior was only surpassed by his hypocrisy. I had not wanted to spend time talking about Gary—if for no other reason than the knowledge that he loved to be talked about—but I was left with no choice.

I said that I had no doubt that his motives were what they always were: to attract publicity and draw attention to himself. It was impossible to concede that he might have any sincere feelings toward my mother for, with the exception of Michael's graduation ceremonies, he had neither seen nor had a kind word for Mother in twenty-five years. As examples of his typical behavior I mentioned his crawling under tables at Sardi's to burn girls' legs with cigars and his appearance at Michael's graduation from Loomis clad in a lady's floppy hat, lady's print blouse, shorts (as a change from his more familiar lady's skirt), and holey old tennis shoes with no laces. He was also carrying a water pistol filled with martinis which—as he cavorted about like a transvestite gnome—he squirted alternately into his own mouth and into the faces of other guests.

To the question "What do you think about his saying on TV that your only motives in writing your book were cruelty and greed?" I replied, "Since he knows more about those two subjects than anyone else I can think of, he obviously wants to attribute his motives in life to me."

Perhaps I should have realized that there was more to the CNN interview than met the eye, but I was running too fast to think about it.

After dealing with Independent Network News and the Associated Press we repaired to the suite for a 2:30 to 3:30 interview with *USA Today*. Lela had a bellman take my bags down to the car so that I could make a quick getaway with

Debra for my 5:15 flight to San Francisco.

Although there is much I would like to say about *USA Today* (sometimes known as "McPaper" and other times referred to as "the home of the investigative paragraph") I will be circumspect and only mention two questions that did not find their way into print. To the first: "Has your mother had sex since her divorce from Gary?" I said that I hadn't the faintest idea. The second was stated as an opinion of the interviewer, but was a question nonetheless: "I think your mother's certifiably nuts and ought to get immediate mental help." I emphatically denied any such possibility. To have done less—let alone to have fallen into the trap of discussing neuroses—would undoubtedly have led to a headline saying, BETTE DAVIS'S DAUGHTER CALLS MOTHER INSANE.

The interview over, *USA Today* accompanied me down to the lobby in the elevator and asked, "What's the strangest question you've had to date?" The answer was simple and I was surprised that he needed to ask. "Has my mother had sex since her divorce from Gary?" I replied.

CHAPTER

As WOULD HENCEFORTH BE THE PATTERN, I WAS MET AT THE
San Francisco airport by a lady carrying a placard bearing my
name. Joyce Cole, like all the escorts who would follow her,
was charming and helpful. In the U.S.A. an entire industry
has sprung up of escorts for people doing publicity tours. She
drove me to the Stanford Court Hotel, where we arrived at
10:00 P.M., local time, and said that she would pick me up at
7:45 in the morning for my live 8:30 appearance on *People Are
Talking*. She also said that I could leave my bags at the hotel
since we would have time to collect them before I emplaned
again.

At the desk there was a message asking me to call the television station and I did as soon as I had unpacked. It seemed
that a woman identifying herself as my half sister had read in
the papers of my forthcoming TV appearance and had called
the station for information on how to contact me. The station,
not knowing whether she was for real or a crackpot, had agreed
to pass along her name and number, but no more than that.

I had only met Jenny Sherry—now married and Jenny Venegas—and her brother John once, that the occasion of my luncheon with my father and Marion in 1964. I was seventeen and recently married at the time; Jenny had been thirteen. Knowing from my father's letter that he and Marion would be in Europe during my brief stop in San Francisco, it had not occurred to me to try to contact his family. I was pleasantly surprised to learn that Jenny was trying to reach me and phoned her immediately. We had a very nice chat but kept it short so that I could call Jeremy and then get a good night's sleep. We agreed to meet at the television station the next morning and I called the station again to make the necessary arrangements.

I arrived at KPIX-TV on Battery Street at 8:00 A.M. to find Jenny, two of her three children—and a friend who had come along to baby-sit her youngest while Jenny joined the audience for the live show—all waiting in the green room. Jenny and I exchanged hugs, then pored over the family photo albums she had brought with her. She gave me a capsule version of her family history and the most extraordinary story unfolded.

"I didn't even know Dad had been married before, let alone that I had a sister, until I was eleven years old. I might never have known if I hadn't stumbled across a picture of Dad, your mother and you in a newspaper one day."

"What did you do when you saw it?" I asked, more than a little surprised.

"I confronted Dad with it. At first he tried to say that it had to be a different William Grant Sherry. We'd always been so close, he knew I was terribly upset. He wasn't telling the truth and I knew it. I just didn't understand why. I felt threatened because he'd had a daughter before me . . . and I felt jealous of you because you came first. None of it made any sense and I went through a terrible time."

"How long was it before he admitted the truth?"

"Oh, I kept at him until he did. After the umpteenth 'This is you, Daddy, I know it is' he broke down and admitted it. He said he hadn't told John or me because he thought it better that we believe he'd never loved anyone but Mom and us. Then, one day—it must have been a few days later—he took me into his studio and unlocked a file cabinet. He took out a folder full of press photos and clippings. There were dozens and dozens of them . . . all about you or you and your mother, none about your mother alone. He talked about you and how he'd had to give you up. He still loves you a lot.

"When I realized that you weren't any kind of a threat to me, I got curious about you. I read all Dad's clippings and everything that appeared about you in the papers from time to time. I stayed a bit jealous because you seemed to have such a glamorous life. When we met over lunch that day, I was so nervous all I could do was sit and stare at you. Do you remember?"

"Yes, I do," I said. "I kept wondering why you were so withdrawn."

"Well now you know. It seems pretty silly now but, at the time, I still found the idea of you completely intimidating. I've hoped ever since that we would meet again under better circumstances. I'm really happy that it's finally happened."

We were interrupted by my being called into makeup but, with the unusual luxury of an hour and a half respite between appointments, I invited Jenny to meet me back at the hotel after the show.

I enjoyed *People Are Talking*. It was the first of many audience-participation, live TV shows, and the variety of the questions kept me alert and, thereby, kept the show interesting, I think. I talked with my two hosts first, then came the questions. Jenny was called upon to stand up and was introduced as my half sister, whom I had just met for only the second time in our lives.

She was asked how she felt upon reading my book and I was surprised by the intensity with which she answered. She said it made her very sad to think that I had undergone such unhappiness during my childhood while hers had been so idyllic; that it was a shame that her family had lived not far from mine in Maine without her even knowing of my existence; and that she was glad that I was happy now and that we had finally met.

Back at the Stanford Court, Jenny and I returned to the photo albums and family reminiscences. The time passed quickly and, when the *San Francisco Chronicle* arrived for its interview, Jenny was obviously reluctant to leave. Joyce Cole, my escort, said she could stay provided she remain absolutely quiet, so the friend took the one-year-old for a walk and Jenny stayed.

As soon as the *Chronicle* learned who she was, they wanted a picture of the two of us. They took many, as usual, and subsequently ran one of Jenny sitting on the arm of my chair in sisterly fashion. The interview ended at 12:30 and, before I did a pre-interview phone conversation with Cable News Network in Los Angeles, Jenny took her leave.

Time heals all wounds, goes the axiom, but it does so by blotting out memory. When the source of the hurt is distant, and the specifics of the pain long passed, the wound is healed. So, unfortunately, it seems to be with love also. I had been thrilled to hear from my real father; I had been excited at the prospect of meeting my half sister. I had liked her immediately upon meeting her.

But we were two strangers come together because of a common link. I was disappointed, I suppose, to find that the link of fatherhood brought no more emotion to the moment than would have the sharing of a grade teacher during our school years. Perhaps that is the way it's supposed to be. Perhaps, one day, there will be more. It's a pity that three thousand geographical miles lie between us as well as so many years.

CHAPTER

SOME TELEVISION SHOWS CALLED ME A DAY OR SO AHEAD OF time to talk and review questions. I assumed they wanted to feel out my attitude toward certain types of questions, as well as to discover whether I was a free talker or a hesitant answerer. Most did not do this but, whatever the case, the hosts had a whole range of techniques with which they worked.

Some hosts did not so much as say hello until thirty seconds to airtime—as in the case of Jane Pauley. Others had me scheduled to arrive half an hour early—and sometimes more—in order that we have time to sit down, have coffee and get to know each other a little. Some went so far as to have a staff member read me the questions before we went on the air. I found it very off-putting, but my protestations did nothing to deter them. No two shows were exactly alike and each, I suppose, reflected the personality of the host.

Joyce and I had lunch during my interview with the *Contra Costa Times*. It ran from 1:00 till 2:00 and, as had been the case with its two forerunners, contained no hostile questions. Everyone in San Francisco seemed to be interested in the emotional and intellectual side of my story rather than the sensational. It was interesting food for thought that cities, like TV show hosts, each had their own personalities.

My last interview in San Francisco was the *Joel Spivak Show*, an hour of live radio from 4:00 till 5:00, which concluded a very pleasant and relatively relaxed day. At 8:15 P.M. I landed in Los Angeles.

Things had been going much too smoothly and something had to go wrong soon. It happened at the Los Angeles airport: my suitcase did not arrive on the plane with me. I fought back the desire to panic indiscriminately, and joked with Ruth Weinberg—my new escort—about how tired I was going to get of wearing the same clothes for the next two and a half weeks. I said a silent prayer for my suitcase while we sought out the lost-luggage department.

God was with me, for when I described the missing piece to the man behind the counter, an image of it immediately came up on his computer screen. The tag had been torn off somehow and it had stayed in San Francisco. The man was very nice and assured me that the suitcase would be on the next flight to Los Angeles—in about an hour and a half—and that the airline, United, would have it delivered to my hotel by no later than midnight. He suggested that I leave word with the concierge if I intended to go to bed before it got there. With all the sad stories about airlines and lost luggage I felt that this was exemplary service.

Checking into the Beverly Hills Hotel was like returning home and, since I always carried my toiletries in my hand luggage, I was barely inconvenienced. Morrow was being very nice to me and I had a beautiful ground-floor suite with sliding doors leading to a charming little walled-in patio. They were treating me like a best-selling author, and I didn't feel like one. There is a world of difference between someone who happens to write a best-selling book and a best-selling author. I said another prayer for my suitcase—this time that United would keep its word—and went to sleep wondering how "Mother's town" would treat me over the next couple of days.

When I arose at 6:00 the next morning I called the concierge and found that my suitcase had rejoined me. I met Ruth under the striped canopy at the front of the hotel at 8:10 to learn that our first stop was what would turn out to be the first of the many additions to my printed schedule. Appointments would be pushed forwards, backwards and sideways. Debra began calling me each evening to let me know the latest batch of changes and my beautifully typed and organized itinerary took on the look of scrap paper covered with random notes.

It was CBS-TV that had wormed its way in ahead of my regularly scheduled events for the day and the questions were, for the most part, standard. The one new area of conversation was movies—not unexpected for Tinsel Town—and whether I had any plans to make one out of my book. They seemed reluctant to accept that I had no such plans and pushed on with questions about whether I would ever consider it. I said that I tried never to say never but that taking such a step would be so far in the future as to make discussion of it at this time utterly pointless.

When I mentioned to Jeremy that night the absorption in L.A. with movie rights, he suggested that I take a different tack to end such speculation: instead of saying, "So far in the future as to be unworthy of discussion," say, "Sure, but only if I get script approval, director approval, cast approval, and last cut." Since no financier of a film would ever agree to such terms, the insistence on them would be tantamount to saying no deal. It sounded like a good idea and I tried it twice the next day. It worked both times. When I thought about it later, it made sense. Hollywood, like the world of diplomacy, operates out of a different dictionary. "Maybe" usually means "yes"; "no" always means "make me a better offer"; "never" means "call me again next week, sweetheart, and we'll have lunch." Deal points, however, are deal points, and insistence on last cut—the right to approve final editing—means that you are prepared to finance the production yourself or, alternatively, that you are an ignorant amateur with delusions of grandeur with whom a tenable deal cannot possibly be made.

We dashed from Sunset Boulevard to Melrose Avenue for *A.M. Los Angeles* at 11:45. The interview was to be filmed with the host and me sitting in director's chairs on a piece of lawn in front of a pretty tree, surrounded by an elaborate flower bed. It was a refreshing change as a setting, but the host was nowhere to be found. The clock kept ticking and Ruth became increasingly nervous. We had to leave by 12:25.

At 12:15 Ruth went for our car and brought it around to the edge of the set for a quick getaway. The host, covered with apologies, burst onto the scene and we did a quick ten minutes, most of it taken up with me pulling the hair out of my mouth. The breeze blew it back in every time I tried to talk while facing the camera.

We reached La Brea barely on time for an hour on *The World of Books*. I remember this show with particular pleasure because it was a family effort. The hosts were Connie Martinson and her daughter, with Connie's son-in-law producing. When I commented, off screen, on how well they all seemed to get along, Connie said that it was one of the greatest delights of her life. She had read my book thoroughly and empathized with me in my predicament. More importantly, though, she joined me in my sorrow that my mother had so filled herself with hate and anger as a result of her belief that the only way to stardom was through fighting with—and humiliating, whenever possible—all those with whom she came in contact. Connie expressed the hope that Mother would see the light before it was too late. I said a silent "Amen."

Back to the Beverly Hills Hotel for lunch and the *Los Angeles Times* at 2:30. The interview turned out to be more of a chat about old times than an interview. Roderick Mann knew all of the players personally—Mother, me, Gary, Jeremy, whom he had known in London—and we swapped anecdotes about this and that and laughed about various episodes in the book, particularly the doves. I gained the distinct impression that Roddy's opinion of my portrayal of Mother was nothing more than a confirmation of what Hollywood already knew or, at least, believed.

We would have been punctual for our 3:50 appointment with *Hour Magazine* at another studio on Sunset Boulevard had it not been for our inability to find the appropriate soundstage. The guard, when we arrived, pointed us to a parking garage on our right and indicated that we should have to walk up a hill and down a side street in order to reach our destination. We found an open spot to park on an upper level of the garage and then jog-trotted our way back down.

We climbed the hill and turned right into the side street

but were unable to find any signs of life. I mean none at all: no people, no sounds, not even any unlocked doors; certainly no signs indicating a potential route to our quarry. We continued to test door handles until we found one that turned. The door opened onto a deserted soundstage, but there was a glimmer of light at the foot of a staircase some hundred feet away.

Ruth and I approached it cautiously—for we had no idea where we were—and were relieved to hear voices at the top of the stairs. We ascended and were happy to discover that we were in the right place. There were no signs on doors or anywhere else, but a passing body confirmed our location. No one seemed in the least concerned that the *Hour Magazine* studio was operating incognito.

When Gary Collins came to introduce himself to me in makeup, I mentioned the trouble we'd had in finding him. He looked surprised and said that *everyone* knew where he was. The interview itself was uneventful.

Friday was very different; it dawned in the depths and ended on the heights. It began with my appearance on CNN, *Take Two*, at 9:15 A.M., and my first experience with "remote" broadcasting. My two hosts were sitting in a studio in Atlanta facing a camera. I was sitting in a studio in Los Angeles facing a camera and with a plain backdrop behind me. My image was projected onto a screen behind my faraway hosts and, whenever it was my turn to speak, they turned to watch me.

The interview started peacefully enough and in standard fashion, but then they began to ask question after question about Gary Merrill. Suddenly, and without warning of any sort, they said they had a film clip they wanted me to watch on the monitor. There was a pause of several seconds. Then Gary appeared.

I recalled, in that instant, that when I had been on CNN in New York, I had been told that Gary was being filmed for his reactions to my interview at a studio in Portland, Maine. Assured that he was in Maine, and not in the studio next-door, I had muttered something to the effect that nothing he did, nor any reaction he might emote, was of the least interest to me.

But now I was confronted with him—even on film he gave

me the willies—and my delightful hosts were waiting with bated breath to film *my* reaction to *his* reaction, etc. As I faced the monitor, the image that hit me was of a frightening, sadistic mask. Gary's famous, resonant voice—which had earned him a good living for so many years doing commercial voice-overs— quickly lost its resonance to harshness as he became infected with his own histrionics.

"Cruelty and greed, cruelty and greed," was the theme. Maniacal laughter was its punctuation. Gary would watch my image on the monitor before him for a few seconds, then bellow, "Rubbish, oh rubbish! Hahahahahaha! Cruelty and greed! Cruelty and greed . . . that's all it is! Hahahahahahahahaha-hahahaha!" He sat hunched forward in his chair, rubbing his hands together in delight with his performance; and, even though I knew it for a performance, I was nauseated by the sight and sound of the man.

Memories from childhood flooded in on me: abuse, threats, drunkenness, beatings. I recoiled as I would from a psychopath stabbing repeatedly at his victim—laughing and stabbing . . . laughing and stabbing . . . the knife and the hand dripping red, yet laughing and stabbing. I felt physical revulsion; a metallic taste in my mouth. I took a gulp of water, but the taste remained.

Even as the film clip was rolling I realized that I would be back on camera at any moment. I could not—I would not— give Gary Merrill the satisfaction of knowing that he had rattled me. I ignored the rest of the clip and prayed for the Lord to strengthen me.

The lions could scent a kill: "Well, B.D., what do you have to say to *that*?"

My answer was a rehash of all that I had said before, in one place or another; essentially that he was a complete phoney. All he had ever wanted was to attract attention to himself, and the role of Mother's white knight was doing that very well. I may not have shone brightly as a star, but I was confident that the lions had been left unfed.

It was only when the interview was over and I stepped down from the platform that I noticed that my knees were weak and I was dizzy. Ruth looked at me and said, "You poor child! I can't believe they did that. That horrible, horrible man!"

I spluttered and Ruth comforted until, at the car, I realized how stupid it was and that the last thing in the world I wanted to dwell upon was my ex-stepfather. There was a little time to spare before our next appointment, so we filled it by going to a toy store where I could find the Transformers that Justin wanted. It wasn't long before Ruth said, "That's better. The color's back in your face."

"I wasn't aware it had left," I said.

"It drained right out of you when your stepfather came on the screen. You managed to regain it somehow when you were back on the air; but it left again the minute you were unhooked."

"They took me by surprise. His projection of hate hit me like a ton of bricks."

Finding the toys, and thinking about Justin's excitement when I got home, were just the tonic I needed. I was fully refreshed and recovered by the time we got to the *Michael Jackson Show* at 11:45. Even Ruth—a very special, sweet person—seemed to have become buoyed in spirit again.

This was a radio show hosted, not by Michael Jackson the singer, but by a charming, gray-haired Englishman who was most disarming. I liked him immediately upon being introduced and, during commercial breaks, he told me about his Andalusian horses and his family. He revealed an extraordinary story about his youngest son who, he said—from reading my book—was the same age as, and sounded very much like, my own Justin.

Several months earlier, when Michael and his seven-year-old son were out riding together, the boy—out of the blue—looked across at his father and said, "You know, Daddy, if you were hurt I wouldn't help you."

"Why not?" Michael asked, startled.

"Because I'm only a small boy and if you were hurt I would be on the ground with two horses and wouldn't be able to do anything for you. So I'd go for help. I just wanted you to know that if you ever get hurt and you see me running away, I'm not running away . . . . I'm going for help."

"That's very wise," Michael said, smiling warmly at his son.

An hour later Michael Jackson suffered a massive heart attack and fell from his horse. The little boy galloped all the way to the stables where they boarded their horses. He convinced someone that his father needed an ambulance and, indeed, an ambulance was at his father's side barely in time to save his life. As I heard the story, I got goose bumps; such prophetic visions come only from God.

The phone lines were lit up with callers but, before taking the first question, Michael displayed a most welcome consideration: he told his audience to remember that when they talked to me, they were talking to his guest; that as my host he would brook no rudeness toward me. After CNN's little game, it felt like a deliverance.

During the break that followed the first few calls the control booth told Michael that Gary Merrill was on the phone, asking to talk to me. Michael looked at me, concern written all over his face, and said, "You don't want to talk to him, do you?"

"No, I don't," I said. "We have nothing to discuss."

"Cut him off," my host instructed the man in the booth.

I was surprised at the calm I felt. I did not want to talk to Gary—I wouldn't even now—but I felt nothing but pity. Not fear . . . not anger . . . not resentment . . . certainly not revulsion . . . just pity for a sad, sick human being. Not love yet, but definitely pity. Thanks to CNN's dirty-tricks department I had been cleansed. Praise God! An indescribable burden had been lifted from my spirit.

It is told that the great turn-of-the-century evangelist Smith Wigglesworth was awakened one night by a great crashing and banging in his house. He lit a candle by his bedside. When he stepped out into the hall to investigate, he was confronted with Satan himself, sitting in an armchair in all his hideous, vile malevolence, grinning at him. Wigglesworth said, "Oh, it's only you." He blew out his candle and went back to bed to sleep soundly.

I know that I have not yet come to a faith as strong as Smith Wigglesworth's, but I also know that, on a memorable day in Los Angeles, God granted me a measure of His grace greater than I had ever known before.

There was lunch with the *Hollywood Reporter* at 1:30 in the Polo Lounge at the Beverly Hills; then a few minutes to relax before the one interview to which I was looking forward with great anticipation. It would also turn out to be the only one that I know for a fact my mother watched.

Scott Ross had called Morrow to say that the *700 Club* wanted to interview me. I had, of course, agreed with delight, but I had, ever since, been puzzled as to why the Christian Broadcasting Network would want to talk about my book, particularly in view of the profanity in it.

When I met Scott and his camera crew in the hotel bungalow provided for the event by Morrow, it was the first question I asked. Pat Robertson and the *700 Club* had played such an important role in my Christian walk—not to mention being responsible for my husband accepting the Lord—that I really cared about their reasons. Scott said that he had felt drawn to interview me after reading in *People* magazine that I was born again. He had read my book with an open mind and had readily recognized that the portrait of my mother would have been incomplete without the profanity; a portrait without a face, as it were.

"That's wonderful," I said. "The strange part of all this is that, even as far back as *People* magazine, I had intended to avoid mention of my faith for fear of clouding the issue. It crept in then, and it keeps on creeping in. So here I am on the *700 Club*, and praise the Lord. I only hope that any Christian who reads *My Mother's Keeper* will see it and accept it as you have."

While the camera crew was setting up, we talked and talked. Scott told me about his own life and promised to send me a copy of his book, *Scott Free*. We talked about my book. We talked about Jesus Christ. The interview, when it began, seemed a natural extension of the conversation we were already engaged in. At the end of it, Scott and I joined hands, the crew bowed their heads, and we prayed for Mother's salvation. People I have met since have told me that when the program aired, they prayed with us and were brought to tears. I was sorry when the interview ended but when I returned to my suite at 6:30, I felt on top of the world and was praising God for His perfect plan.

It was some weeks before I heard, on good authority, that Mother had seen my *700 Club* interview. I freely admit that her reaction was a disappointment. After sitting through it stone-faced, her only comment was to hiss, "She didn't even *apologize.*" But that was alright; my confidence remained undiminished that God—at the time and in the manner of His choosing—would guide Mother's footsteps to the narrow way. Thousands—perhaps millions—were praying for her. When she took that first, tentative step, she would find a friendship and a family that she never dreamed existed.

CHAPTER

I spent a lovely weekend with old friends in Los Angeles and Lake Arrowhead and then flew to Houston on Sunday afternoon. On Monday I did *Good Morning Houston* on KTRK-TV, *Hour Houston* on KIKK radio, and the *Warner Roberts Show* on KRIV-TV. Bart Connors was touring to publicize his book, *Go for the Gold,* and I bumped into him in a green room for the third time in as many cities. I suggested that we would have to stop meeting like this lest people start talking. A lady host achieved what I am still convinced was world-class devious reasoning when she accused me of writing *My Mother's Keeper* for no other purpose than to promote the book she had heard my mother was writing.

I flew to Chicago in the afternoon and arrived at the hotel to find a huge package of news clippings that Debra had sent there to await me. I showered, ordered dinner and sat down to read.

The clippings were from newspapers in the East. Many were from newspapers to which I had given interviews; many were from newspapers I had never even heard of. There were multipage articles, short articles, and some book reviews. The content ran the entire gamut from evenhanded—occasionally flattering—reportage, to the hysterical demand that I be lynched at the earliest possible moment. Some accepted that I had done what I had done for the purpose stated; many did not.

I now had to concentrate on putting out of mind—and ignoring as best I could—the accusations and unkind comments about my motives. I had to focus on the only thing that really mattered. The opinion of the world was irrelevant; the sole relevancy was my mother. She—no matter what she might say—would know it was the truth; and knowing it, would one day come to understand that I'd had no viable alternative than to write and publish. That was the only thing that mattered. The slings and arrows would inevitably continue to fly, but I would smile my way through them and pretend that they did not hurt.

My reverie was broken by the telephone. Pastor Wayne Pitts had called Jeremy for information on how to reach me and was bursting with enthusiasm about my upcoming appearance in Louisville. He wanted Serafino Fazio's phone number so that he could invite him to come too. At the end of a lengthy conversation he told me that my coming to speak at Evangel Tabernacle was being advertised in all the local media and, for the third time, stated that he knew something important was going to happen. I was too intimidated by the thought of addressing four thousand people to be able to give much attention to his prophecy.

An hour later I called Serafino in West Virginia to see whether he had heard from Pastor Pitts. He had, and he, Joan and all three daughters were making rapid plans to meet me in Louisville. I was thrilled at the news and said so. It had been eight or nine months since I had last seen the Fazios and I missed them. I was sorry that Jeremy would not be there with us.

The next day I did two print interviews, two radio shows and a TV show before appearing on *Kup's Show* on WTTW-TV. When we were seated, Irv Kupcinet began with, "In your book, B.D., you call your mother 'mean-spirited and vindictive.' Now . . . how can you say—"

"I call her nothing of the kind," I interrupted. "That is not a quote from my book. It's a quote from *USA Today* about my book. I read it last night." Kupcinet turned to his assistant. "Is that in her book or not?"

"No, Mr. Kupcinet. That isn't in the book. She's right . . . it was in *USA Today*."

"Are you sure?" Kupcinet said. He was visibly upset at being deprived of his opening gambit.

"Yes, sir, I'm sure."

"Rewind the tape," he ordered. "We'll start again." What a shame, I thought, that all shows were not live. It would be nice if the audience could see it when the interviewers made fools of themselves, rather than just the interviewees. The next day was Detroit, Thursday was Cleveland, and Friday was Boston.

Peter Meade, on WBZ radio, a preppy in his mid-thirties, was thoroughly charming—as so many of my hosts had been—and his interview followed what I had come to regard as "the friendly format." It was only when he opened the show to callers that events took off in a singular direction.

I wish, now, that I had kept an accurate count, but—among many others—some ten or twelve elderly ladies called in. Every one of them had been to school with Mother and Aunt Bobby—at Crestalban, Newton High or Cushing Academy—and every one of them had approximately the same thing to say. "My name is _____. I went to school with your mother and Bobby at _____. I just wanted you to know that I thought your Aunt Bobby was one of the sweetest people I ever knew. We all thought it was horrible the nasty, mean way Bette treated her. We all knew Bette was going to be something great one day and we felt sorry for Bobby. I'm glad you've written the book about Bette and shown the way she really is. Anybody that mean shouldn't get away with it. Good luck, dear, and have courage. You're doing the right thing."

With such sentiments coming so unexpectedly—and live on the radio at that—I was hard-pressed to think of anything to say. I believe I responded in much the same way to each of them: "Thank you for your interest and support. Aunt Bobby was an absolute sweetheart and I'm glad to know she had so many friends." There wasn't much else I could do.

Another call was from a man in Lowell, Massachusetts. He was very put out and wanted to tell everyone about it. "When we had our Bicentennial celebration in Lowell back in '76, we invited your mother. She was born in Lowell, you know?" I said that I knew that and he went on. "Ed McMahon was born here too, and *he* came. Your mother never even answered the invitation and I think it was pretty rotten. I'm glad you wrote your book. Your mother is always carrying on about her New England upbringing and her Yankee principles, but she doesn't even have any manners."

I apologized on Mother's behalf and tried to suggest that the invitation might not have reached her. The man from Lowell would have none of it.

I flew to Philadelphia that night, had an interview with the Philadelphia *Inquirer* on Saturday morning, and then spent the long weekend with friends. Monday was Memorial Day and I only had one radio show in the evening prior to one TV and two more radio shows the next day.

My flight from Philadelphia to Washington was delayed for a few hours and I was, consequently, stranded for that long at the airport. I was by now well accustomed to total strangers coming up to me and saying that they had seen me on this or that television show. I had also become pleasantly accustomed to the fact that—contrary to my original expectation of being accosted by hordes of outraged Bette Davis fans— every single person who approached me was either sympathetic or downright flattering.

The scene at the airport that evening, though, was unqualifiedly strange. It felt as though half the population of the United States were there, and that no less than half of *them* came to say hello and shake my hand. I don't think I have ever shaken the hands of so many strangers in my entire life. It reached the point where I was giving serious thought to sunglasses and a dark wig.

To cap off the experience, Mike Love was on the same flight to Washington as I. To have the lead singer of the Beach Boys recognize *me*, and then come over to introduce himself, was almost too much. His opening remark was original too: "Hi. I'm Mike Love and you're the person who's written that naughty, naughty book."

CHAPTER

A HAND WAS GENTLY SHAKING MY SHOULDER AND A VOICE FROM far, far away was saying something about being in Louisville and having to get off a plane.

Pastor Pitts and his wife, Evelyn, were at the airport to meet me. They took me straight to the hotel—only accepting with reluctance my repeated avowal that I was not hungry—and then insisted on seeing me safely to my room. The Fazios were in the room next to mine, and once Serafino, Joan and I were in full conversational flow, the Pittses took their leave. They arranged to pick us up at 8:30 the next morning.

Serafino wanted to know all the gory details of my tour. Then we talked about Jeremy and the boys; then about our church in Freeport and the building thereof. By the time we stopped talking it was midnight and we were all hungry, so we went out for pizza. So much for the early night I had planned.

Before we called it a night, I told the Fazios that Pastor Pitts was taking all of us to Prayer Mountain first thing in the morning, followed by a visit to the new Christian television station that would soon be going on the air. "Hopefully," I

added, "we'll get a few hours to relax before the service tomorrow night."

"Are you nervous?" Serafino asked.

"Dreadfully," I admitted. "I've never spoken to thousands
of people before. Somehow it seems almost impersonal on radio or TV . . . you just talk to the microphone or the camera.
I'm praying that I don't make a complete fool of myself."

"I'm nervous too," Serafino said.

"I don't know why you should be," Joan interjected with
a big laugh and a loving squeeze of his arm. "You've been
rehearsing your speech day in and day out since Pastor Pitts
called. Just do it the way you said it while you were shaving
and you'll be fine." We all laughed, but I wished Joan were
doing this instead of me.

Pastor Pitts and Evelyn were in the lobby punctually at
8:30 A.M. and we set out for Prayer Mountain, a retreat in
Shepherdsville—half an hour outside Louisville—where people come to pray and seek the Lord in solitary, bucolic surroundings. After showing us around, Pastor Pitts surprised
Serafino and me by asking us each to speak for a few minutes
to the people assembled for the morning prayer meeting.

From there we were taken on a guided tour of the ten-
thousand-seat sanctuary under construction in Louisville, the
almost-completed Christian television station and, with a stop
for lunch first, Evangel Tabernacle itself.

By the time we got back to the hotel my ankles were swol-
len to bursting point. They had been bothering me for days
and, with all the walking we did with Pastor Pitts, they felt
like burning balloons. Putting them up for two hours felt like
heaven but did nothing to reduce the swelling. When it came
time to leave for the evening service I tried to put on my high-
heeled shoes, but it was no use . . . the pain was excruciating. Sandals felt much better and I judged that if they were
good enough for Jesus, they certainly were good enough
for me.

Joan and the girls were seated at the front of the church
while Serafino and I were led behind the platform to an office.
There we were introduced to two of the resident pastors—
Wallace Cauble and Greg Holt—and enjoyed a time of quiet
prayer together before the service began.

The sanctuary was at near capacity and the choir was singing when we took our places on comfortable sofas off to one
side of the platform. My feet appreciated the comfort even if
I was too nervous to be aware of it at the time. There was a
beautiful service, and then—all too soon, it seemed—Pastor
Pitts went to the microphone to make the introduction.

"Tonight we have two very special guests with us: a person whose name has been mentioned many times lately in the
media. You've read about her in the newspaper and seen her
on television programs. There are probably a lot of question
marks in your mind in regard to this person . . . in regard to
her faith and her belief in the Bible and what she knows about
Jesus Christ. And along with her is a Businessman, a Full
Gospel Businessman that—through the Full Gospel Businessman's ministry—he and his entire family were converted, were
really born again, to a miracle of God. We're going to hear
about it tonight.

"I want you to listen closely. We will hear afresh how the
Holy Spirit can guide us and work in our lives that we might
be soul winners, that we might be able to reach and win
somebody else to Jesus. Don't you love to hear testimonies of
conversions?" There was loud applause.

"Amen! I'm not talking about just joining a church; I'm
talking about a change that comes about in a person's life.
These are the things we believe in. The Bible teaches us this.
I'm just looking here in the Book of Acts, chapter nine; something is said here in regard to Paul; that right after his marvelous conversion a lot of question marks were in many people's
minds when he first accepted Christ. We notice in verse twenty-
six, 'And when Saul was come to Jerusalem, he assayed to
join himself to the disciples: but they were all afraid of him,
and believed not that he was a disciple.'

"It's a tremendous verse of Scripture when you get to
thinking about it, isn't it? But the thing is, we put no limits
on the Grace of God; and we recognize that people of all walks
of life come to a place where they need to know Jesus, just
like everybody else; and God is no respecter of persons.

"And so tonight, in just a few moments, I'm going to introduce to you B. D. Hyman; she's the daughter of this well-
known movie star—Bette Davis. The question is asked, 'Is

B. D. Hyman really born again? Is she really a Christian? I want to know.' Well, praise God, I personally believe that she is.

"Some weeks ago I was in the Bahama Islands, at Freeport. I did not know anything about this person. I arrived in Freeport and the missionary met me at the airport. He said some people had come by to meet me. He said they had moved to the island and he told me a little bit about them. Then, on Sunday morning, B. D. Hyman, her husband and two sons were in the second pew, right in front of the church. They were right there with open ears and you could tell by the look on their faces they wanted to hear what God had to say. They shared in the meeting, worshipping God like everybody else.

"I was invited to go fishing with them and I found they were ordinary people, like all the rest of us. Then they asked me to come to their house and eat with them, and I came to know some people where there was love in their house; where there was love between the wife and the husband; where there was a deep appreciation for their two boys, for their children, and I like things like that. Praise God!

"I'm not a person who's familiar with movie-type people, Hollywood people—in fact, I'm not much at seeing many movies—so when I heard her mother's name, it didn't mean anything to me. I had to learn something about who Bette Davis was. But the thing tonight is, B. D. Hyman is not here at this service to sell a book. In fact this is the first time she's ever been in a meeting like this.

"For the past two or three weeks she's been on a special tour for the ones who are promoting her book and, when she's had a chance and the right questions were asked, she's put in a word about Jesus. When I invited her to come here, before I knew anything about her tour, I felt impressed in my heart to invite her to come to Louisville. Then she called me and said, 'They've asked me to go on a tour. When that's all over with, I'll let Louisville be my last stop.'

"She was at Prayer Mountain this morning and oh what a blessing her testimony was to the people there. And I'm glad to have her with us tonight. Since this is more or less the first time—not her first time to talk about Jesus—but the first time to be invited into a church, a building, a congregation of people like this, to give her testimony, I think first I should invite

Businessman Fazio from Parkersburg, West Virginia. I'd like for him to come and more or less lay a basis for how this woman has come to know Jesus. Brother Fazio, would you come?"

Serafino, looking very dapper and self-assured—despite his earlier protestations of nerves—did beautifully. He talked about how he and his family had found the Lord and then the extraordinary way in which our two families had come together. Having him go first made it a little easier for me, but when my turn to take the microphone came, I found that I was so nervous I had to lock my knees back to stop them from shaking.

After a few introductory sentences I plunged into the story from the point Serafino had left off. "We talked to Serafino a great deal that day; asked him a lot of questions. I was a typical agnostic; I felt there might be a God, but that it didn't matter a whole lot, one way or the other. You see, I thought I was about the happiest person in the world. My husband and I had a fantastic marriage; we'd been married for twenty years at that point. Now it's almost twenty-two. We had two beautiful sons; we had, we thought, everything that could be asked for in life. We were grateful for it, but we didn't know the source. We didn't think we needed anything, and I think there are many people in that position.

"They aren't in a desperate situation; they feel they are really together, they have a good life, they feel they are good people; and indeed they are good people. But they don't think they have any more needs than that. I know we didn't think we did. I thought it was nice for people to care about God; if it suited them, I was very happy for them and thought it was wonderful . . . but it didn't have anything to do with me. I didn't need that. It was for other people. I really believed that.

"Then Serafino began talking and I remember one of my first questions to him. I was kind of bristly; I'd had many people witness to me over the years and they'd always quoted Scripture at me without any personal story, without any evidence of what God had done in *their* lives. So it always seemed very empty to me. I can recall, as I said—in a bristly fashion, which Serafino's too kind to mention—I said, 'Well, look, if this God is really as valid as you say, and if Jesus Christ is our advocate, then what about all this religious strife? What about all this bigotry? Bigotry makes me ill; it always has. And what about the situation in Ireland where one way of worshipping is killing the other way of worshipping? And what about the Middle East and all these horrible situations?'

"Serafino waited till I'd wound down, smiled at me and said, 'That's Satan's way of twisting what God wants for the world. Religion is of man . . . faith is of God.'

"That startled me, and got both my husband and me thinking. We'd never heard it put that way and it was the first time it made sense to us. We went from one thing to another and I, at least, discovered that I had an incredible thirst for knowledge."

I continued on with the story and talked about the dinners with the Fazios, keeping them up till all hours in the morning, the endless questions and answers, Jeremy's dinosaur-plex, my revelation and salvation in the middle of the dirt road one morning, Jeremy's "deal" with Serafino regarding the healing of my back, the healing which came through a Word of Knowledge from Pat Robertson on the *700 Club*; Jeremy's acceptance of the Lord; the blizzard, the flood, and our trip to Akron to see Ernest Angley; the miracle healing of the man with the crushed hand; Ashley's visions and healings; the rest of my healing; and the fact that both boys have continued to grow stronger in the Lord just as my husband and I have. In closing, I said:

"Just as Serafino said, our lives have continued with these endless miracles; miracles we've been able to participate in with friends, with other people, within the Body of Christ in our church. The Lord led us to Freeport through a whole series of circumstances and our pastor down there, Ernie DeLoach, is one of the most beautiful Christians imaginable and has such love and such caring for the people there. We're blessed to be able to participate in that church, to help build it and watch it grow. It's something that I believe began at the beginning of time with every other plan that God has ever had. God's perfect plan for all our lives and all our seasons is just overwhelming to me. I praise the Lord every hour of my life and will continue to do so.

"Thank you for the honor of being able to share with you this evening."

Pastor Pitts took center stage again. He asked me a few

questions about my faith, made a few comments, and then asked the congregation whether anyone doubted that I was truly born again. I gained the impression that he had perhaps, prior to the service, come under criticism for inviting me. It was entirely possible that the advertising had brought forth some potential hecklers. It was even possible that some regular members of Evangel Tabernacle were less than pleased at my appearance. Whatever the case, it was strictly an impression and I did not seek to verify it.

The good pastor need not have worried anyway: it would not be long before God addressed the question Himself.

The questions continued and we talked about my interview on the *700 Club*. Then Pastor Pitts called upon Brother Greg Holt to lead us all in prayer. Brother Greg spoke for a few minutes before asking the congregation to join with me in prayer for my mother. Having four thousand people agree with me while I prayed was a memorable experience.

"Oh Heavenly Father, in the precious Name of Jesus Christ, who can do all things, I pray that you leave my mother's heart open. Break down the walls around her heart, Lord. Let her hear, let her be able to hear, let the wonderful, wonderful miracle of salvation begin in her heart. Let her find you, and let her know what true love is. And let her know your love, and your promises, and all the wonders that you have for the whole world. In Jesus' Name, amen."

Brother Greg then led us in prayer. When he asked if there were any needs, a healing line formed. It was ministered to by several pastors who went to the foot of the platform for that purpose, and there were several healings. One in particular that I remember was a woman who was healed of lupus.

Praising in tongues began. Then something occurred that I had never witnessed before: singing in tongues. It was the most beautiful sound that I could imagine. All those people; all singing in different tongues—each in his own prayer language—but all singing in harmony as if it had been rehearsed. It was so incredibly beautiful that I just stood there and wept.

When God spoke, the import of His message escaped me. It wasn't until the service was over and hundreds and hundreds of people came forward to shake my hand, hug me and talk that I understood; it wasn't until the first few well-wishers had all said the same thing that it got through to me: God had been speaking about *me*.

His message, as always, came first in tongues. A lady to my left, and two-thirds of the way back in the sanctuary, received it. Her tone of voice, as she spoke the words that none of us could yet understand, was very chiding. She sounded like an angry parent reading the riot act to a disobedient child.

The interpretation was given by a man sitting in the center and halfway back.

> Oh, my people: shall he that has created you instruct not? Yea, shall you come and shall you tell me whom I will use? I shall use you. Though you seek me not, I shall use you. When you have yielded to me, I have used you. When you have resisted me, yet have I used you.
>
> I shall use whom I shall use; and I shall bless whom I shall bless; and I have given my son to die on the cross that I might bless all things and that I might use my servants.
>
> Yea, you have seen me work in your midst tonight; and yea, you will see me work in your midst again; and you shall not teach me, nor shall you tell me whom I will use.
>
> But yea, I shall magnify and I shall bless you. If you will yield in Christ, then will you see greater things, and you will know my love; yea, for my love and my secrets are with them that fear me.

CHAPTER

11

THE FLIGHT TO FREEPORT TOOK FOREVER—CUSTOMS TOOK LONGER than that. When I finally emerged onto the sidewalk outside the baggage area it was 10:00 P.M. Justin hugged me and jumped up and down simultaneously. He allowed me to hug and kiss his dad, but only briefly.

Once at our apartment I flopped on the couch and let out a long sigh. I had never felt so physically and emotionally drained in my entire life. Jeremy made coffee and Ashley, following my directions, opened my bag and found Justin's Transformer toys and the presents for himself and his father. I lay there with my feet up and said over and over again how happy I was to be home.

Jeremy shouted questions from the kitchen, Ashley grumbled about having to unpack Justin's toys for him—when he would rather be eating—and Justin showed me how each toy became something else as his brother unearthed it for him. It was total confusion. Boy, it felt wonderful!

With the last of the presents extracted from the jumble Ashley had made of my things, and a cup of coffee in my hand, I told the boys to be quiet so that I could talk to their father. Justin went a few feet away and transformed; Ashley withdrew to the kitchen to make himself another in the unending stream of grilled-cheese sandwiches that seemed to be as intrinsic to his survival as breathing; Jeremy sat down in a chair opposite the sofa.

I could talk to him without holding a telephone to my ear. It seemed incredible after the past three weeks. "Boy, I'm glad to be back!" I said with another long sigh.

"I know," my husband said. "That's the seventh time you've mentioned it. But will you please stop saying it and tell me what happened at Evangel Tabernacle? You only gave me the barest outline last night."

As I recounted what had happened the previous night I realized that I was only just beginning to assimilate the full impact of the events. By the time I came to the end of God's message the tears were flowing down my cheeks. Jeremy was smiling broadly but there was a catch in his voice, and he too looked a bit teary when he whispered, "Praise God."

He sat quietly for a few moments, then leaped out of his chair and said, "We have to get a tape of the service! They did tape it, didn't they?"

"I don't know. It didn't occur to me to ask. Why do we need a tape anyway?"

"Because I want to put God's message in the book. He spoke directly about you. Don't you see? It's the definitive answer for any Christians who may still be troubled by what you've done. But we can't do it without a tape of the message. Far be it from me to risk changing God's word."

Jeremy's excitement at the idea began to infect me and I promised to write to Pastor Pitts the next day. I went to my suitcase and got the envelopes of news clippings that Debra had sent me and gave them to my husband. While he was reading I glanced through the letters that had come in from readers of *My Mother's Keeper*.

We occasionally stopped to compare notes and, being now among those I loved, I found myself amused by comments I had earlier found hurtful. There were few truly vile articles, but Jeremy—who had long held an unshakable conviction, which I wholeheartedly shared, regarding the nature of the majority of my mother's most ardent male fans—read a couple of them aloud with a Truman Capote–like accent. He thereby reduced the writers of the articles to caricatures and me to helpless laughter. He also succeeded in changing forever my reaction to the utterances of the most strident among my detractors.

It was late and the boys went to bed after a few minutes of family prayer. Then I told Jeremy how amazed I was that I had managed to keep it all together through eleven cities. I had always been such a homebody—reluctant to do anything on my own—that it now felt as if someone else had been out there for the past twenty-one days. That God had given me the strength, both physically and emotionally, went without saying. But I found it so improbable that I had done it. After only an hour or so at home, the tour had begun to take on an air of unreality.

Almost as great a relief as being home was the knowledge that I could finally stop answering questions. I would not have to spend most of every day analyzing my mother and our relationship. I would not have to endlessly define and defend my reasons for writing my book. I had been through it all so many, many times—interview after interview, city after city—and now I could let go of it. I could relax and reclaim my niche in the real world.

When I awoke the next morning it was to the sound of the typewriter clattering away in the den. I suddenly realized that I had been so full of my own experiences that I had not even asked how the new book was coming along. We had made copious notes before I left, and Jeremy, during our phone conversations, had seemed very pleased with his progress.

I dressed hurriedly, grabbed a cup of coffee and went to the den. I read what my husband had done during my absence and proffered a couple of comments. We worked together for an hour or so and then packed it in for the day. It was baking-hot outside and the boys wanted to go out to the reef to do some diving.

My excitement with our new work was fully renewed. It was so different this time. We were telling the continuing story of my relationship with my mother—yes—but that part was entirely secondary to our testimony. I certainly wanted Mother to read this one too, but only in the hope that she might find answers to questions from which she had always shied away. It occurred to me that it might be God's plan that both books be finished before He touched Mother.

There was so much Jeremy and I wanted to say; so much we wanted to share with others, particularly those who were still in the darkness from which we had escaped. The wonder of the events at Evangel Tabernacle came to me again. God had called me His servant and had proclaimed that I was doing His work. As I sat in the back of the boat I was filled with an overwhelming joy.

I wanted everyone, particularly Mother, to know that joy, to know that oneness with the universe and its Creator. It suddenly became important that I write to my mother. My book was in stores everywhere but it wasn't enough. I had to let her know where I was and what I was doing. I had to remind her that nothing was over unless she wanted it to be over. I had to write to her and keep on writing.

She wouldn't answer my letters—I couldn't even be certain that she would read them—but it was important to tell her that I loved her. Perhaps she would save the letters and take them out in moments of loneliness. She would know that I was still thinking of her. She would know she was not abandoned—even if it did suit her sense of drama to say that she was.

I wondered whether she would be angry that my life was better than ever and so full of joy. Would she try to figure out why? Was there really a chance that something, sometime, would awaken in her the knowledge that there was a gaping lack in her life?

Given Mother's singular determination to deny even the obvious when it fails to suit her; given the ease with which she transfers to others her own shortcomings; given her ability to see her fantasy world as reality—what can convince her that our time on earth is but a stepping-stone to eternity? What can convince her that we have to measure up now in order to inherit the future? What can convince her that fame cannot work a ticket to heaven, that Oscars will not fit the keyhole? What can possibly convince her that the only way is to say, "I accept you, Jesus, as my personal Lord and Savior"?

I don't know what will convince her, and it doesn't matter

that I don't know. God knows. I'll write to her from time to time. I won't preach—I won't even try to witness—I'll just let her know what's going on in my life and that I love her. Publishing my book has solved my problem but not hers. Praying for her isn't enough. The least I can do is give the Holy Spirit the opportunity to work in her through the expression of my love.

CHAPTER

IT WAS NOT ONLY MY SURROUNDINGS THAT HAD CHANGED SO dramatically with our move to the island, it was also my pattern of living. I had for so many years been used to a life regulated by animals to be cared for and chores to be done that it took me a long time to become accustomed to doing almost everything on the spur of the moment. Since Jeremy had decided that writing was fun and had declined to become involved in any other business ventures, and since the only fixed requirement in our days was to deliver and retrieve the boys to and from school, we fell into the habit of doing whatever we were in the mood to do without preplanning.

For the most part we began each weekday with the idea that we were going to work diligently. We would lay out our notes—or write new notes—drink coffee and discuss what we were trying to say. Sometimes creativity was present in full force and pages rolled out of the typewriter. At other times the words just did not want to arrange themselves satisfactorily. We quickly found that pushing it for the sake of looking busy only produced work that we threw away the following day.

It wasn't long before the adage "If we can't earn it, we better go catch it" became our excuse to go lobstering and/or fishing on noncreative days. It sounds a bit lame, even to me, but the fact is that it worked. We would sometimes go for days without producing anything, then turn out a mass of material we liked in nothing flat.

Whenever we were fishing on what should have been a work day, Jeremy would always think of one subject or another relative to the book that ought to be discussed. The discussion might last only for a few minutes but it seemed to lessen the feeling that we were goofing off. Of course, his unfailing "Is this the way to hold a story conference, or what?"—as he was reeling in the fish that had ended the discussion—did little to add dignity to the argument that we were actually working.

The Regency Theater, home of the Freeport Players Guild, held a meeting on the first Monday of every month to discuss business matters and plan upcoming productions. Jeremy and I enjoyed set painting and also lent a hand with "front of house," which is ticket sales, door tending and so forth. It was fun and we enjoyed getting to know the diverse personalities that made up the group.

Over a period of a few months we developed some wonderful friendships in the Guild. Cay (pronounced "eye" with a "K" in front of it) and Andrea Gottlieb were the first to invite us to their home for dinner. They had five children, seldom less than five dogs—including a Great Dane and a Saint Bernard—chickens, ducks and cats. My kind of people.

Andrea also had a couple of horses which she kept at a boarding stable but brought home and allowed to graze on the lawn at Christmastime. Cay always threw a fit when he saw the horses chewing on his palm trees, but Andrea couldn't stand the thought of her babies being all alone during the holiday—which makes her as wacky about horses as I am.

Cay's father had become very famous in the Bahamas as the first doctor with a medical degree to set up practice in the Out-Islands. He and Cay's mother had come from Germany after World War II. Cay, therefore, despite his German heritage, was Bahamian. He was a lawyer who owned a recording studio and wrote and performed his own music. (Ask anyone in town where to find "the singing-honkey-lawyer" and they will give you directions.) Andrea was from Cardiff in Wales, originally coming to the islands as a contract teacher but then staying on.

A young couple—both in their mid-twenties—moved into our apartment building and it was not long before we formed a very close friendship. Colin Evans was from Wales and his wife, Lynn, from England. They were both teachers and had been on the island for a year when we met them. They were greater spear-fishing addicts even than we but, when it came to investing in a boat, had drawn the line at an inflatable with a small outboard. It seemed quite natural when we found ourselves coordinating our longer boating trips with the Evanses' availability.

Our investigation of every inch of fishable reef and every blue hole within reach led in due course to my absorption with seashells and the search for them. I bought some books on the subject and quickly learned to give up trying to memorize the names in favor of remembering the terrain in which I was most likely to find them. There was plenty of time to figure out what species the critter was once I had found it.

Every available surface in the apartment became covered with my treasures and I began to long for shelves to keep them on. I had six species of conch, four species of helmet, three species of triton, and uncountable tuns, tulips, bonnets, murex, whelks, cones, nerites, star-shells, cowries, top-shells, scallops, oysters, chitons, arks, clams, tellins and what-have-you. The Lace Murex, incidentally, has to be one of the most beautifully intricate of all of God's creations.

I ceased being of much help to Jeremy and Colin in their constant quest for food. I was always shuffling about in the sea grasses or poking among holes and caves in the coral looking for shells. Worse than that, when it came time for cleaning the catch of the day I was much too busy cleaning my latest shell to be able to attend to anything so mundane as the wherewithal for dinner. I mean to say, it looks like I may have found a Lamellose Wentletrap, people! Let's keep our priorities straight!

Ashley's interest stayed strictly with spearfishing, but Justin became infected with my enthusiasm for shelling. Not that he didn't enjoy spearing—he did, even getting thirty lobsters one day—but finding a shell off Sandy Cay (pronounced "key") which turned out to be an Atlantic Yellow Cowrie, and relatively uncommon, made a convert of him. Whenever someone came to visit, Justin was sure to show them his cowrie and point out that it was rarer than anything else in the collection.

I must state at this point that neither my husband nor I are among those who feel that Christians must shun, or perpetually try to shove their faith down the throats of, non-Christians. We treasure the friendship of Christian and non-Christian alike, believing that it is just as important to live a witness as to merely talk a witness. Anyway, Colin and Lynn were with us one day when Jeremy surprised even himself. We were well off the north shore of the island and had spent the entire day searching for coral heads, and the lobsters that frequent them, without much luck. We had found dozens of heads and speared a few grouper, but the lobsters were successfully eluding us. There has to be bright sun and a light chop on the water to be able to spot the heads. The day was wearing on and the sun was getting too low in the sky.

Colin who, like Jeremy, had grown up being bored to death in the school chapel six times a week and twice on Sunday, was standing on the bow of the boat with my husband, squinting out across the dazzling aquamarine ocean. Jeremy prays aloud when he goes for his long walks at night; he prays aloud in the privacy of our home and in church; he is not much given to praying aloud before non-Christians—except for saying grace at mealtimes—lest he make them feel uncomfortable in the wrong way and at the wrong time.

Nevertheless, he suddenly began to pray aloud, and an unusual prayer it was: "Lord, I haven't come all this way and spent all this time just to go back empty-handed. You've always looked kindly upon fishermen, Lord, and you promise all of your children the desires of our hearts. This may not seem like the time or the place, Lord, but I claim your promise. Lead us to a head that has fifty to a hundred lobsters on it so that I won't have burned all this gasoline for nothing. And you'll have to do it quickly, Lord, the sun will be too low in another half hour. In Jesus' Name, amen."

The expression on Colin's face, when he looked back at Lynn who was standing next to me in the cockpit while I steered, was a study in bewilderment. He obviously thought, as Lynn probably did too, that Jeremy had gone completely around the bend.

It was only a matter of minutes before Colin spotted a coral head two hundred yards ahead of us and to starboard. He clambered back across the bow, down into the cockpit, and went to the stern to put on his gear. Jeremy stayed forward to direct us to our quarry. When we reached the head Colin, spear in hand, jumped over the side. We awaited his findings with bated breath, Jeremy looking supremely confident. When Colin surfaced and shook his head—signifying there was nothing there—I expected my husband to be crushed. Quite the contrary, he was hopping up and down and signaling that there was another head less than a hundred yards away.

Colin stayed in the water and held onto the diving step while we towed him the short distance. Down he went again, this time to reappear within seconds with his thumb up. We anchored the boat and went to work.

By the time we had the head cleaned out there was less than an hour and a half of daylight left. The loran showed that we were twenty-three miles northwest of Dover Sound and the entrance to the Grand Lucayan Waterway, the man-made canal that cuts through the center of Grand Bahama to connect the north and south shores. We had to get to the waterway, go the eight miles down it, and then go another eight miles west along the south shores to our home canal. We would have to get a move on.

Jeremy drove, pushing the boat up to thirty knots before we were even finished stowing the gear. Lynn, Colin, Justin and I beheaded and deveined the lobsters while Colin kept the count. We were within sight of land when Colin announced the total: eighty-three. My husband grinned from ear to ear. "Thank you, Lord, for the bountiful harvest," he shouted to the dimming sky. Lynn and Colin exchanged a private glance. One could not tell what they were thinking.

We are not good cliff dwellers—Jeremy's name for people who live in apartments—and, with our lives beginning to take shape, the restrictiveness of our apartment was wearing on us. The amount and unending nature of the maintenance required by Ashdown Farm had been such that a few months away from it had been a welcome respite. But we were beginning to itch for gardens to tend, lawns to mow, elbow room, and homegrown vegetables.

Elbow room was not the least of it. Forty-four cartons of our belongings were still in storage for lack of space in the apartment; there were no garages or outdoor sheds, so the boys had to keep their bicycles in their bedrooms. To leave them outside would be to see them "tiefed" the very first night. And our black Dachshund, Beasley, would be much better off without the traffic of an apartment-building parking lot. Then there was the matter of shelves for my shells and the German shepherd I wanted to get.

We let it be known that we were looking for a house and awaited the workings of the grapevine. Jeremy had learned his lesson about local real estate agents back in October. It was not long before we heard that the wife and family of a Scotsman, who had been on the island sixteen years, wanted to move to the mainland. We went to see their house and fell in love with it.

It had four bedrooms and a den that could be used as a fifth if needed, a big kitchen with dozens of cabinets, a huge high-ceilinged living room opening onto front and rear patios that was typical of the houses we had liked so much in Jamaica, a two-car garage and a storage shed (Jeremy and I were happy). It was only a two-hundred-yard walk down a private lane to the beach (Ashley was happy). The swimming pool had a water slide (Justin was happy), and it had a fenced-in mowed field beyond the gardens (Beasley was happy even though she hadn't been invited to vote).

Beyond all that, it was a very pretty white stucco house with gray cornerstones and a red tile roof. The gardens were lush and fully mature and the bougainvillea festooning the overhead trellises on the back patio was breathtaking. The only thing it did not have was a canal in which to keep our boat but, with a nice marina only a mile away, we felt that that was a compromise well worth making.

A few weeks before we were due to move into our new home Cay Gottlieb's sister decided to move to New York. She had a beautiful German shepherd called Casino . . .

Moving day arrived. The house was less than a mile from the apartment building so, with the help of two friends, the Harmons, and the use of Andrea's pickup truck, we decided to dispense with the services of a moving company. It was a pain in the neck but we saved a lot of money and avoided all the packing and unpacking that attends professional movers. Jeremy, Ashley and Dave Harmon emptied the apartment, stuffing things into the car and the pickup—sometimes in cartons we had saved, sometimes loose—while Linda Harmon, Justin and I put everything away in the house. The most exciting day came when the forty-four cartons were delivered from storage. It had been a year, and opening all those cartons and finding our books, paintings, sculptures, good china and crystal, not to mention the rest of our clothes, was like a giant Christmas party.

Dave and Linda, with their children, Freddie and Lisa, had arrived on the island a few weeks after us and represented the Salvation Army's first venture onto Grand Bahama. Jeremy met Dave at our church one day and took an immediate liking to him. They had come from a two-year posting to Trinidad and our first dinner together quickly grew into a lovely friendship. Apart from anything else, neither Jeremy nor I had the faintest idea what the Salvation Army actually did. Like many people, I suspect, our image of the Army was one of soup kitchens, Santa Clauses with kettles ringing little bells, and dark-clad people with trombones playing "Bringing in the Sheaves." We did know that they accepted old clothes which they distributed to the needy, but beyond that we had never given the matter any thought.

Dave and Linda were intelligent, witty, well-educated and well-spoken people, both hailing from Chicago. Their ministry, we learned, was to bring enlightenment in both the spiritual and the worldly senses to—to put it bluntly—the dregs of humanity. A more selfless calling than that of the Salvationist cannot be imagined. He ministers to the poor, the illiterate, the unfortunate of every description. The environment in which he works is frequently so desperate that the best he can do is to concentrate on convincing the children that there is more to life than alcohol, drugs and filth. Anyone lacking the humility that God demands of us should spend just one day following a Salvationist on the rounds of his ministry. It is a humbling experience.

Dave stopped by the house one day with his boss from Nassau, Henry Arrowood. They could not stay for long so we invited them to come back for dinner, Linda and the children too. Henry was a charming man although a bit reserved and formal among strangers. He seemed a little more comfortable when he joined us again a few months later, but did not completely relax until the third time he came for dinner.

It was then that we got to know more about him. We were surprised to discover that he was a southerner. He did not have a southern accent and we might never have learned that he was from Tennessee had not the afterdinner conversation turned to pastors with interesting—or downright odd—speaking styles. Henry had us in stitches with an impression of his father—a classic southern preacher—and that was only the beginning.

The high point of his commentary came when he started doing impressions of singers and singing groups he had encountered at a Gospel music get-together in his home state. Mention that one man had sung a song entitled "Drop-Kick Me Jesus Through the Goalposts of Life" led to an anecdote about a group of "good old boys" who sang a very special song.

The good old boys delivered a short sermonette before each song but, when they came to the very special song, their leader went on at considerable length. Henry did it in a wonderful southern drawl that I wouldn't dream of trying to reproduce in print—except for "the thray most prayshus wurds," that is.

Those three words, the speaker explained, were the three most precious words that God ever spoke. Those three words had turned the speaker's life completely around. They quite obviously were the most wonderful three words in the universe. And so he was going to sing a song, the title of which was these three most precious words: "Ah Fawr Give."

CHAPTER

13

WE RAN INTO TROUBLE AT CHURCH. WHEN IT HAPPENED WE WERE so taken aback that we dealt with it very badly at first.

We loved our church family and had come to know more and more people individually through joining in various church activities. Picnics were my favorites. Pastor had a pet spot on Fortune Beach where we could drive in under the pine trees to set up the food tables, charcoal grills, volleyball net, and domino tables (dominos is the national sport of the Bahamas). It was a lovely setting for a picnic in that it was completely shaded, yet right next to a gorgeous sandy beach.

During one such outing I went snorkeling with Jeremy and Justin and discovered that it was also a good shelling ground. There was a big barracuda that had claimed territorial rights near the church's chosen area and when he cruised past and made his presence known, dozens and dozens of children ran shrieking from the water. Justin took great delight in continuing to swim, trying in fact to keep up with the 'cuda. When he emerged, to admiring glances from the girls and jeers from the embarrassed boys, he launched into an authoritative talk on the behavioral patterns of the barracuda. "You don't have to be frightened of them. They only feed on fish smaller than themselves. They follow people around because they're very inquisitive. If you swim straight at them they run away."

There were giggles from the girls, but from the boys, "Not me, man!" and, "You crazy!" My little one looked so cute standing there and holding forth to his peers I couldn't stand it.

"But you shouldn't wear any kind of jewelry," he continued. "They'll go for anything shiny no matter what."

"You crazy what you say. My daddy says barracuda the most viciousest fish in the sea. You gonna get eat up, that's what you gonna get."

"No, I'm not. I've been with my dad when he chased them. They just run away—unless you have a fish on a spear—then they'll come after the fish just like the sharks will."

"Eeeek!" This was too much, even for most of the little girls, and they promptly ran for their mothers, chattering about Justin and sharks all the way. Most of the boys moved off grumbling about Justin being "crazy in de head" and not knowing "what he talk about." A few of each stayed, though, saying, "He brave, you know?"

"I think you went too far," I said. "You had them with the barracuda but you lost them with the sharks."

Our trouble derived from our irregular church attendance. At first we went on Wednesday nights and Sunday mornings. We stopped going on Wednesdays because the services frequently continued until well after nine o'clock and it was too late for Justin. He had to go to school the next day and it wasn't fair to keep him up until ten or later; nor was it fair to leave him out of our family worship.

Then we began to miss the occasional Sunday. Sometimes it was the only day of the week with seas calm enough for diving. Since the boys could only go boating on weekends we would forgo church in favor of the reefs. Once in a while our failure to attend was due to nothing more than being too tired to get up early enough to go. We had long since elected the 8:30 A.M. service since it had to end by 9:45 at the latest— though it frequently ran until 10:00—to permit of the Bible study class that followed. We had attended several 11:00 A.M. services and found them much too long for us. They often went on until 1:30 and 2:00 P.M.

The church of Jesus Christ consists of all those who have accepted Him as their personal Lord and Savior and who have done their best to follow His teachings. The church of Jesus Christ is not restricted to those who sit in buildings. Attending church the edifice is something we do because we want to. We do it because we feel a need for the fellowship of other Christians and a need for the blessings that attend a large group of people joined with one mind and one purpose: to praise the Lord.

We do not go because someone is taking attendance. Nor do we go in the belief that the going is a bonus point on Judgment Day.

Faith, like the human body, must be exercised regularly if it is to stay fit. Regular exercise is a discipline. Faith, too, requires a discipline. For some, going to church regularly is the only discipline that is acceptable, but there are many, many others who do not agree. My family and I are among them. For us, going to church is the frosting on the cake; it is not the whole cake.

Our daily prayers are the basis of our discipline. Jeremy's long walks along our dirt road in Pennsylvania every night—no matter the weather or how tired he might be—have been replaced by long walks on the beach. That is when he feels closest to God and that is when he conducts his most serious prayer and worship. My favorite time is our daily family devotion which usually takes place right after dinner.

We have an opening prayer and then a discussion of anything that may be on anyone's mind. We read the Scripture for the day, discuss what it means, then close with a request for divine help where it is needed and a prayer of thanks. It is wonderful and is as much church as is church the edifice. Jesus said, "For where two or three are gathered together in my Name, there I am in the midst of them."

We also have a nondenominational Bible study group in our home once a week. Our leader is a Bahamian Bible scholar—who happens to be a Methodist—whose understanding of the Word is as great as that of any seminarian and vastly enriching in its insight. Anyone is welcome to join us and many do. It is not that our church does not have Bible study—it does—but it does not engage in the Socratic method of teaching that we so enjoy.

So that is our discipline. We go to church frequently and thoroughly enjoy our times of worship; but we go when we want to, not when we are expected to.

It was a shock, therefore, when people started asking where we had been the previous Sunday. If we had been off the island they looked relieved, but if we had been out in the boat they looked deeply troubled. When two ladies I was particularly fond of took me aside to discuss our absences I was hard-pressed to be polite. When we got home that day Jeremy and I talked about it.

The more we talked, the angrier we became. How dare anyone presume to judge us on the basis of our church attendance? It was precisely the reason that Serafino's answer to Jeremy's question, "What church do I have to go to?" had been so important to him. If going to church was to be the measure of his faith he would never in a million years have accepted Jesus.

The crowning blow came when we heard through the grapevine—accurately or inaccurately as the case may have been—that Pastor and Kay had felt led to pray for our deliverance. We were furious. We even contemplated finding a different church to attend—one that would accept us as we were without seeking to impose its ideas upon us regardless of our personal wants and needs.

We loved Pastor and Kay dearly and probably reacted so badly because of it. We felt betrayed by friends who, we thought, understood us and owed us better than that. It had not yet occurred to us that we had an obligation to understand them.

Pastors, regrettably, are judged—and judge themselves—by "jahave?" and "jaget?" It is a terrible shame that this is the case but there doesn't seem to be any way around it. What other simple measure of a pastor's efficacy is there besides, "How many did jahave?" and "How much did jaget?" There are other, more important yardsticks, but they are subtler and only discernible over long periods of time. How successful is the pastor's family counseling? How successful is he at leading the young people away from drugs and other foul temptations of the times? Much more important yardsticks both. But jahave? and jaget? are the visible measures and so it will probably remain.

It was several days before Jeremy and I calmed down enough to think clearly and like Christians. If people we loved were troubled and asking questions—intrusive though we might feel them to be—might we not owe them an explanation? If Pastor, by the simple yardstick, thought we were falling by the wayside in our faith, should we not, perhaps, bring the matter into the open and discuss it with him? Did we not have an obligation to explain to him—as our pastor as well as our friend—that we saw things differently and exercised our faith in a manner that suited us, and seek his acceptance of us the way we were? Wasn't that more appropriate, not to mention more Christian, than muttering to each other about invasions of our privacy and talking about going to a different church?

Trying to talk to Pastor at his home or in his office was a waste of time. The phone never stopped ringing and the knocks on the door were endless. We called and invited him and Kay for coffee on the first morning convenient for them. We got together a few days later and, after a few minutes of niceties, we blurted it all out: the lateness of the services, the length of the services, our private devotions, our prayer life, our resentment of being criticized—even prayed for—because church the edifice was not the focal point of our faith.

I would like to be able to say that the meeting went swimmingly; that everyone stated his case and that we parted with smiles of relief, each understanding and respecting the other's point of view. Unfortunately, this was not to be—at least not for a few weeks.

The tension at the meeting was palpable. It was obviously the next best thing to impossible for anyone steeped in church—let alone the pastor of one and his wife—to accept that anyone's faith can remain strong, even grow, other than in church. They were clearly ill at ease in trying to appease balky members of their flock without compromising the most fundamental of their beliefs.

Time proved that we had done the right thing, however, and Pastor and Kay now accept us as we are. We enjoy our private devotions and our Bible study group. We go to church frequently, but only when we really want to go to church. It can be argued that we are being selfish, but we do not think so. If the exercise of one's faith is insincerely motivated, then it is not an exercise of faith but merely an exercise.

The love and friendship between the DeLoaches and us is alive and well and we each accept the other's need to do it his way. I have recently learned that there is great concern among many Christian leaders that the church has failed the "baby boomers." Apparently that generation—of which I happen to be a member—is having difficulty finding spiritual fulfillment in any church and is, therefore, turning away from faith altogether.

Wrong!

Faith is to be found in our own hearts, not in a building. If what goes on in the building does not suit us we must go to another building or, better than that, stand on Christ's own words: "Again I say unto you, That if two of you shall agree on earth as touching any thing that they shall ask, it shall be done for them of my Father which is in heaven. For where two or three are gathered together in my Name, there am I in the midst of them." What more can we ask? Two or more of us together are a duly constituted church. There is time to find a building we like and services that we find inspiring. Sustaining our faith is nobody's responsibility but ours. Losing or turning away from it cannot be blamed on others. When we stand before our Lord Jesus Christ we shall stand alone and we shall be answerable for our own deeds and our own consciences.

Another lesson we had to learn involved false prophets. The Bible is full of warnings but, in our infinite naïveté, Jeremy and I actually believed that if someone called himself an evangelist he had to be an evangelist. If he stated that he had a healing ministry it followed that he had a healing ministry.

Lorraine, an acquaintance from church with a congenitally deaf two-year-old son named Joey, rang us one day to say that an evangelist had come to the island to hold healing services and that she was going to take Joey. We had never heard of this particular evangelist and agreed to meet Lorraine at the opening-night service.

When he arrived at the hall we saw posters depicting the evangelist preaching to thousands of people and testimonies of all kinds attesting to the miracles that had been performed during his services. Hundreds of folding chairs were lined up but only half of them were occupied when we filed in. A jolly fellow was making the rounds of the arrivals, introducing himself as an assistant and inquiring as to special needs that people might have. We found this last a little puzzling since we had never encountered anything like it before.

The service began with organ music, a few well-known hymns and a period of prayer. The evangelist spoke and a collection was taken, then people with infirmities were called forward for healing. Lorraine took Joey, fast asleep in her arms, and stood in line with a few others. Jeremy and I were surprised at how few there were. The evangelist obviously was too, for he promptly delivered a pep talk on how the first night in any new city was always a bit slow and that everyone should return the following night if they really wanted to see God's blessings pour forth.

He prayed over a lady with a heart condition and two or three others. Then he came to Lorraine. Jeremy had already whispered to me that something was wrong. "I don't feel any anointing at all. I don't think anyone's being healed of anything. They keep saying they feel the healing power but I don't believe it."

"I don't either," I whispered back. "I'm afraid it's just wishful thinking, but let's see what happens with Joey."

The "evangelist" touched the still sleeping child and prayed, "Lord, heal this child. Bring a full measure of hearing to him. In Jesus' Name, amen." He clapped his hands loudly next to Joey's head and said, "Joey, can you hear me?" The child slept on. The "evangelist" proclaimed, "He's healed! He's just too tired to be aware of it yet." He looked at Lorraine. "You know he's healed, don't you?" The poor woman seemed on the verge of tears but she wanted to believe, so she nodded her head vigorously.

My husband and I whispered again. We had seen children healed of deafness in Akron. Little ones, particularly those with congenital deafness, are all but frightened out of their wits by the sudden inrush of unfamiliar sound. Most of them cry. None of them go right on sleeping in their mother's arms, unable to be roused even when shaken.

Lorraine returned to her seat and the "evangelist" preached for a while. He thanked God for the "miracles" He had performed and called for another collection. We felt like jumping up and telling everyone to hold on to their money, but the man we were now convinced was a fraud was on the island under the auspices of a local pastor. As non-Bahamians—and guests on the island ourselves—we had no right to interfere.

With the collection taken, to the encouraging sounds of inspiring organ music, the "evangelist" stepped down from the platform and walked among the seated congregation. He stopped at different people and announced that they had this or that need. He laid his hand upon the head of each one and prayed for their need to be met. We were obviously supposed to believe that he was receiving Words of Knowledge. Jeremy and I were convinced that the jolly fellow had matched up needs and faces for him from behind the curtain before the service began.

The clincher came when he stopped behind Jeremy and placed his hand on his head. We can only believe that God led him to do it so that not a shred of doubt could remain in our minds. "Lord, please bless this brother," he solemnly intoned. "He has important decisions to make and he needs your help and guidance. Lift from his shoulders the burden he feels. His decisions will affect the lives of many besides his lovely family who are with him here tonight."

We left as quickly as we could and talked in the privacy of our car. The "evangelist" had picked a pretty safe prayer for most men. There is hardly a man alive who does not have decisions to make. Some have weighty ones that could affect the lives of others outside their families. Even if not so weighty, the man would probably be flattered by the implication that his concerns loomed so large in God's mind.

There was only one problem: at that moment in time Jeremy had nothing more pressing on his mind that what to order for dinner. Through God's grace we hadn't a problem in the world beyond my weight and Jeremy's thinning hair. Neither of those required decisions, let alone decisions that would affect the lives of many.

We had no way of knowing what effect this sham had on others who attended for they were all—including the local pastor who imported the "evangelist"—strangers to us. We do know that it was sad for poor little Joey and, perhaps, a tragedy for Lorraine. We tried to console her. We told her about God's healing power that we had witnessed for ourselves at Ernest Angley's services and elsewhere. I told her about my back and varicose veins. But it was no use. We never saw her at church again and she left the island a few weeks later for business reasons. We fear that her disappointment was so great that she lost her faith and blamed God for not healing Joey.

It was several months later when Jeremy called me to the television set one night. He had been for his walk and was watching Johnny Carson while I tidied up in the kitchen. "There's a man coming on called the Amazing Randy. Apparently he used to be a magician and now spends his life debunking frauds. He's written a book exposing phoney TV evangelists."

When the man came on he was introduced as James Randy. He was self-assured and the evidence he presented regarding one so-called television evangelist was convincing indeed, particularly in light of our own recent experience. He averred that this personality used a radio receiver disguised as a hearing aid to receive transmissions from his wife—hidden out of sight of the audience—in order to perform the same Words of Knowledge fraud that we had witnessed. The same trick had been used of interviewing people as they arrived, only this lot had gone so far as to have them fill in cards. In response to a question from Johnny Carson, James Randy stated that such people were taking in as much as twenty million dollars a year.

With that much money at stake it is not surprising that frauds have cropped up. I truly hope the Amazing Randy keeps after them and does not become mired in lawsuits that stop his good work. I hope that his work is honest and thorough. His motivation is irrelevant—whether he knows it or not, he is doing God's work by exposing Satan's lies.

Beyond that, I hope that people who are duped by a fraud do not weaken in their faith—or lose it completely—as may well have been the case with Lorraine. Our faith is tested constantly. A phoney evangelist—the basest of all confidence men—is serving Satan as surely as if he had signed a contract with him. We must use the power of discernment that God gave us. We must recognize evil when we see it.

If James Randy is God's instrument in helping us, then let us pray for his continued success. Above all, let us beware of putting our faith in men rather than in God.

CHAPTER

I HAVE A NATURAL, THOUGH NOT EARTHSHAKING, GIFT FOR painting. I had long wanted to do an oil of our Lord to hang in our own home. The problem was that I wanted to do one that was entirely original, one that I had not seen anywhere before and that could really be mine. I was reading Revelation one day when I knew that I had found my painting.

It is the moment when Jesus—clad in a blood-red robe with KING OF KINGS AND LORD OF LORDS embroidered on the hem—rides forth astride a white horse at the head of the armies of heaven to slay the beast. It is one of the most electrifying moments in the Bible and I was so excited that I dropped everything in order to paint. Dinner was frequently very late and Jeremy was at his wits' end trying to get me to confer with him regarding the book.

I left the face of Jesus until the very last, afraid that I would not be able to do it at all. When I ran out of excuses for further delay I prayed. I have no doubt that the Holy Spirit guided my brush for it was done in mere minutes. I stood back and gazed at it in awe. It was so far superior to anything I had ever done before that it left me breathless. Tears came to my husband's eyes when he looked at the finished work and he insisted that we hang it in the living room for all to see.

* * *

So much had happened during the past year that it was difficult to accept that the holidays were upon us again. Once more in a real house, and with all our belongings out of storage, I was able to cook my head off and invite lots of friends to join us. There were twenty for Thanksgiving—including six house guests—and I served dinner on the patio on iron tables covered with checkered cloths and arrangements of hibiscus. The guests helped themselves from the dining room where the table groaned under the weight of the huge turkey and all the side dishes.

It was the way I had always imagined that holiday feasts should be. There had been large gatherings in the past, to be sure, but Mother's dark presence had inevitably hung over them like a lowering cloud, raining or threatening to rain whenever conversation became too genial or gaiety dared raise its unwelcome head.

Ashley had a great time appearing in the Christmas musical at the Regency Theater and Justin, sitting with his father and me at the last performance, drove us crazy by whispering, "There's Ashley, there's Ashley," every time his big brother came on stage.

We were nine for Christmas dinner, but were forced indoors by the temperature making a sudden descent into the low sixties. Friends dropped by at random—something else my mother had never countenanced—and it was the most joyous Christmas of my entire life. The candlelight service at church was beautiful and extremely moving. I thought of Mother with sadness. I wondered what she was doing.

It was a few days later that I found out what she was thinking—if not what she was doing. A package arrived from her. Jeremy, wearing a big grin because he had already seen the contents when clearing the package through Customs at the post office, set it on the dining room table.

I folded back the layers of tissue paper and revealed a lovely wicker, horseshoe-shaped basket. There was a tiny chintz-covered cushion on top and the basket was full of all sorts of fragrances: soaps, sachets, bath salts and bath gels. The whole thing was festooned with brightly colored ribbons. Jeremy's grin had given way to a chortle by the time I found the card.

"I know it'll be something snide," I said to him, "but I

don't care. It's really beautiful and I love it."

"Yes, it is. But read the card."

Even the card was pretty. On it was written, "By now you both must need this plus a pillow on which to try to sleep. Ruth Elizabeth."

I broke into gales of laughter and Jeremy joined me. The more I thought about it, the funnier it became. The boys rushed in from the pool to discover the cause of so much hilarity. They looked at the basket and Ashley took the card from my fingers and read it aloud. He looked puzzled for a few seconds, but then grasped the point. "I guess she's saying she thinks we stink. But why the cushion?"

"It's axiomatic that people with guilty consciences can't sleep," his father answered. "She's sent us a pillow on which to rest our sleepless heads."

Justin took the card and frowned at it. "Why is it signed 'Ruth Elizabeth'?"

"I'm not absolutely certain," I said, "but I think it's because I made such an issue in the book about Ruth Elizabeth being my mother—the person I love but hardly ever see—while I find Bette so obnoxious. She probably thought that if she did something she considered nasty—and did it as Ruth Elizabeth—she would shoot down my contention that she is two distinctly different people." We discussed my analysis and then Jeremy said, "I know you're going to write her a thank-you note, but what are you going to say?"

"That's easy," I replied, "I'll thank her for the lovely gift. I'll tell her how much I'm going to enjoy using all the fragrances and completely miss the point. She'll be furious. She'll probably go crazy trying to find out whether the shop really wrote what she told them on the card." I chuckled at the mental image of Mother raving at the shop, and then raving at her secretary over my inability to grasp the point of so obvious a put-down.

"One thing's for sure," I said. "She hasn't managed to completely blot me out of her thoughts. That's a good sign." Jeremy looked at the basket and its contents again. He tossed the tiny cushion in the air and caught it a few times. Clear in his voice was the same touch of sadness that I often felt when he said, "Your mother may be nuts, but she certainly has style."

CHAPTER

15

AT SIXTEEN ASHLEY HAD ATTAINED A HEIGHT OF NEARLY SIX AND a half feet. He was extremely handsome and had a mane of blonde hair that could only be likened to pale corn silk. It was the envy of every woman who saw him, including me. He had never enjoyed team sports but had proved proficient—and enjoyed—individual ones like riding, skiing and swimming. He was a loner and always had been. He refused to join groups and all too often suffered the inevitable consequence of loneliness and boredom. No amount of coaxing by his father or me had convinced him that his life would be fuller and more enjoyable if he would just become a joiner. In addition to this he had two major problems.

The first was that he saw no reason to work hard. His teachers found him so attractive, polite and charming that they never flunked him at anything, even when it was apparent that he had bent no effort at all to accomplish his assignments. The worst report he ever got was, "Ashley would do much better if he worked harder." This would accompany a C or C plus. On the odd occasion when something really captured his attention and he actually gave it his best, the teacher became ecstatic and gave him a rave.

His other problem was me. He was quite willing to accept the authority of men, particularly his father, but had become more and more infected with machismo as he grew older. He saw no reason why women should have the right to order him about.

It was the one area in which Jeremy and I were at odds. Ashley had the ability to make me so angry that I shouted at him, but he was careful to provoke me only when his father was well out of hearing. The minute Jeremy entered upon the scene, Ashley's entire demeanor changed from pugnacious defiance to charming confusion at my lack of self-control in the face of some trivial—not to mention wholly accidental—boo-boo on his part. He would look his father squarely in the eye and say pathetically, "All I did was make myself a grilled-cheese sandwich and Mom went right off the deep end."

Since it wasn't the making of the sandwich that had sent me off the deep end—but the incredible mess that Ashley had wrought in the kitchen and the defiance with which he had rejected my criticism—it was difficult for his father to do anything but look from one of us to the other in total bewilderment. Ashley always seemed to have a point. I always seemed to have overreacted. My defense was never persuasive.

"Why didn't you make lunch for him if you didn't want him in the kitchen?" my husband would ask.

"Because I was busy. I told him to wait a few minutes but he went right ahead and did it anyway. I work very hard at keeping a clean house and I won't have Ashley destroying the kitchen every time he's hungry. It isn't fair and you know it!"

"I couldn't agree more, but it also isn't fair to make him wait forever for lunch. We're completely willy-nilly about meals around here—except for dinner—and we all know it. It's the way we like it. We eat when we're hungry."

"But I told him I would make lunch for him as soon as I was finished flea-bathing the dogs," I would insist.

"Is that true?" Jeremy would ask of Ashley, knowing that it was.

"Sure, Dad," Ashley would answer, all wide-eyed innocence, "but I waited ten minutes and then went ahead. I thought I was helping Mom by doing it myself."

Whenever this scene—in its infinite variations—played,

Ashley knew he had me. It was impossible for Jeremy to remain anything but undecided regarding who was right and who was wrong. He would sometimes wander off about his business and make me twice as angry by exiting with a line like, "It seems to me that you two children must learn to play nicely together." On more than one occasion I yelled at his departing back in utter frustration, "You wait . . . one of these days Ashley's going to forget himself and do it to you. Then you'll know what I'm talking about."

As I said, Jeremy and I were at odds. Ashley was the weak link in our love for each other, the only gap in God's hedge around us through which Satan could occasionally tiptoe. My husband felt that I was lacking in tolerance; I felt that he was lacking in sensitivity and understanding. The situation persisted until Jeremy had to go to the mainland for our new boat.

We had enjoyed our first boat, but after a year, we had begun to feel that we had peered into every coral cave and looked under every rock within safe sailing distance of home. We began to yearn for a bigger boat, one we could sleep on comfortably and on which we could cruise to other islands. We found just what we wanted and, when the day came to take delivery, Jeremy and Colin Evans flew to Ft. Lauderdale to sail it across the Gulf Stream.

Ashley had more or less behaved himself for several months. I was, nonetheless, apprehensive about his father being away for days. I had the feeling that whatever drove Ashley to defy my authority was going to come to the surface again the minute his father was gone. I kept my feelings to myself and overlooked any number of reasons to pounce on Ashley for his behavior, but it was no use. My misgivings had been well founded and there was nothing I could do or say that would prevent the inevitable showdown.

It came to a head on Sunday night, the day after Jeremy's departure. The boys and I went to evening services. We had dinner at a restaurant first—which we all enjoyed since we seldom dined out—and then went to the church. As we were taking our seats, Ashley spotted some friends and announced that he was going to sit with them. I said that I preferred that he stay with Justin and me since I wanted to leave promptly when the service was over in order that Justin would not be too late to bed. Ashley totally ignored me, defiance oozing from his every pore as he swaggered down the aisle.

He had chosen his moment with the same exquisite sense of timing that his grandmother invariably displayed. He knew with certainty that I would not make a scene in church. He knew that he had me and I was heartsick. I asked God to prevent things from going too far but, even as I was praying, I knew that nothing good could come of this unless it first got worse.

After the closing prayer I beckoned to him, held my watch high and gestured at it, then pointed towards the doors. He scowled at me, shook his head and turned away. A boy sitting near him—Kenny, whom I knew and liked—mouthed that he would bring Ashley home.

Not a single nuance had been lost on Justin. On the way home he said, "Ashley's doing this because Daddy isn't here to make him behave." I reached an arm across to give him a hug. "I know, Sweetheart. Lord preserve us from the teenage macho syndrome."

It was after nine when we got home. As I was tucking Justin in he said, "Mommy . . . I promise I'll never be a teen-ager. I couldn't do it to you."

I sat and watched television. Since the older kids usually went for pizza after evening services it would be at least an hour before Ashley arrived. Because of his size, no one ever remembered that he was only sixteen. The twenty-year-olds accepted him as one of them and gave not a thought to his needing parental permission for things.

There was nothing on the tube that managed to distract me. What had begun as annoyance gave way to anger. On top of that I was tired. Shortly after ten I locked up the house and went to bed. I checked the dish in Ashley's room where he kept his house key. The key was in the dish but there was no need to worry about hearing him return—any noise near the house would set the dogs off.

It was after midnight when I awoke to the knowledge that Ashley had raised the stakes. I had to be certain, so I un-locked the patio doors to see whether he had been too stub-born to knock and had gone to sleep in the hammock or on one of the chaises. There was no sign of him. I wandered about for a while, wondering what to do and becoming increasingly worried. I should have called Kenny much earlier; I could not bring myself to wake him up at half past midnight.

Prayer recommended itself as the best course of action. I asked Jesus to keep His hedge tightly around my wayward son, no matter where he was or what he was doing. I went back to bed but slept poorly, waking every hour or so. Whenever I thought of the scowl on Ashley's face, and his turning his back on me in church, I became angry. I wished the big jerk would stay wherever it was he had gone. Life would be so peaceful without him!

Then I felt guilty about being so angry at him and prayed again for his safety. The conviction would come over me that nothing bad was going to happen to him and I would doze off. An hour later I would wake up and go through it all again.

It was one of the longest nights I have ever spent. I loved him, I resented him for his insolence, I prayed for him, I forgave him, I was angry with him again. Around and around I went, never able to get my emotions in order.

I prayed for my own peace of mind.

The alarm clock went off and I roused Justin. At quarter to eight I called Kenny. He said that he had dropped Ashley at the foot of our driveway at 10:30. He was horrified to hear that he was missing. On a whim I rang Lynn Evans to see whether Ashley had gone to her house. I realized too late that Lynn would have called me immediately had he done so, but the damage was done.

Lynn became hysterical and could not understand why I wasn't. I assured her that God would not let any ill befall Ashley, but she was determined to do something. She said she would call in a replacement teacher so that she could drive around the island looking for my son. I insisted that she do no such thing. "He'll turn up somewhere and driving around won't accomplish a thing. Maybe he's decided to walk to school to prove how independent he is. I appreciate your concern, really I do, but I'm convinced that I have to sit still and wait it out."

Lynn was aghast. "Aren't you even worried about him?"

"Of course I am, and maybe a lot more upset than I sound. But I know he's in God's hands. Jesus won't let him come to harm."

"But anything can have happened," Lynn protested. "Druggies, thiefs, anything."

"There's only so far he can go on the island and I have absolute faith that nothing's happened to him. The Lord has His angels around the darned fool in spite of himself."

There was a long silence before a thoroughly befuddled Lynn said, "I hope you're right."

I rang Pastor to let him know what had happened and to ask him to be on the lookout for Ashley. Then I took Justin to school. I half-expected to see Ashley strolling along the road somewhere. Shortly after I got home Kenny stopped by to see if there was anything he could do to help. He left at ten and then Lynn called.

Despite my injunction she had taken a quick spin around the beach area. She had found Ashley ambling sedately on his way to school. She had offered him a ride and he had jumped into her car, chatting happily about this and that as though nothing out of the ordinary had taken place. He had not said a word about his adventure and Lynn had felt it best to keep her counsel. I thanked her, breathed a big sigh of relief, and promised to stop by when she got home from work.

I spent the next few hours going about my normal routine as well as I could. I thanked the Lord for taking care of Ashley and for giving me such peace of mind as I had. I thought of calling Jeremy, but decided against it. There was nothing he could do from where he was, and it would be ridiculous to ask him to fly home to deal with something that I should be able to handle myself. There was certainly no purpose to be served in making him worry from afar.

When it was time to collect the boys from school I asked the Holy Spirit to minister to me and allow me the objectivity I felt the situation demanded. I was determined to keep my temper in check and to avoid argument.

Justin was the first to reach the car. "Ashley's in school," he burst out.

"I know. Lynn Evans found him and gave him a ride."

"What are you going to do to him?"

"Absolutely nothing. Please don't even mention it until Ashley does."

Justin fiddled with things in his satchel and we waited in silence.

Five minutes passed before Ashley sauntered jauntily through the front gate of the school, jacket flung over his shoulder and held with one finger. He opened the car door and tumbled into the front passenger seat without looking at me. "Boy, oh boy, what a day!" He threw his head back and laughed loudly. "Boy, oh boy, what a day!"

I clenched my teeth, drove out of the parking lot, and turned into the side street heading east. Ashley spun around to look at Justin in the rear seat. "How are you, little brother?" Justin stared at him wide-eyed—as I could see in the rearview mirror—but did not answer. I returned my eyes to the road and continued driving. Then Ashley turned to me and uttered the immortal words, "Hey, man, what's *your* problem?"

"Now you've done it," Justin said quietly.

I do not really know what went through my mind at that moment. I think my entire life may have flashed before my eyes. Despite all my good intentions I fairly erupted. "*My* problem? *My* problem? I don't have any problems except you!" Apparently this was the funniest thing he had ever heard. He let out a loud guffaw, then lunged forward in his seat and drummed on the dashboard with his fingers and the heels of his hands.

That's when I lost it completely. I slammed on the brakes at the Stop sign on the corner and screamed, "How dare you? How dare you? You insolent, thoughtless, selfish, stupid, irresponsible child! You have the unmitigated gall to disappear for the night, ask me what my problem is, then laugh in my face when I say it's you. Now I'm going to tell you something. I don't want to hear another sound out of you unless it's constructive or enlightening. Do you understand me?" He muttered something unintelligible, shook his head and rolled his eyes toward heaven.

A minute or two passed in silence. I was turning off Settler's Way into Coral Road when Ashley spoke. "I knocked on the door when Kenny brought me home but you refused to open it."

273

"Tommyrot," I said. "You did no such thing and you know it. Don't lie on top of everything else."

I ignored the inane protestations that followed. Finally he said, "O.K., so I lightly touched my knuckles to the side of the house so I could say I knocked."

"Why?"

"Well, I figured that with Dad away and you in bed it was a good opportunity to stay out all night—go down to the Holiday Inn disco and party. I sang hymns all the way down the beach. God was really with me. It was great, really great."

I had to stop for the light at East Sunrise. I took a careful look at my son's face. He was grinning cheerfully, evidently unaware of anything but his sense of personal achievement at defying me. I was suddenly frightened for him. "Do you mean to tell me you actually believe that God is applauding what you did? Do you really believe that God wanted you to run away, defy your mother, not give a single thought to the worry and concern of your family and friends? Do you think God wanted you to hang out with a bunch of tourists, partying at a resort hotel? Where did you sleep, by the way?"

"On the floor of the water-ski instructor's apartment. He didn't mind."

There were more exchanges concerning what he had done and where he had been. It had all been quite harmless, thank God, and I pulled into our driveway feeling much relieved. At least the macho routine had given way to reasonable conversation. Ashley made no move to get out of the car. Thinking that he might have something else he wanted to say, I waited patiently. Suddenly he began to weep. Through his sobbing he said, "It was Satan, wasn't it? Boy, did he have me fooled. God wouldn't tell me to do those things, but I didn't stop to think about it."

He continued to weep quietly. The barrier had been broken and I thanked the Lord.

"How did I let Satan in?" my son asked with an anguished expression on his face.

"He got his foot in the door when you decided to defy me in church. He used your defiance to influence you. He never stops trying, you know. Not ever. You opened the door and invited him in. It's up to us to recognize him for the disgusting, hateful liar he is and be sure to avoid his temptations."

We got out of the car, Ashley's eyes still wet with tears, and hugged each other. He asked if it would be alright if he took a nap. He had been up until six in the morning, first at the disco and then on the beach, and was exhausted.

The whole unfortunate episode seemed to have ended satisfactorily enough, but I was worried about Ashley's state of mind. One hears so much about teenagers and their problems that I wondered whether there was more to my son's behavior than met the eye. I called Percy Kemp, the youth pastor of our church—who was great with teenagers—but he was out. I was about to put off further action until I could locate Percy when I remembered that all of the Out-Island missionaries were in for a convention. One of them was Percy's younger brother, Sobig, who was also very good with teens and their troubles.

Sobig was staying at Pastor's house and I rang him there. I explained what had happened and what I thought might be the underlying cause of Ashley's behavior. Sobig felt that it would be beneficial if he and Ashley got together for a chat—immediately if possible—and he asked to speak to him on the phone.

It was just at that moment that Justin came rushing into the kitchen. "Ashley's gone again! I heard him say that he wasn't a good Christian and that if Satan was the only person who wanted him, he could have him. He undid the screen and went out his bedroom window."

A cold chill ran down my spine. I was really scared. I ran to Ashley's bedroom, saw the screen out and the window open, and ran back to the phone. I told Sobig what had happened. He heard the panic in my voice and said the first thing we had to do was pray for Ashley's safety and for Jesus to take hold of his heart and bring him home quickly. We bound Satan's power over Ashley and then Sobig asked the Holy Spirit to assure me that my son was safely in God's hands.

A complete peace came over me. I knew Ashley was safe. I was about to thank Sobig when he said, "Now, there's one thing that's very important. I'll tell Percy what's been going on, and he and Ashley must get together, but in the meantime you have to do one thing. You may find it difficult but, believe me, it's remarkably effective. You have to tell Ashley that if he ever takes off again, don't come back."

*   *   *

I had promised Lynn Evans that I would go to see her in the afternoon, so I locked up the house and Justin and I drove over there to visit for a few minutes. Her first question, naturally, was, "How's Ashley?" I had to tell her the truth, poor thing, and she flew into another panic. She said we had to do something; call the police; anything. She all but shouted at me not to just sit there looking so complacent. Didn't I know all the horrible things that could happen to him?

"Calm down," I said. "God is in control. I don't know why He let Ashley take off again, but there's a reason for it. No harm's going to come to him."

Lynn looked really angry with me and I wished she could understand. She said, "How can you just sit there? You have to do something."

"I already have. I've done the best thing I can do. I've committed Ashley's safety to Jesus."

"What in the world are you going to say to him if . . . when he comes home?"

"A friend who has a lot of experience with teenagers says that the best thing to do is tell him that if he runs away again he shouldn't bother to return. He says it's very effective."

It was less than an hour after Ashley's second departure when Justin and I came back from Lynn's. Ashley was standing on the front terrace. "Hi," he said rather sheepishly.

I unlocked the front door and walked into the living room, then turned to address him. "I'm glad to see you back so quickly, but I'm curious as to what you have to say for yourself this time."

Ashley closed the screen door behind Justin and then faced me. "I feel like a jerk. I was halfway to the Holiday Inn beach when I realized I was turning my back on God again. So here I am. Where were you?"

"Over at Lynn's. I'm glad to see you're making sense at last. Are you going to stay this time?"

"Yes."

"Good, because if you decide to leave again, you'd better take a suitcase. You won't be welcome back."

We did a great deal of talking that evening, perhaps the most we ever had. Ashley admitted, for the first time, to his loneliness. He also admitted that his hanging around the Holiday Inn beach with all the tourists was a way for him to have company without getting involved or leaving himself vulnerable. He agreed to talk to Percy and join the church youth group. A short time later he did exactly that and has never looked back.

Jeremy and Colin arrived with the boat the next day. They took eight hours to make the crossing—instead of five or six—due to encountering six- to nine-foot seas and having one engine go sick halfway over. They had also run through thunderstorms most of the way. To say they were tired is an understatement; they were completely wrung out.

Ashley wanted to unburden himself the minute his father got in, but I suggested he let him get ashore and recuperate first. The boat was in under quarantine and it turned out that the Customs man had just left the marina, thinking his work was done for the day. We had to wait for him to come back. It was too much for Ashley and he blurted out the whole story. Perhaps it was for the best. Jeremy was too tired and too frazzled to become angry. He mulled it over for a few seconds, then said, "Your mother seems to have handled it as well as anyone could, so there's only one thing left for me to say: if you ever do it again, don't bother to come back."

Ashley looked from his father to me, then back at his father. "What is it with you two?" he yelped. "Mental telepathy or something?"

CHAPTER

16

JEREMY AND COLIN EVANS SAT AT THE DINING ROOM TABLE SUR-
rounded by navigation charts, meticulously plotting courses
and tides for our first major cruise on the new boat: a day of
lobstering west of Mangrove Cay, overnight in a convenient
lee shore; another day of lobstering going east from Mangrove
to Sale Cay, that night to be spent in the protected, horseshoe-shaped cove at Sale; a final day of lobstering—the season
would close that night for four months—as we made our way
from Sale to Walker's Cay to spend a few days fishing.

Lynn and I were in the kitchen rechecking the menus and
provisions lists, making sure that we would not run out of
anything in midocean. Justin bustled from here to there—
looking very busy and getting in everyone's way—carrying the
little nylon bag that contained his diving gear. He was so afraid
of forgetting to take it aboard that he had not let it out of his
sight for days. Ashley packed and unpacked his grip in a fe-
ver of anxiety that he might not have the right clothes. He
was unwilling to accept his father's assurance that all he needed
was razor, toothbrush, swimming trunks, shorts and T-shirt.

He knew that Walker's Cay was a renowned haven for game

fishing. If there were to be game fishermen on hand, so might their daughters be. Ashley was going to be prepared—clothing-wise, that is—regardless of his father or anyone else.

Into the midst of these final preparations came a knock at the front door. Justin answered it and brought me an Easter lily in a pot. Lynn looked over my shoulder as I opened and read the card: "I still can't break the habit."

"Who's it from?" she asked. "Do you know?"

"Oh, sure," I chuckled. "It's from my mother."

"A bit weird, isn't it? I mean, she didn't even sign the card."

"Yup. That's my mother. Last year she signed the card; this year she didn't. Next year she probably won't even send a card, just the lily."

"Do you know what it means?"

"Not really. The only certainty is that she hasn't been able to forget me. I guess, to that extent at least, it's an encouraging sign."

I stood the pot in a dish of water in the hope that the beautiful plant would still be alive when we returned in a week. The buds were not yet open and I love Easter lilies. I then went back to the business of preparing to sail at dawn the next day.

Except for a few days of rough weather the trip was wonderful. We speared enough lobster to last us through the summer, but not as many edible fish as we had hoped for. We had much to learn about where and how to fish. We were proficient with spears and never lacked for grouper—which are readily spearable—but we seemed to be deficient in knowledge when it came to the subtleties of line fishing.

The Easter lily was alive and in full bloom when I entered the living room. I sniffed its delicious fragrance and thought of my mother. I wondered where she was and how she was. I wondered what went through her mind when she sent the lilies each year. Jeremy had gone for the mail and my musings were interrupted when he burst through the door waving a letter over his head and shouting, "Look at this!"

It was an invitation to go to a seminar at the *700 Club*. Scott Ross, who had interviewed me for the Christian Broadcasting Network during my book tour, had said that he would try to have us invited, but we had not actually believed it would come to fruition. When I realized that it had, I was as excited as a child at Christmas.

The *700 Club*! Pat Robertson! I could not believe it. I had watched the show whenever possible for two years. I owed the healing of my back to a Word of Knowledge received by Pat Robertson. Jeremy had come to the Lord because of that healing. And now we were going to be there. We might even meet Pat Robertson. It was thrilling.

We went; and we spent a weekend that I cannot describe. It was the most exciting and spiritually enriching time that I have ever in my life experienced. We met the most beautiful people and forged friendships with a few that I know will last for a lifetime. We met Ben Kinchlow and Danuta Soderman. We met Harald Bredesen. And we met Pat Robertson.

For a man who, for Christ, gave away everything and began again with nothing, his achievements boggle the mind. And it was all done with love, hard work, self-sacrifice and faith in God and His Word. No arrogance, no self-satisfaction at the accomplishments. Nothing but love and humility. By the time we left to come home, we were on a high that lasted for weeks and which I doubt that any drug addict has ever experienced. If that sense of joy, love, peace and oneness with God could be bottled and merchandised by Madison Avenue, there would be no more strife in the world.

We had only been back in Freeport for a few days when Linda Harmon called to tell me that my mother was about to be interviewed by Rona Barrett on *Entertainment This Week*. The interview had just started when I turned on the television set.

I sat down on the sofa in front of the set and was astonished to discover how intensely interested I was in how Mother looked and what she had to say. The first thing I noticed was that the slight droop in the left side of her face—the result of her stroke—was not only still there, but turned toward the camera. The stage was set with Rona Barrett to the viewer's left and Mother to the right. The droop would always be toward the camera.

I felt guilty at first for making the observation. Then I realized that it was not a criticism, merely an observation. I was evaluating a new performance and trying to understand the actor's motivation. I read it as a clear statement: "See the droop? I had a stroke. I fought another good fight, and don't you dare forget it." I tried to put it out of mind but it was there, right before me. And so it would be during two subsequent appearances I was to see shortly thereafter. She posed herself the same way for each.

Aside from the deliberate featuring of her left profile and the droop, she appeared and sounded vital and strong. She wore a long, red sequined dress which had been made for her, she said, to wear for a French award ceremony. She displayed a statue and made a point of how heavy it was. Indeed, when Rona Barrett took it for a moment, her hand dipped with the weight. Mother hefted it with ease. She seemed her old self.

When it became apparent that the interview was going to be a long one, Jeremy offered to make milk shakes for the boys and they wandered off to the kitchen. Suddenly there was the infernal racket of the blender echoing into the living room and obscuring the voices on the television.

"Shut the door!" I hollered. "I want to hear and I can't." The sound of the blender stopped and my husband's head appeared around the corner. "I didn't know you were so riveted."

"Neither did I," I said.

The peculiar thing was that, although I was truly interested in what she had to say, I felt no emotion.

I examined myself as I sat there and watched. She never referred to me, even when she talked about Michael or her children in general. I searched for inner feelings and could find none. But I knew I had them. It was emotional anesthesia. I loved her as I loved every one of God's children. Her soul was of major importance to me, as was the soul of anyone else. But I could not rationalize my interest in this interview with my complete lack of emotional response.

I told myself that here was my mother whom I had not seen for eighteen months, yet I felt nothing. I knew that I had cut all practical ties to my mother when I published my book, but what was becoming clear to me as I watched and listened to her image on the television screen was my tremendous sense of release and freedom. It had never been there before.

Here was this woman who had permeated every facet of my very existence; whose wishes had been my commands long into my adulthood; against whom I'd had to struggle even to keep my husband and children—unto the last dire step of writing a book—and now I was free. I had been healed of my bitterness and resentment long since, but now I was free of the emotional bondage that had dogged my footsteps.

There she was and, yes, I cared. But she had no more power over me. The rush of freedom was profound. I had no regrets, no guilts; I was truly free. Free to be whom I wanted without having to justify it to my mother. Free to plan holidays without worrying that she might have some conflicting plan. Free from the omnipresent lawyer informing me of my obligations. *Free, free, free.* It was the first time that it had hit me in this way.

I had often commented that the past eighteen months, without my mother breathing down my neck, had been, sadly, the happiest and most peaceful of my life. But now I was really floating free! Thank you, Lord.

I would never again have to suffer her glowering presence in my home. I would never again have to take Valium to cope with that presence; or become ill out of reaction to that presence when it left. If and when she should ever be in my house again it would be on mutually acceptable terms, not her terms. She could either accept Jeremy and me as one or not, but if she decided upon acceptance it would have to be sincere.

No more role-playing, no more pretense. It would not be as before, when I persistently fooled myself into believing that I had some vestige of control while actually being under absolute emotional bondage without knowing why, let alone how to break free.

With all people like my mother, when the break comes it is like the messiest and most bitter of divorces. It is nasty. That is the only way it can be. If reason and reasonableness were available options, the problem requiring the exercise of those options would not exist.

The freedom from such oppression can only be appreciated by someone who has been the object of such oppression.

Even my husband, who stood by me through the thick and the thin for twenty-two years, did not fully comprehend my final release. I felt like an eagle that had been caged all its life—except when occasionally taken out on a string for short, controlled flights—who had finally cut the string. No matter what anyone does to recapture him, he knows he can fly higher and soar longer than any of his pursuers. Even if faced with nis previous captor, he knows he has his measure.

Jeremy returned from the kitchen and offered to share the milk shake, the blending of which I had hollered at him for. I kissed his cheek and we grinned at each other.

"Has she said anything interesting?" he asked.

"Not really. Just this and that. It's mostly the old over-awed-interviewer-graced-by-the presence-of-the-living-legend bit. Apparently she's making movies in Europe now. The French gave her that big sprout that's sitting on the coffee table next to her. Michael's now her wonderful son. That's about the size of it." Jeremy nodded, sat down next to me, and said it was nice that my brother was finally being appreciated.

It was obvious, at least to me, that Rona Barrett had been enjoined from asking any questions about me or the fact that I had written a book about her illustrious guest. She suddenly asked a very clever question: "If you had to choose one thing, what would you say was the biggest disappointment in your life?"

Jeremy and I exchanged glances. Mother looked at the ceiling of the studio with a wistful expression. "Without further comment, I would have to say my daughter's book." Despite her exclusion of further comment, Mother went on to say that it did not matter to her what I had said; just the fact of my saying anything at all was terrible.

At that moment I became certain that, despite my cherished hope—even tentative belief—that Mother had read what I had written, she hadn't. Nor did she ever intend to. It was a sad moment for me. It was no great surprise, Mother remaining true to her lifelong form of having selective hearing, but sad nonetheless. Perhaps my disappointment was as great as hers.

Something very funny happened next, and I dare say

Mother was as angry as I had been when confronted with a tape of Gary Merrill out in Los Angeles. The cover of *My Mother's Keeper* filled the screen for a few seconds. It was only two weeks before I was due to start my paperback tour and Mother had unwittingly engineered a free plug for the book. Jeremy and I laughed so hard that I don't know whether there was any more to the interview. When I regained control of myself I said, "Oh, is she going to have a fit when she finds out what they did. I'd hate to be on the other end of the phone when she calls Rona Barrett's producer."

"Poor beggar won't know what happened to him," my husband chortled.

We both stopped laughing at the same time. The sheer, wasteful, unnecessary absurdity of the entire situation returned to us simultaneously. Jeremy switched off the television set and took the dirty glasses to the kitchen. The boys were at the other end of the house. They had not had sufficient interest in their grandmother to watch more than the first few minutes of the interview.

I continued to stare at the blank screen. I thought about God's plan for Mother. I was confident that her salvation was assured. I had no idea how or when; perhaps at her final hour, perhaps today. The how and the when were not important.

I was not at all sure about the possibility of reconciliation anymore. If she had read the book, we would have had a chance—slim, I admit—but a chance. Without her reading it . . .

It was inconceivable to me that God would have used me in the way He had if Mother's salvation were not part of His plan. Our lives here on earth are so short compared with eternity with Jesus in heaven. The only matter of moment here is that we recognize and accept the one great truth. Eternity is what matters, life as opposed to death, and that life only available through Jesus Christ.

If my mother and I shall one day come to know each other as a mother and a daughter should, it will be wonderful. I continue to pray that it will happen. But to know each other in heaven is what really matters. We are all, in Christ, a family.

My mind was, as it so often had been during the past year, drawn back to that night in Louisville, and the momentousness of God's message. I had so often listened to the tape recording of it sent to me by Pastor Pitts—and had played that tape for so many friends—that I almost knew it by heart.

Oh, my people: shall he that has created you instruct not? Yea, shall you come and shall you tell me whom I will use? I shall use you. Though you seek me not, I shall use you. When you have yielded to me, I have used you. When you have resisted me, yet have I used you.

I shall use whom I shall use; and I shall bless whom I shall bless; and I have given my son to die on the cross that I might bless all things and that I might use my servants.

Yea, you have seen me work in your midst tonight; and yea, you will see me work in your midst again; and you shall not teach me nor shall you tell me whom I will use.

But yea, I shall magnify and I shall bless you. If you will yield in Christ, then will you see greater things, and you will know my love; yea, for my love and my secrets are with them that fear me.